THE
EVERYTHING.
Personal Finance
in Your 40s & 50s
Book

Dear Reader,

Congratulations! You've taken a vital step in building the financial security that will support you through the rest of your life. As you'll see, it doesn't require expensive, complex strategies—just a clear understanding of your goals, a carefully crafted plan to reach them, and the tools to make adjustments when life throws you a curveball.

Whether you're starting over from scratch after a divorce or the death of a spouse or hitting your financial stride with an exciting career and a full family life, there's a lot you can do now to make the next twenty years and beyond the best they can be. Time can be your ally if you use it wisely.

For more than a decade, my clients at Compass Planning Associates in Boston have helped me refine the financial planning strategies that work best when you're busy with work and home and still need to keep the financial part of your life moving forward. This book will introduce you to, or help you perfect, money management skills with simple but powerful strategies. Most important, you'll emerge from the planning process with a sense of power over your finances. Starting now, you're the boss!

Jennifer Lane, CFP

Bill Lane

Welcome to the EVERYTHING® Series!

These handy, accessible books give you all you need to tackle a difficult project, gain a new hobby, comprehend a fascinating topic, prepare for an exam, or even brush up on something you learned back in school but have since forgotten.

You can choose to read an *Everything*® book from cover to cover or just pick out the information you want from our four useful boxes: e-questions, e-facts, e-alerts, and e-ssentials. We give you everything you need to know on the subject, but throw in a lot of fun stuff along the way, too.

We now have more than 400 *Everything*® books in print, spanning such wide-ranging categories as weddings, pregnancy, cooking, music instruction, foreign language, crafts, pets, New Age, and so much more. When you're done reading them all, you can finally say you know *Everything*®!

QUESTIONS?
Answers to
common questions

FACTS
Important snippets
of information

ALERTS!
Urgent
warnings

ESSENTIALS
Quick
handy tips

PUBLISHER Karen Cooper

DIRECTOR OF ACQUISITIONS AND INNOVATION Paula Munier

MANAGING EDITOR, EVERYTHING SERIES Lisa Laing

COPY CHIEF Casey Ebert

ACQUISITIONS EDITOR Lisa Laing

DEVELOPMENT EDITOR Brett Palana-Shanahan

EDITORIAL ASSISTANT Hillary Thompson

Visit the entire Everything® series at *www.everything.com*

THE
EVERYTHING®
PERSONAL FINANCE
IN YOUR 40s & 50s BOOK

A comprehensive strategy to ensure you can
retire when you want and live well

Jennifer Lane, CFP® with Bill Lane

Aadamsmedia

Avon, Massachusetts

To the Compass Planning team.

An Everything® Series Book.
Everything® and everything.com® are registered trademarks of F+W Media, Inc.

Published by Adams Media, an F+W Media Company
57 Littlefield Street, Avon, MA 02322 U.S.A.
www.adamsmedia.com

ISBN 10: 1-59869-860-5
ISBN 13: 978-1-59869-860-2

Printed in the United States of America.

J   I   H   G   F   E   D   C   B   A

Library of Congress Cataloging-in-Publication Data
available from the publisher.

This book is available at quantity discounts for bulk purchases.
For information, please call 1-800-289-0963.

Contents

Acknowledgments

I owe an enormous debt to my clients and advisors who continue to share their lives and insights with me and help me perfect my craft by candidly sharing their thoughts and experiences. I'm grateful for their confidence, and my joy in seeing their success is immeasurable.

And as ever, thank you to William C. Lane for starting this whole thing.

Top Ten Keys
to a Successful Financial Plan

1. Understand the difference between appearing rich and being rich. Don't spend yourself into financial disaster by trying to put up a wealthy front.

2. Be open to change. Your 40s and 50s are a time of transition. Embrace change and welcome the chance to prioritize your goals.

3. Let your kids fly on their own. Don't set your kids up in a lifestyle they can't maintain by themselves. Save your money for your retirement.

4. Understand your asset allocation. Get educated about the market and understand how the growing global economy will affect your nest egg.

5. Use technology to simplify your life. Use direct deposit, auto-invest, auto-pay, and online banking to maximize your time.

6. Establish monthly money meetings. Review your finances and your financial goals with your family on a regular monthly schedule to be sure you stay on track.

7. Get your will, health care proxy, living will, and power-of-attorney documents completed or updated.

8. Never be too busy for fitness. Medical expenses in retirement could claim a huge part of your budget if you don't take care of yourself now.

9. Hit your savings targets. Even if you're just starting retirement investing now, you have at least ten years until retirement—maybe more.

10. Save outside of work. Building investments outside of retirement plans will give you better flexibility and save taxes in retirement.

Introduction

▶ EVERY DAY, MORE than 10,000 people turn 40 and another 10,000 or so turn 50. While you have been called the most affluent and financially powerful generation in history, you are also the first American demographic segment in decades that is moving toward late career and retirement without traditional pension plans backing you up. You've been forced by government policy and workplace trends to go it alone, or nearly so, as you prepare financially for retirement. Without the corporate pension safety net that protected your parents and grandparents, it is important that you take responsibility for your own financial security.

In addition to its financial heft, your generation makes up a significant portion of the Sandwich Generation, which finds mid- and late-career adults raising children while caring for parents. The Sandwich Generation put off having children until their careers were firmly rooted and thriving, meaning you're far older than the new parents of a generation ago. At the same time, advances in health care are keeping your parents alive, though perhaps not in full health, far longer than their parents lived. You're more likely to be coping with financial challenges from two family generations—in an assisted-living residence, a dorm, or your home—as well as your own upkeep. Never has financial planning been more vitally important to Americans in their 40s and 50s than now.

New college curricula and the media are giving your kids a much broader financial education when they're young enough to take advantage of it. You can learn the same lessons, but your focus needs to be tighter and your plan must be executed more rigorously. Your time is shorter to accomplish with modern investment tools what your parents were given in the American workplace of most of the twentieth century. You're not alone, but it will take your individual initiative to go into retirement with the financial resources to let you accomplish your most cherished goals.

While traditional retirement remains the goal of many in their 40s and 50s, with its emphasis on leisure time and rewarding yourself for a career of hard work, this book approaches the question of retirement with the understanding that many of you are too intellectually and emotionally engaged in your life's work to cut it out of your life entirely. You'll find the discussions surrounding retirement in this book continually applied to the possibility of a "selective retirement" that enables you to customize your personalized balance of work, charitable involvement, and leisure in ways that your parents and grandparents wouldn't have recognized. Your generation is blazing new trails in defining retirement, just as it has in everything else it has touched.

Knowledge is, indeed, power. This book will help you uncover the unknowns that surround your late-career years: shifting social security benefits, career changes, building your retirement nest egg on your own without a secure pension, balancing your life with the demands of your kids, and caring for parents. You have a limited amount of time in your day, and this book gets directly to the most important points and gives you straightforward, actionable guidelines.

Whether you've been watching nervously from the financial sidelines or you feel comfortable with your money and want ideas on how to maximize your resources or you want to help a family member or friend gain control of his money, this book will simplify such complex topics as budgeting, investing, helping kids with money, and talking to parents about their finances. It's a holistic approach to healthy financial planning that, if you commit to it, we know will help you achieve your financial goals.

CHAPTER 1

It's Never Too Late to Start Planning

Financial planning—being in control of your money instead of letting it control you—is a lifestyle, not just a one-time exercise. Learning about your money and how to manage it well falls clearly in the category of helping yourself succeed. Getting to your 40s or 50s without a financial plan is not uncommon. Earlier, you started a family, raised kids, and built the career that supports them. Now it's time to start thinking about you. Let's get started!

The Planning Process

Financial planning has always been a part of your daily life, but you may not have always realized it. When you've made decisions about what kind and how much insurance to buy for your car and your home, you've been doing personal financial planning. When you contemplate the tax implications of a purchase, that too is a form of financial planning. And of course, the way you manage your income and your spending is clearly financial planning. Your finances affect virtually every aspect of your life. Choices you make in one area affect the choices that are available in others. Realizing this and creating an easy-to-follow plan around each process is an important part of reaching your goals.

Keep It Simple

Maybe you've put off financial planning for fear of what you'll discover about yourself and your finances. Or you may have been scared off by the idea of complex cash tracking systems or detailed daily spending diaries. But by ignoring your money, you miss investment opportunities or make mistakes that financial planning could help you avoid. Getting in touch with your finances and creating a simple plan for staying in control is the best way to keep your money working for you, not against you. You're about to learn which methods are right for you—and which to run away from! Let your financial planning process be as individual as you are.

Think Holistically

Most people think of financial planning as merely starting a retirement account or creating a budget, but it's a lot more than that. In fact, financial planning really touches almost every part of your life—and it connects almost every part of your life. What you're spending on now affects the ability to acquire things you may want to spend on later. How you feel about your money affects your overall stress level, and therefore your health and your relationships. Whether you've planned for college costs or for life insurance or emergencies affects your security when large or unexpected expenses arise. You probably think you have an intuitive feeling about how secure your finances are. Creating a financial plan or reviewing your personal finances regularly either confirms this intuition and gives you the chance to plan ahead and get the most out of what you have or provides an opportunity to take corrective action right away.

Parts of Your Plan

Your financial plan covers seven general areas:

- Goal setting
- Managing your cash and your budget
- Risk management and insurance
- Tax planning
- Investing
- Retirement or planning for a job transition
- Planning for what happens when you're sick or when you're gone

Once you've created your plan and filled in the missing pieces, you can come back and review individual areas separately. Remember, your plan will always be changing. You make a plan, set a course, and, like a ship navigating across an ocean, you adjust your course as the currents change.

Financial Planning Is More Important than Ever

By their 40s and 50s, many people are in both their peak earning and peak spending years. This generation has an additional strain: being at the tail end of the baby boom. The effect the boomer retirement wave will have on the economy, interest rates, and the stock and housing markets makes personal financial planning very important to 40- and 50-somethings. These economic factors, coupled with the significant reduction in company pensions, make focusing on managing your own money even more important.

Following the Baby Boom

The baby boom generation—those born between 1946 and 1964—has had a historic effect on the economy and culture as its members have grown up. The first baby boomers are now turning 62 and are eligible to collect social security benefits. The boomers are expected to put enormous strain on the economy and on social security resources as they retire, start selling their investments for retirement income, and draw against government benefits. Many people in their 40s and 50s expect social security benefits to end altogether before they're eligible to collect, based on the well-publicized strain on the Social Security Trust Fund. That's unlikely, but it still makes sense, more than ever, to be sure your financial plan is ready for any contingency.

Planning in the New, Unknown Economy

Planning for contingencies is the mantra of financial planning, especially in your 40s and 50s. Investment advisors are forever reminding you that past performance doesn't promise future results. This can also be said of financial planning in today's economy.

The boomers have fueled a prolonged period of economic growth. This has created a comfortable standard of living and the expectation that the growth will continue. As you think about your plan, think about ways you can build in contingencies if growth starts to slow. For example, when you make retirement projections, reduce the historical returns that some formulas and software programs recommend by a percentage point or two; be extra sure that you have cash available for emergencies; budget in savings at the same time that you're paying down debt; don't refinance your house to the maximum the bank will allow, as that will leave you without equity to sell if you need to. The strong economic past has encouraged people to focus on short-term wants rather than long-term needs. A strong financial plan is about planning for your future goals and being excited about them, but also about balancing current wants with savings so you have the important resources when things don't work out as expected.

Pensions Versus Personal Savings

Personal financial planning is important today because this generation is truly working without a financial safety net. Few employers offer corporate pensions anymore, and fewer people stay with a company long enough to become eligible. The federal government continuously sends the message that they won't be there to help by increasing incentives for individuals to save on their own. Increased limits on retirement plan contributions and lower taxes on investment earnings are among the policies that call attention to the individual need to build financial security. Politics aside, this is a reality that can't be ignored. Fortunately, along with increased urgency to plan and save have come innovations in technology and information that make it easier.

Financial DNA

Fashion advisors say everyone has a body type. They see some as apple shaped, others resembling pears, some lean and slender, others thick and muscular. Knowing your body type is helpful because you can dress to flatter yourself and minimize flaws. The same can be said of your money type. To decide your type, think of a horizontal line moving between the extremes of saver on the left and spender on the right. Where you fall on the scale will indicate how you interact with money.

Reading Your Type

One of the key things to remember about money types—as with body types—is that there is no bad type. Most people don't live at the extreme; they are typically more moderate. People who tend to be savers don't save constantly and never spend. People who tend to be spenders do often save for their goals, if they're clearly defined. Knowing where you fall on the money type scale is important not so you can change your type, but so that your self-understanding lets you think about how to implement your financial plan in a way that will work best for you.

What Is Your Money Type?

Check the following statements to decide where you fall on the money type scale. Then, just like planning your wardrobe around your body type, you can build your financial plan around the way you behave with money. Start at the center of the scale. Review each statement below and then move to the left or right depending on your answer. Move one step to the left for each Yes answer and to the right for each No answer.

	Yes	No
You give up short-term extras in order to invest or save.	❏	❏
You're the last person you know to buy the new "thing" everyone else is buying.	❏	❏
You review your account balances regularly and keep your checkbook up to date.	❏	❏
You spend cautiously and can remember your last five major purchases.	❏	❏
You try not to boast about new purchases to your friends.	❏	❏
You seldom help your adult children with expenses.	❏	❏
You know how much money you spent on entertainment last month.	❏	❏
When you buy something on credit, you think of the total cost rather than only focusing on whether you can handle the monthly payment.	❏	❏
You plan ahead for large expenses.	❏	❏
You open your account statements as soon as they arrive and decide whether to pay, file, or shred them.	❏	❏
You update your budget regularly and plan your expenses around your income expectations.	❏	❏
An unexpected expense fits easily into your budget.	❏	❏
Financial windfalls and gifts seem to come fairly often and you apply them to fun extras or invest them.	❏	❏
You maintain your car and home regularly.	❏	❏
You paid off your credit cards and now use them for convenience rather than to make ends meet.	❏	❏

Financial Planning by Money Type

You may find that you tend to be more of a saver or more of a spender depending on your current circumstances. You may also find that you'll tend to be less of a spender as you gain control of your money and start focusing on longer-term goals. Also, keep in mind that your partner is probably not the same type as you. Spenders and savers often get along great together, except when they discuss money. Remember, you're together because you have common goals. Financial planning to achieve these goals together will help you understand each other better.

Tips for Spenders
- Spend money with deliberation. Wait forty-eight hours (or walk down the block) before making a purchase.
- Create a saving and spending plan in small incremental steps—don't try to stop spending cold turkey.
- Track your expenses in an easy-to-follow system.
- Hire a financial planner.
- Give an emergency fund more importance than retirement investing, to start.

- Review your accounts as they come in and pay bills right away.
- If your partner or spouse is a Saver, be patient.
- Set up an automatic savings plan.

Tips for Savers
- Don't be overly conservative in your investments and in your spending.
- Balance fun life activities with investing.
- Stay closely involved with your money/investment manager.
- Beware of long work hours.
- Teach your children financial independence.
- If your partner or spouse is a Spender, be patient.
- Try to stay balanced. Beware of binge spending.

Assessing Your Situation

Your net-worth statement and income-and-expense plan are two very important tools to help establish your current situation and your progress toward your goals. Each should be a one-page report that you can review once a month.

Net-Worth Statement

Your net-worth statement establishes what you own and what you owe. Think of it as a personal balance sheet. It lists the balances of all your asset accounts and your debt accounts—the current asset value or the total owed. The net-worth statement helps organize the list and makes easier the job of managing and tracking.

To start, gather copies of all your account statements: checking, saving, mutual fund, brokerage, life insurance, credit cards, mortgage, equity loan, car loan, school loan, and anything else with a balance. Organize the statements into two piles—one for assets that you can liquidate for value and one for liability balances that you owe. Organize the asset pile in order of safety or ease of withdrawal. This would put cash accounts such as bank and money market accounts and life insurance cash value on top. Then list the riskier, but still easy to withdraw, investment accounts next.

Don't Stop Now

List the restricted accounts next—the retirement accounts. These might include individual retirement accounts (IRAs or Roth IRAs), employer accounts (401(k), 403(b), or deferred-compensation accounts), or self-employment accounts (SEP IRA or SIMPLE accounts). Finally, list your assets that are not liquid—the things that would be difficult or expensive to sell. These are so-called use assets such as your home, car, boat, business interests, and personal property.

Use assets are difficult to value because you don't get a statement every month listing their value. Home values can be estimated by using tools available online and through real estate brokers. A quick Internet search using "what is my home worth" will bring up the most common home value estimators. Don't be tempted to overvalue personal assets unless they are special collections or antiques that can be appraised. Online resources to value your car, boat, or airplane can be found with a quick web search.

Set up direct deposit to savings to build your emergency fund. You should eventually have three to six months' expenses in an account, depending on your job security and the waiting periods on your disability insurance coverage. Start today by directing 1 percent of your pay to an account. Increase the amount when you get pay raises.

Check Your Results

Once you've finished your net-worth statement, step back and examine the breakdown of your assets and liabilities. Do you have enough cash available in case of emergency? Do you have high-interest debt that should be paid down with cash or targeted with extra monthly payments? Do you have old retirement accounts that could be combined or rolled into new accounts to make them easier to manage? Do you have both liquid investment accounts as well as retirement accounts?

NET WORTH STATEMENT AS OF _____

ASSETS

Cash/Cash Equivalents

Checking account	
Saving account	
Money market account	
Total Cash/Cash Equivalents	

Invested Assets

Total Invested Assets	

Retirement Accounts

Total Retirement Assets	

Use Assets

Residence	
Automobile	
Personal Property	
Total Use Assets	
TOTAL ASSETS	

LIABILITIES

Liabilities

Mortgage Principal	
Auto Loan	
Credit Card	
TOTAL LIABILITIES	

Net Worth	$

Income-and-Expense Plan

Your income-and-expense report lists all your payments broken down by month or by paycheck, depending on how you prefer to think about them. These are not the account balances, but the amount you regularly pay toward each expense or receive from each income source. Tracking where your money is coming from and where it is going is very important from an everyday budgeting standpoint, but also in planning for retirement. It's hard to know how much you need to save for retirement when you don't know what your current lifestyle costs or how much you can allocate in your budget toward investing.

Start your income-and-expense list by gathering your bills and your pay stubs. Not all bills come monthly; be careful not to miss the quarterly or annual bills. Not every expense results in a bill; pull together credit card and bank statements so you can calculate the amount you spend on variable expenses such as groceries, clothing, entertainment, and holiday spending.

Getting It Right

The trick to a good income-and-expense plan is to boil everything down to its monthly or per-paycheck equivalent. The regular bills are easy because you probably have a recent statement to refer to. List the cost of each next to the appropriate category. Annual or quarterly bills need to be divided down into their monthly or per-paycheck equivalent. Remember that there are four and one-third weeks in each month, so if you're adjusting a monthly expense, such as the electric bill, into a weekly per-paycheck equivalent, you'll need to divide by 4.33.

Credit Purchases

List the expenses that you pay with your credit card separately in their correct category. For instance, if you went out to eat and paid with your card, put that expense under entertainment or dining. Payments toward paying down an old credit card balance are listed under credit card payments. So the $500 you sent to your credit card company last month might contain both current expenses—such as dining—and debt reduction through payment on the previous balance.

Both the net-worth statement and income-and-expense plan should be updated monthly.

INCOME AND EXPENSE PLAN

Monthly Pay 1	
Monthly Pay 2	
Other income	
Total monthly income	

Fixed Expenses

Income Taxes

Federal	
State	
Local	
Social Security	
Medicare	
Subtotal	

Savings and Investments

Retirement account	
Emergency fund	
Investment account	
Other	
Other	
Other	
Subtotal	

Housing

Rent or mortgage (incl. real estate tax)	
Renter's or Home insurance	
Storage	
Maintenance or repairs	
Supplies	
Other	
Subtotal	

Utilities

Phone	
Electricity	

Variable Expenses

Food and Cash

Groceries	
Dining out	
Cash	
Subtotal	

Children's Expenses

Day care	
School tuition	
Fees and dues	
Lessons	
Clothing	
Other	
Subtotal	

Personal Care

Hair/nails	
Clothing	
Dry cleaning	
Health club	
Organization dues or fees	
Other	
Subtotal	

Pet

Food	
Medical	

Water and sewer		Boarding	
Internet		Other	
Subtotal		Subtotal	

Transportation and Automobile		**Entertainment, Gifts, and Travel**	
Car payment		Video/DVD/CDs/Netflix	
Auto excise tax		Movies/concerts/live theater/sporting events	
Car insurance		Holiday gifts	
Registration		Extra holiday spending	
Fuel		Birthday gifts	
Maintenance		Weekend travel	
Parking		Annual vacation	
Subtotal		Other	
		Subtotal	

Insurance and Medical		**Charity**	
Health insurance		Charity 1	
Life insurance		Charity 2	
LTC insurance		Charity 3	
Disability insurance		Subtotal	
Medical expenses incl. prescriptions		**TOTAL VARIABLE EXPENSES**	
Subtotal			
TOTAL FIXED EXPENSES			

| Total Fixed Expenses + Total Variable Expenses = Total Expenses | |
| Balance (Income - Total Expenses) = | |

Managing Cash

Creating an easy way to keep track of how much of each paycheck is getting allocated to each expense is key in creating a strong financial plan. Most people manage one or maybe two accounts: paycheck goes into the checking account, and then the month's bills are paid out of the checking. That's a hard way to manage expenses because you can't see at a glance how much of the money in checking needs to be saved for quarterly or annual expenses. A better way is to create money baskets. Money baskets are separate savings or checking accounts that hold money specifically earmarked for a particular financial goal.

Managing Fixed Expenses

Not all fixed expenses come due each month. Rent, mortgage, and loan payments come frequently enough that they are easy to remember. Quarterly and annual expenses are easier to forget until the bill comes in the mail. When this happens you find yourself saying, "This month would have been fine if it wasn't for that real estate tax bill that only happens once a year," or something along those lines.

Set up an account that will be your fixed expense savings basket. When it comes to fixed expenses, there should be no surprises. A part of your paycheck needs to be allocated to your real estate taxes, insurance bills, mandatory auto inspections, school tuition, and car registrations. Divide all annual expenses by the number of paychecks you receive in a year and have your employer direct deposit the per-paycheck sum into your fixed expense basket account. For example, if real estate taxes are $3,000 per year and you get twenty-six paychecks (you're paid every other week), then $116 per paycheck ($3,000 divided by twenty-six) should go into the fixed expense account. The same simple math can be done for all other fixed expenses, and the combined amount of all will be part of the same direct deposit into the fixed expense savings basket.

ALERT!

Some people even go the extra step of opening smaller checking accounts with individualized names to keep money for annual expenses such as real estate taxes and tuition separate from more frequently paid fixed expenses. Many online banks such as ING Direct will let you nickname your accounts so they are easy to keep track of.

If you become aware of a new fixed expense, figure the per-paycheck amount right away and start allocating it into your fixed expense money basket. You'll find it much easier to manage your month-to-month budget and to stick with an investment plan if you figure out how much of each paycheck is already committed to fixed expenses.

Planning for Variable Expenses

Variable expenses are difficult to plan for because they don't come with a regular bill. Fortunately, though, most people are truly creatures of habit and the expenses that might seem variable are somewhat predictable under close inspection.

Take the urgency and pain out of unexpected expenses by planning ahead. With an old car, for example, you should anticipate a regular amount of maintenance. Make an educated guess about how much repairs could cost each year, then create a money basket. This trick works well for other expenses, too. Be creative!

Variable expenses are all those costs that are not fixed. These might include: utility payments, which tend to increase and decrease seasonally; entertainment expenses; fees for children's lessons or sports; clothing costs; and pet costs. The key to managing these expenses is to check your last twelve months of records—or three months at a minimum—and then estimate an average per-paycheck amount for each. These expenses may seem to fluctuate—e.g., higher electric bills during the winter if you heat with electricity—but if you total all your bills over the past twelve months and take an average, it will be clear how much you should allocate to the variable expense money basket. Entertainment and dining out may seem to fluctuate, and might rise during the holidays, but if you take an average of the total annual amount you spend, calculate a per-paycheck amount, and then deposit that into your variable expense money basket each payday, you won't be surprised.

Can I create money baskets without separate checking accounts?
Yes, you can track your money baskets separately on a spreadsheet, with index cards, or in an online tool such as Mvelopes.com. The key is to easily know how much of your money is already accounted for before you spend it.

Spread Out Long-Term Expenses

Establishing a long-term money basket for the things that you foresee but that won't occur for some time is the last step in managing your cash flow. Long-term expenses are much more easily handled if you can start planning for them well in advance. Take some time to list long-term expenses; a family vacation, a major home repair such as a new roof, or school tuition are common expenses that are too big for most people to pay from their regular paycheck, and instead are often paid by credit cards. Credit card interest significantly increases the final costs and reduces the resources you'll have available for future spending.

Wouldn't a vacation be more relaxing and exciting if you weren't thinking of the big credit card bills you were going to have when you got home? To take the stress out of vacation costs, and other long-term expenses, create long-term money baskets. Calculate the per-paycheck cost of each long-term expense as soon as you become aware of it. If you're not yet sure of the total cost, make an estimate. Start building individual money baskets right away. And if you miscalculate and save too much, reallocate that surplus to another money basket.

Check the amount that you are paying toward consumer debt such as credit cards each month. If your payment is more than 20 percent of your take-home pay, it's time to pay extra attention to getting the debt paid down.

Budgeting Tips and Guidelines

Most people say they're surprised when they first create an income-and-expense report and can clearly see all the easily forgotten expenses. Remember, when you're looking at your spending, there are no inherently bad expenses, and your expense pattern will be very personal and unique. Examine your income-and-expense report for expenses on things that hold little value for you, and minimize that spending. Know why you spend. Understanding your habits and reasons for spending will help you allocate your resources toward your goals—the things you think are important.

Budget-Busters

Once you've worked on planning your fixed- and variable-expense money baskets, the biggest budget-busters are no longer a threat. But your money baskets won't be fully funded overnight. Managing the big budget-busters until you've accumulated your emergency and other baskets is important to your final success.

Many people grow frustrated by their income-and-expense plan because they make it too complex to stick with. Once every few years, they spend a lot of time setting up a plan, calculating their expenses and drilling down into very fine detail. They set up their baskets or another similar plan, and they start. But problems arise when they get too busy to revisit their plan and make adjustments. They underestimate a particular expense and don't readjust their money baskets. Or they borrow from one basket to cover another and don't ever get back to readjusting the baskets. Before they know it, they're falling behind in their tracking and can't get caught up.

QUESTION?

How do I get the budget to balance if my total expenses are more than I make?
Everyone lives on limited resources, no matter how rich they may seem. Be sure you're spending on what's important to you. Check your list and see if there's anything you can reduce. Entertainment, vacation, and holiday spending are places people often find they can cut back.

Don't fall into this trap. Make your baskets as simple as possible. No matter how carefully you research your expenses, you won't have everything perfect the first time. Allow room in this initial money basket plan for missed or misestimated expenses.

Baby Steps

A goal may be to put aside money for your young child's college education, but your budget, with the new expenses of a child, is too tight to start. Start a money basket for their current expenses (day care, diapers, etc.) and plan to reallocate those expenses to a college savings plan as they decrease. You may also find that you don't need to use an amount equal to all of their current expenses to meet the college goal. If your child is older and you don't have the expenses of a newborn, but the school and sports fees are in your budget, think of continuing to set aside that amount toward tuition once the kids move on to college.

ALERT!

Keep total housing costs (mortgage or rent, real estate taxes, and insurance) below 30 percent of your after-tax income. If your income is relatively low, try to get housing down to 20 percent of your take-home. Remember, you need to have money to save for retirement and emergencies—becoming "house poor" isn't the way to do that.

Saving on a Modest Income

Money baskets and savings goals work well whether your income is high, moderate, or low. The real trick is managing within your resources and being clever about stretching them if your income is relatively low. Take a close look at what you spend your money on. Are you spending to meet your goals, or are you spending to appear more affluent than you are? Beware of trying to keep up with the Joneses!

Working a good budget on a low income takes extra finesse and attention. Work through your budget first and be sure you're not spending on anything you don't value. Next, check your regular expenses to see if there is any way to reduce the cost of each. Here are some things to think about:

- Compare prices online versus what you pay in the store.
- Are there any brand changes you can make to save money?
- Are you paying extra fees on banking, check cashing, investment accounts, or credit cards because of late payments, overdrafts, or sales charges?
- Can you change your utility payments to a budget program so that the monthly cost is always the same?
- Would a cell phone only rather than a cell phone and a landline save money? Do you need a cell phone, or just an emergency phone with prepaid minutes?
- Do you buy food your family doesn't eat? Can you adjust the menu to less-expensive whole foods rather than prepackaged foods?
- Don't ignore your health. Quitting smoking, losing weight, and planning regular dental and health care visits are more important to a balanced budget than you would think.

CHAPTER 2

Set Your Goals, then Stay on Track

Everyone lives on limited resources, so it's very important to be sure your resources are applied toward your most important goals. Being sure that you're making choices to spend deliberately so you can manage an achievable goal is key to good personal finance. Regular, positive communication about money between partners or setting aside time to focus on your money if you're single is a critical part of getting and staying on track.

Where Do You Want to Go from Here?

By now, you've created a list of your assets and liabilities—a net-worth statement—and you set up money baskets to help track and manage monthly expenses. The next step toward achieving your financial goals is establishing a balance between work and life, spending and saving, keeping up appearances and building targeted savings.

Being Rich Versus Appearing Rich

It's been said that many people keep themselves poor trying to appear rich. Nothing could be more true. So many people have gone into debt trying to appear as successful as their peers or their neighbors that it has become a vicious cycle. Your neighbor or colleague is trying to appear better off than you; you spend to appear as well off as, or better off than, them. And on and on, until both of you are so deep in debt that the only winners are the credit card companies charging you interest. Few people are able to resist the temptation to appear wealthier than they are. The credit card companies are happy to help out with easy credit and growing credit lines.

People who succeed in building strong personal finances are not necessarily those with high income, but those who have targeted their habits and their resources toward achieving those goals. Balancing spending now with spending later is a key part of this.

Making Choices

One of the best ways to manage the want-versus-need debate is to develop clear goals—and write them down. Post-It notes or notes on your computer desktop are ways to keep your goals in the forefront of your mind. Day-to-day life is busy, and people make decisions based on what they want now; tomorrow seems so far away and convenience takes precedence over planning. Having your goals written and displayed where you'll see them often will help you stay on track.

People establish spending patterns that eventually seem unchangeable. These habits are often a source of contention between partners. Identifying these unproductive behaviors isn't always easy, and changing them often involves dramatic lifestyle changes. But don't let this keep you from examining your financial life. Remember, these are the ways that you might be sabotaging yourself. Depending on what you're doing, these unfocused habits might be the only thing keeping you from really getting in control of your money.

Your Money Journal

The best way to identify how you feel and behave around money is to keep a money journal. This doesn't have to be an elaborate "dear diary" nightly exercise. Your journal can be as structured or unstructured, detailed or casual as you want. Many people find it easier to avoid trying to write in paragraphs and start with lists and random thoughts or fragments of sentences.

Your journal can be very specific or abstract. Start by writing down thoughts about your money and your goals. Think about how your goals relate to your day's saving or spending. Your journal can list your purchases and the purchases you thought about making or might once have made, but bypassed because you decided that you placed a higher priority on another use of your money. List budget-extending purchases such as items you bought on sale or lower-cost versions of more expensive name-brand items. If you splurged on a purchase, record it and acknowledge that you treated yourself. Be sure to record your thoughts about buying that luxury, and maybe revisit that purchase later and record whether your enjoyment of the item or experience was, in hindsight, worth its cost. If so, congratulations! If not, that reflection will guide your future spending and help you prioritize.

Your money journal doesn't need to be written. Use a more visual format if it will help you express your thoughts. Try pasting pictures onto a poster board or, if you're more talented, sketch or paint in any medium you'd like. The idea of the journal is to get your thoughts down in a way that lets you examine them.

Once you've kept your journal for a few entries, you can go back and look for patterns or themes in what you've communicated. Jot down thoughts about what you think the journal shows. Look at the way you interact with your money—are you more of a saver or a spender?

Planning with Achievable Goals in Mind

Defining your goals in specific, clear, and measurable terms is the foundation of your financial plan—deciding whether they are achievable both psychologically and financially and allowing for adjustments as you get older are important parts of making the plan real.

Making the Goals Specific

Most people start with fairly undefined financial goals. After reviewing their notes from their money journal, they might decide that the goal is "to retire comfortably." Making the goal more specific will allow you to calculate specific savings goals and will help measure whether or not you're on track to achieve them.

To make the goal specific, put some precise measurable facts within it. For instance, "I want to retire at age 67 with my current income" is a specific goal. "I want to retire from this job at age 55 and then transition to part-time and work until I'm 70" would be another specific goal. Make sure the goal has both a timeline and a financial aspect specifically stated. The previous goal might go further and say, "At 55, I want my job to provide enough income to cover my expenses, but I don't necessarily have to be able to save at that point. I will work part time to avoid withdrawing from my retirement nest egg until I'm 70." Further planning will help you define that goal more specifically—in this case, by adding a monthly income target.

FACT

People are living longer, but society's norm of retiring workers in their mid-60s hasn't really changed. Think about whether you're ready to be in retirement for thirty years or more. Faced with this, many people are planning for a transition into retirement that will keep them active longer.

Decide Whether a Goal Is Achievable

The next step is to check whether your goal is both psychologically and financially achievable. Think about your personality. If the money works out, can you picture yourself actually living the goal? If you've decided that you will work part time for a number of years, can you see yourself doing that, or are you too much of a workaholic to cut back? If part-time work means an entry-level job, are you willing to do that at an older age? Lifestyles are difficult to change. Don't expect that you'll want to live in a way that is dramatically different from the way you live now.

It's a little easier to check whether a goal is financially achievable. In most cases, once you've calculated the monthly savings requirement to meet the goal, you'll see whether you can afford it. The catch is being sure that you have considered all options. A goal that may seem out of reach now may, in fact, be achievable by investing future increases in pay, reducing nonvalued current expenses, or pushing the goal out a few years to give you more time to save.

Planning in Real Life

John Lennon once wrote, "Life is what happens to you while you're busy making other plans." Considering real-life issues such as your career, your kids, and your parents is critical to creating a financial plan that will weather the inevitable unplanned changes in your relationships.

What's Next in Your Career or Business?

Your career and your finances are more closely linked in your 40s and 50s than they were in your 20s and 30s. When you were younger, you had more independence that enabled you to make changes and take chances that might be more difficult now that you're tending to financial and family commitments. Thinking about how your finances and your career fit together at this stage will help you make sure your financial goals are achievable.

Make an outline of how you envision your career path looking from now until full retirement. Will you continue doing the same thing you do now? Would you like to change to a new field or maybe transition to a different set of responsibilities in the field you are in? Do you expect a promotion that will increase your pay or are you considering changing jobs to something you're interested in but that will pay less? Will you continue to travel as much as you do now? Will you move for your job or your partner's job? Do you believe age discrimination will be a factor for you in your field? Do you need to be sure to be settled in a position by a particular age?

Where Are the Kids?

Whether your kids are young, in grade school, teenagers, or grown, their timeline and finances are an important part of your planning. Allocating the money you were spending on their childhood expenses back into college saving or tuition, and later into your own retirement savings, is a good first step, but you should also consider what they will be doing after they graduate. Setting your kids up for financial security isn't necessarily just writing them a check—in fact, in most cases that is the worst thing you can do. Being sure the kids are set is more related to how they function with money.

Think about your own planning in light of whether your kids are savers or spenders. Will they need your financial help in the years after they leave college? Should you start now to encourage them to plan for themselves? What will you want to do financially for your grandkids in the future? Bring your kids into the planning loop with you. Talk to them about what you are doing and what they are doing financially. Keeping the communication lines open between you will help everyone plan.

What's Happening with Your Parents?

Thinking ahead about your parents' financial situation will avoid the frustration of your financial plan being thrown askew because they unexpectedly need your help. Many people in their 40s and 50s are juggling raising their kids and helping their parents. Often parents are in good shape financially, but the time needed to care for parents should be considered as you start your own planning.

Start an ongoing dialog with your parents. Most families don't talk about money. Starting early and discussing money often will slowly start to change this habit. Being able to anticipate issues will help everyone deal with them when they are small and relatively inexpensive. Start by sharing your own planning process with your parents. You might mention that you're starting, or reviewing, an investment plan or that you are having a will created. Talk about the financial planning books you're reading or financial stories you saw on TV or on the web. Most parents want to talk to their adult kids about money, but don't know where to start. They may not be comfortable revealing all to you right away—and you don't need them to—but an open dialog, at the very least, will help you create your own plan with as many contingencies in mind as possible.

QUESTION?

My parents are very private about money. How do I talk to them about their finances?
Ask them to write you a letter detailing their finances. Tell them to put the letter away and that you won't read it unless something happens. Their information will be private, but you'll know where to find it if you need it.

Family Money Meetings

Keeping your goals on your radar screen is difficult considering day-to-day pressures and busy schedules. Writing down your goals and posting them where you can review them often—inside a closet door, perhaps, or on a home office bulletin board—is a terrific idea. Planning monthly reviews and family "money meetings" is another important habit to keep you on track to your financial goal.

Divide Responsibility, Set Regular Schedules

In most couples, there is one person who manages the day-to-day bill-paying. He or she functions as the family's chief financial officer, or CFO, the person who has a fairly clear picture of the family's financial state of affairs. This person may not be the investment tracker or the big-picture planner, but the position of family CFO gives him or her an intuitive sense of family spending that the other family members don't have. Unmanaged, this assignment of duties—while logistically desirable—can cause arguments and stress when other family members spend money unilaterally or begin to form financial plans that might not coincide with the family CFO's expectations. Holding regular family money meetings can reduce family strife, avoid miscommunications, and help keep the plan on track.

ALERT!

Don't think that you can skip family money meetings if you're single. Reviewing your finances and your goals on your own using the same agenda that a couple would use will help you keep your sights on your goals and reduce the tendency to get bogged down in the day-to-day budgeting.

Your First Money Meeting

The family CFO should prepare a fresh net-worth and income-and-expense statement for the meeting. Attach the investment, bank, and debt statements that factor into the net worth. This won't be as time-consuming as it sounds.

The meeting should start with a review of the financial goals—long-, mid- and short-term. Starting with a goal discussion will help you focus more on the purpose of your planning and less on the monthly expense detail.

Next, review the net-worth statement together. Discuss the savings goals for each account and decide if your accounts are still organized the way you want them. Did the balance in any accounts change? Did debt increase or decrease unexpectedly? How are your investments doing? Is it time for an annual investment review or can your accounts go on unchanged for the time being?

Check the income-and-expense report and check the money baskets. Is everything as it should be here? Should the budget for any expense category be increased or decreased based on recent experience? Should money baskets be changed based on upcoming expenses?

When Money Talk Is Difficult

Many people, and especially couples, avoid talking about money because it can be a tense subject that exposes varying values and desires. The important thing to remember when communicating about money and financial planning is that one of the reasons you are together is because you share common goals. Focusing on those goals rather than on personal short-term spending is the best way to start a family money meeting and keep it from turning contentious.

Too often, couples start by talking about current spending, and this can quickly descend to finger-pointing. If your budget is tight, this can be an especially difficult place to start. People seldom have the same short-term tastes, so the spending habits of each of you will probably be different. But be reassured: you can still have a successful financial plan together even if you both have different short-term goals.

Busy people often get drawn away from their true long-term financial goals by short-term convenience and spending whims. These short-term fixes can be important for keeping the fun in life, but you have to look at them very closely if they're hurting your long-term goals. Sit down and make a list of the things you spend on for short-term needs that are unrelated to your long-term goals. Double check the income-and-expense report to be sure you cover everything. Are you comfortable with what you're spending? Is your short-term spending reducing your ability to save for the long term? Now, come back to the family money meeting with ideas about how you can adjust your short-term spending in favor of the common long-term goals.

QUESTION?

My partner doesn't want to merge our accounts. Should I be worried about his commitment to our relationship?
No, many people have had difficult experiences with money in the past and feel that keeping money separate will avoid anything happening again. Mixing your money will make tracking easier, but it's more important to honor each other's feeling about money.

Separate Accounts

Planning while keeping each partner's money separate adds a bit of complexity, but it's manageable if you create joint accounts for each savings goal and for monthly expenses. Partners should contribute their salary to the household account, less a separate allowance. The allowance for both partners should be the same regardless of income. Both of you will spend time between jobs and you're each likely to take a stint making less than the other, so it's better to avoid the "I get more allowance because I make more" trap. Fund your money baskets from the household account and continue the family money meetings together. Many couples who start with separate money eventually mix their income completely, but some never do. Some stay with the allowance habit and others merge spending completely. Whichever structure works best for you, it's important to keep in mind that adjustments can always be made at the next monthly family money meeting.

Planning for Life Transitions

The decades of your 40s and 50s seem chaotically full of transitions; kids are growing, parents are aging, jobs are maturing or changing, and your personal health starts to be more of an issue. Planning your money around these changes is essential to making a strong plan and staying on track.

Goal Mileposts

Think of your financial life as a process, and your goals as mileposts. Don't think of the goal as a finish line. After all, retirement is still a long-term goal even when you're in your late 50s and it seems to be getting nearer. Allow your goals to be flexible to accommodate your inevitable life transitions. In fact, think of each goal as a transition itself, not a finish line.

For example, many people think of their retirement goal as a fixed point in time. They might say things like, "I'm retiring at 60 next year, and I need to change my investments today so they are not too aggressive." If she retires at age 60 this woman may live another thirty-five years! Supporting an income during more than three decades in retirement is a long-term goal. If she's flexible in her goals, this woman may decide that it makes better financial planning sense to retire at age 61 or even later. Thinking of retirement and all of your financial goals as transitions will help make them flexible enough to fit into everyday real life.

Finding Balance

Think of building your financial security as creating a three-legged stool. Make sure that your financial plan leaves space for three important "legs": money, health, and mind. Getting control of the money category is what this book is all about. But a fully satisfying financial plan must also provide sufficient time and spending on those things that help you stay healthy and fit. Spending now in your 40s and 50s on gym memberships, enjoyable sports and physical activities, and preventive doctor visits will pay dividends for years to come. And the health of your mind and emotions relies on the proper balance of work and life, as well as hobbies and community or intellectual interests.

All three legs of the stool are critical to building a financial plan that will provide the flexibility you'll need as you transition toward retirement, or at least the late-life work that you choose to do.

Job Flexibility

Layoffs and job changes are a hard reality for today's 40- and 50-somethings. Building extra emergency cash into your plan, avoiding the urge to increase your housing and other fixed expenses up to the very top of your now-peak career earnings, and preparing emotionally for being replaceable at work will create more options within your plan and allow you to be flexible. Being hit by a layoff just as the kids are starting college can be stressful. As you hear of an impending layoff, or if you fear you might be next, prepare by reducing consumer debt, opening (but not using) a credit line on your home equity, and keeping auto and home repairs up to date so that they don't come due just when your budget is under pressure.

If you are laid off, avoid the temptation to jump back into the work force too quickly. Step back and examine your goals. Is there work that will bring you closer to achieving the three legs of the retirement stool? Is there a way to make the transition work for you in a way that gets you closer to your long-term goals?

Losing Parents, Partner, and Children

Losing people that you love is a difficult part of being in your 40s and 50s, and it unfortunately occurs more frequently with time. People under 40 experience it less often and people older than 60 have had a chance to think more about preparing for loss. People in their 40s and 50s are often losing very close loved ones for the first time and are not always prepared for it emotionally, let alone financially.

It's critical at your life stage that you discuss with parents and older loved ones the financial details that are important to end-of-life planning. Open discussions now can prevent the potentially disastrous lapses that leave estates in chaos for years, or cost heirs significant money or other family assets when all is finally put in order.

You should look closely at loved ones' estate plans. Do they have a will, a health care proxy, and a power-of-attorney document? Do they have, or do they need, a trust? Have they discussed their final wishes with you and others in the family? Review their life insurance to be sure it is enough and appropriately structured for their family.

Many people don't think of estate planning until they get married. Your single adult children need estate plans, too. Have your lawyer create a will, health care proxy, and power-of-attorney document for your children as soon as they are of age. Not having these documents could make helping them during a medical crisis especially difficult.

Now spend time thinking about these same things, but as they apply to you. It's important that your partner, children, grandchildren, and other loved ones understand how you're planning your finances to take into account the possibility that you might pass away unexpectedly. No one enjoys the thought of his own passing, but that's not a sufficient reason to ignore this critical planning step for the sake of your loved ones.

Technology Makes Planning Easier

Keeping track of income, expenses, account balances, and liabilities can take time if you don't have a process, and time is something you can't spare. Using the ever-growing technological resources at your fingertips is a key part of creating and implementing a strong financial plan. Many people hesitate to get online for fear their financial information might be stolen. In reality, the information is already available online and is no more or less accessible to thieves simply because you accessed it. Being a savvy Internet user and accessing online tools is the best way to protect yourself. Access to online tools and planning resources puts more power in your hands.

Auto-Pay and Direct Deposit

Setting your money baskets so they receive direct deposit—or, for the smaller baskets, electronic transfers—from your paycheck will save you time going to the bank and waiting for checks to clear. What's more, the ease of managing your money baskets will increase the likelihood that you'll continue to implement your plan and reach your goals. You may already have your paycheck direct-deposited into one or two checking or saving accounts. Take this a step further by calculating how much should be deposited in each money basket, set it up in your next family money meeting, then sit back and relax as the money baskets fund themselves. You can change the amount of your transfers any time, with usually only a day or two advance notice, so there's no fear that you might overcommit and not be able to reverse a transfer.

Take the direct deposit step one level further and arrange to have as many of your bills as possible paid via auto-pay through either your bank or your service provider's credit card payment system. You'll be sure the payment gets made on time—avoiding late fees and boosting your credit rating—and have fewer checks to write.

Online Banking

Fewer and fewer banks are charging for online banking, and virtually every bank does business on the web. In most cases, services are free for all or fees are waived for accounts with direct deposit or a minimum balance. Online banking makes tracking payments and deposits easier. And transactions usually carry more information if you are downloading them into bookkeeping software such as Quicken or MS Money. Online banking saves you the time you'd spend writing and mailing checks, and there are fewer checks to lose or be delayed by mail.

Web Resources

Information-gathering is made easier thanks to web resources called *consolidators*. These web services—such as Yodlee (*www.yodlee.com*) or similar services provided through your bank or investment company—maintain a list of your accounts, user names, and passwords and when prompted log in to your accounts and display balances and transaction information for as many accounts as you manage there. This could save you enormous amounts of time preparing for family money meetings and on routine account tracking, and can help in remembering your passwords.

Bookkeeping services such as Quicken, MS Money, and Mvelopes gather information from online and either downloads it into a program that sits on your computer or, in Mvelopes' case, stores it online for access from any computer.

Make sure your passwords are secure. Don't use familiar names or words that someone else could guess. Combine letters and numbers where possible. Don't keep the list of passwords in your wallet, on your computer monitor, or anyplace else where they could be discovered. Try basing them on personal events with the year of the event mixed or reversed.

Don't Expect Perfection

Any technology you use is only as good as your efforts to set it up and maintain it. Don't work without some form of backup and alternate ways to access your account information. Still, the ease of using online systems makes creating a computer-based plan and sharing it with family members much more efficient than having a paper-based system. As long as you remember to back up your information, technology is a tool worth using in your financial plan.

CHAPTER 3

Credit and Debt Management

Your credit report is the closest thing in real life to the permanent record your grade school teachers warned you about. How you manage your debt and the way it's reported on your credit report affects your loan rates, credit availability, job opportunities, utility account access, and, in many states, insurance rates. You can improve your credit score and start saving interest almost immediately by making small positive changes in your debt management.

Maintaining Good Credit

A big part of maintaining good credit is keeping your eye on the ball. Making payments on time, checking your credit report regularly, and fixing errors quickly are as important as balancing the type and amount of credit you carry.

How to Check, What to Look For

The three primary credit reporting companies—Experian, TransUnion, and Equifax—are required to give you a free copy of your report once every twelve months if you ask for it. Take best advantage of this by ordering your report from one company at a time and stagger your requests out across the year. This way you'll get a look at your file more frequently and will catch any wrong or fraudulent information more quickly. Reports are available through *www.annualcreditreport.com*.

As a memory hook, check your credit report through *www.annualcredit report.com* when you change your clocks in the spring and the fall and then also in January when you're gathering your information for your tax return. Request your free report from one of the three credit bureaus each time.

The report itself will guide you on how to correct errors. Check your personal profile, addresses, work history, accounts, and payment history. Look for anything that doesn't seem to be yours. Old accounts that suddenly have a payment due, incorrect addresses, payments that weren't credited, other social security numbers, or strange names connected to your account could indicate fraud.

The credit report is a list of all your accounts; while you have everything listed in one place, take the opportunity to clean up your record. Close all but two or three credit card accounts. (You'll need to pay them off first, of course.) Keep at least one long-held card because the length of your credit history matters. Minimize the credit lines on your credit cards and make sure they are correctly reported on your report. Credit card companies often increase your available credit line without your request. High credit card limits—even if you haven't borrowed against them—can reduce the amount a mortgage or auto loan lender may be willing to offer.

ALERT!

Don't close your credit card accounts or minimize your credit lines if you're working on paying your cards off. Keeping the ratio of the amount of credit used to the amount available is important. Also, banks recommend that you don't close cards too closely to applying for a loan. This extra activity could raise a red flag to a lender.

When Report Data Is Wrong

Maintaining a watch over your credit file is important because errors or fraud can have a dramatic negative effect on your financial health without your even being aware of it. Many credit card companies and some other lenders will increase the interest rates on accounts you have with them if a late or missed payment is reported on another account.

Credit reporting agencies want their information to be correct. Unfortunately, they are only information collectors; they rely on their sources of information—sources such as court filings, real estate records, reports from lending and credit card companies—to be accurate. A mistake in a record will show up in your report. The Fair Credit Reporting Act, available at *www .ftc.gov/credit*, outlines your rights and how to correct information. Each agency will have slightly different procedures for disputing information, but in general you'll need to contact the agency about the error. The agency will report the dispute to the original source of the information. The source must reply within thirty days and any incorrect or unverifiable information must be removed from the report. The key point to remember is that you need to identify the incorrect information in the first place.

Good and Bad Credit

The type of credit you have and how you use it is as important as making on-time payments and not maxing out your credit card limits. Check through your credit report and make sure you've considered the following:

- Keep your credit card balances low—account balances are reported to the agencies at the end of each month. Even if you're paying the balance off each month, if the balance on the statement is large it could negatively affect your score.
- Use an old card—accounts that you've stopped using will stop being updated at the credit agency. Pull out your old card now and then to keep its long history fresh in your report.
- Don't apply for new credit if you already have enough—avoid the temptation to chase cards with lower rates by opening new accounts. Each new account is a negative on your report.

If you'd rather use a credit card than a debit card for monthly expenses, you're not necessarily hurting your credit score, as long as you're keeping your balances low. Check your account online midmonth and pay down the balance before the statement closes. Use a couple of different accounts and avoid using more than 30 percent of the limit on each card.

Become Debt-Free on Your Own

Many people, even those struggling with midlife financial disasters and challenges such as divorce, widowhood, layoffs, and high college tuitions, are able to become debt-free on their own, without using a consolidator, credit counselor, or bankruptcy attorney. Going it alone might take a little more effort, but in the end your debt-management skills will be highly honed and your sense of accomplishment will keep you from getting back into bad debt again.

Plan and Priorities

First, you need to set your priorities; decide what your longer-term goals are. Focusing on longer-term goals such as retirement or starting a business will make the short-term pain of changing your lifestyle in order to pay down debt more tolerable. Most people who struggle with their monthly budget haven't clearly set longer-term goals. They make decisions in the present moment rather than setting aside resources for a greater, but longer-term, goal. Write down your long-term goals. These goals are the reason that wasting money on high loan interest and revolving debt is harmful to your financial security. Write them down and post them where you'll see them often—in your checkbook, on your computer desktop, or even on the bathroom mirror. When you're tired of the sacrifices you're making to pay down your debt, glance again at your goals and remember why you're doing it.

Next, set your sights on your accounts. Refer to your credit report and account statements and make a list of your accounts, their balances, interest rates, and minimum payments. Look back at your budget and decide which of your current expenses are of lower priority right now than the goals you listed for yourself. Add up the money per paycheck or per month that you can apply to debt principal. Get ready to apply 90 percent of that—call it your "pay-down fund"—to your debt and 10 percent to a new savings account. Not putting everything against the debt is part of the strategy for staying out of debt once everything is paid down. The 10 percent that you're planning to save is your personal "freedom fund" that assures you'll never be in debt again.

Pay all your accounts at their minimum payment except the "target" account. Target the smallest account first; pay the minimum balance plus the pay-down fund amount to that card until it's paid. When that card is paid, add its minimum payment to the pay-down fund, then set your sites on you next target, accounts that are over 50 percent of their credit limits. Pay them down in turn the same way you did the smallest account. You'll be debt-free before you know it and your growing freedom fund will keep you from using new debt when you encounter an emergency.

Negotiating with Companies

Contact the companies to which you owe money as soon as you expect you'll miss a payment or need to make a payment late. Many companies will work out a payment schedule with you if you're up-front about your situation. Too many people wait until they've missed a payment or two—or more—before calling their creditors. By that time, the negotiations are much more difficult.

If you're in the situation where you've waited to call your creditor and are now faced with the awful taped messages they play after you've entered your delinquent account number into their phone directory system, it is important to keep your cool. Don't get angry with the call-center representative. Tell them that you would like to negotiate a payment plan. If they can't negotiate, ask to be transferred to a supervisor.

FACT

Calling your mortgage company before you miss a payment won't hurt your credit score. If a financial emergency has happened and you think you'll miss or be late with a payment, call your mortgage company and let them know. It's easier to work with them early, while you are still up to date on payments.

Creditors do not have the right to call you at work or to threaten you in any way. If a creditor is calling you at work, tell them that they've dialed a work number and ask them to stop. (Review the checklist at *www.ftc.gov* for help managing creditor relationships.)

Focus on paying secured loans first. Loans that use your home or car as collateral are important to maintain. Keeping your utility payments up to date is more important than paying unsecured debt such as credit cards. As a last-ditch measure, many creditors—or collection agencies representing your creditor if the creditor has charged off the account and sold it to the collections agency—will accept a lump sum payment that's less than the total owed. Use this option as a last resort. Keep comprehensive records of all correspondence with the company—yes, don't negotiate by phone with a collection agency—and don't let on that you need to settle quickly. Time is on your side by the time you deal with the collection agency.

Out of Debt: Now Stay that Way

Now that everything is paid off, go back and look at your growing freedom fund savings account. All along, you have been putting 10 percent of your extra income per month into that account. It should have built up to a nice amount by now, something you can be proud of. Double check that you've budgeted so you're sure your fixed expense and variable expense baskets properly cover your expenses. Keep your freedom fund going into savings until you have accumulated an amount equal to between three and six months of total household expenses. When you reach that level, reduce the direct deposit to savings down to a comfortably small amount, say $50 or $100 a month. Now, with that small amount replenishing the account you can feel safe that if you need to use it for emergencies you won't fully deplete it and you won't sink back into debt.

Getting Help with Debt

In some cases, your debt will be too great to manage a pay-down program by yourself. If this is your situation, it's important to understand whom you are working with, what their motivations are, how they are compensated, and whether they are truly acting in your best interest.

Credit Counseling

Advisors experienced in credit counseling and budgeting often help you at no cost. They offer services focused on helping you work through a budget program and debt repayment. In many cases, these folks are honest and truly have your interests at heart. Be sure your counselor outlines any fees or other obligations on your part prior to engaging him. Also, be sure he is a member in good standing at one of the organizations listed in Appendix B.

If the counselor hesitates to answer any of your fee questions or seems to want to move too quickly to a debt management plan or debt consolidation, stop the relationship right away and either take on the program yourself or find a new counselor.

Debt Management Services

Under a debt management service, you pay the management company a preset amount and they, in turn, distribute your payments to your creditors. In theory, this sounds like the perfect solution. They deal with creditor phone calls, you just have one payment to make, you have a set schedule to follow, and you can see a light at the end of the debt-payment tunnel. Unfortunately, this is not always the case in practice. Many debt management services charge monthly fees that would be better off paid against the debt instead of to the service administrator. Payments can be lost or miscredited by the creditor receiving them. In some rare but frightening instances, disreputable debt management services have made no payments to creditors at all, and have simply made off with clients' money.

Will using a consumer credit counseling service hurt my credit rating?
Probably not more than making late payments or having credit card companies write off your accounts for nonpayment. Your credit rating will start to recover as soon as you start making on-time payments, whether or not you use a credit counseling service.

Deciding to use a debt management service doesn't mean you're off the hook for the payments. Keep a close watch on your statements. Make sure they reflect the payment agreed to through the debt management service. Make sure payments are credited on time, and be ready to send money quickly if they are not. Check in regularly with the management company and keep them up to date if your credit accounts are sold and the payment locations or amounts change.

Debt Consolidation

Consolidating your debt—paying down multiple balances with one account and then paying down that single account—can be convenient if you have many accounts. It can also save money if you have a way to transfer to tax-deductible debt such as a home equity loan. It's important to do a little bit of homework before deciding whether this is the best course.

First, have you adjusted your budget so new debt won't simply rebuild in the accounts you're paying off, leaving you in worse shape than you are now?

Second, can you really deduct the interest so it's cheaper than what you're paying now? Many people incorrectly think they can deduct 100 percent of their mortgage or equity-line interest. Income phase-outs and alternative minimum tax rules often reduce or eliminate this option. And don't forget that by converting the unsecured, high-interest debt into debt secured by your home, you may be putting your house in jeopardy.

Third, will consolidating save you money in the long run? Consolidating debt into a single loan with a lower interest rate or stretched over a longer pay-down schedule may make your minimum payments lower, but will it save you money? Lower interest might not help if the duration of the loan has been increased. You'll pay less interest per year, but adding years increases the total cost of the loan over time. Also, having one loan account full while other credit lines remain empty has a negative effect on your credit score. Creditors like to see good loan management. Moving to a consolidated loan or dumping all the balances into one credit card should be a last choice.

Where to Find Help

Check Appendix B for a list of organizations with advisor members that can help. Once you've decided what type of advice you need, it's important to interview two or three potential advisors. Don't be shy about asking tough questions. Before starting a relationship, you should know the advisor's experience with clients like you, how she is compensated, and what other alliances or incentives she may have. You should also feel that she is approachable and will be accessible if you have questions during the process. Her fees should be outlined in advance and should not be related to the amount of your debt or the type of debt.

Bankruptcy 101

Recent changes in bankruptcy laws have made this a less accessible option than in the past. Many bankruptcy filers are given a payment plan rather than the clean-slate debt liquidation they might have hoped for. There are, however, very difficult circumstances that can make bankruptcy the best option.

FACT

All bankruptcy filers are required to receive credit, budgeting, and debt counseling from approved sources. In the end, many filers are put on Chapter 13 repayment plans that last about five years. Bankruptcy stays on your credit report for ten years.

Rules

There are two types of personal bankruptcy, named after the chapters in the law that defines them. Chapter 7 bankruptcy establishes a clean slate by removing most of your debt so you can start over. Access to Chapter 7 requires that you pass a means test to see if you can afford to pay down more of your debt rather than get most debt forgiven. Under Chapter 13 bankruptcy, much of your debt remains to be paid back on a schedule.

Some debt that can't be discharged in bankruptcy includes:

- Overdue child support
- Alimony
- Some kinds of tax debts
- Student loans, unless repayment would be an "undue burden"
- Other debt that your creditor convinces the court should remain

Bankruptcy's Consequences

Filing for bankruptcy creates what's called an automatic stay that stops your creditors' efforts to collect your debts, can halt utility disconnections and wage garnishments, and will temporarily delay foreclosure. The filing stays on your credit report for up to ten years and can make getting a mortgage or other credit more difficult and more expensive in the form of higher interest. Still, if you have tried to negotiate with your creditors yourself, and you've tried to present a payment plan yourself without success, filing bankruptcy may be your only choice.

How to Find Help

Referrals are the best way to find a bankruptcy attorney or advisor. Talk to your financial advisor, lawyer, or accountant for a referral to a bankruptcy attorney. Check with your local Bar Association or with your employer if they offer a confidential employee assistance program. There is an additional list of resources in Appendix B.

The Liquidity Solution

No matter how diligently you plan, life seldom follows a script, and events frequently take you by surprise. Using credit to give you added liquidity—access to cash when you need it—is important.

Equity Lines, Loans, and Second Mortgages

Getting your home mortgage paid down is a great feeling, especially if you're in your 50s and looking forward to retirement. The irony of having equity in your home is that the value isn't easily accessible unless you sell the home. Make your equity accessible with an equity line of credit, but don't overdo it. Many banks will encourage you to take a line equal to the total equity in the house. That much liquidity isn't necessary, but having one or two years of salary available in the form of a home equity line can create great peace of mind.

An equity line of credit on your home is like a checkbook against your home's value. Lenders typically charge a variable interest rate that can increase or decrease your payments. Equity loans don't have the same borrowing and repayment flexibility as equity lines, but their fixed interest and payments might be a wiser option to fund specific home-improvement projects.

Borrowing from Retirement

Money has a powerful psychological hold on people. No matter how hard you try to think of your finances as cold, hard numbers, your feelings about your accounts will continue to affect your money decisions. Borrowing from retirement accounts is definitely one of these emotionally charged cases.

Your employer may allow you to borrow against your 401(k) or 403(b) plan. In some circumstances, you can withdraw from your individual retirement accounts (IRAs) or Roth IRAs without penalties. This can seem a ready source of money. But is it? Your retirement savings is there for you when you stop working. Once you've psychologically lowered the barrier to withdrawing your retirement nest egg before you retire, it will be difficult to stop. Don't start down this slippery slope unless you absolutely have to.

If you absolutely must access retirement money, remember that IRA withdrawals are usually taxable and carry a 10 percent penalty if withdrawn before age 59½ and not replaced (in full, including any tax withholding) within sixty days. If you're sure you'll have the cash to refund the loan within sixty days, this can be a helpful way to gain quick cash. Employer retirement-plan loans are usually payable over five years but become due quickly after leaving that employer and are taxable if not repaid.

Margin Loans

Your brokerage firm will offer you the option to borrow money against the value of the investments you hold in your account. In some cases, this can be a quick, helpful source of liquidity. Be careful to keep your loans well below the margin limits set by the brokerage firm. If you've maxed out your margin loans and the value of the securities in the account drop, your broker will issue a margin call. That means you'll need to add money to the account to restore the margin between what's owed and the value of the account. If you can't meet the margin call, your securities will be sold to cover the loan, possibly at a sizable loss.

Margin loans are not necessarily the lowest-interest loan available—you might pay lower interest on a personal loan from a bank, or on an equity loan. On the plus side, having margin capability on your brokerage account doesn't count toward your open credit line as an equity loan would, and once established, margin capital is available very quickly.

Credit Card Management

It's helpful to have a variety of credit card brands—MasterCard, Visa, and American Express—since you should limit yourself to only two or three cards once they are paid off. Some areas of the world have more merchants that only accept Visa cards while others prefer MasterCard. Other cards, such as American Express and Discover, offer services and perks to card holders. Some cards offer travel awards and points or credits toward future purchases.

Be sure that the credit card you use fits your needs. Don't pay extra for gold or platinum status if you don't use the related services. Don't pay the membership fee for travel awards if you never travel. If you do, be sure to use the miles or points quickly—the credit card doesn't pay you interest on them.

CHAPTER 4

Planning for the Unexpected

Insurance was created to share risk among all the members in a group, easing the burden on an individual when a loss occurs. It's impossible for an individual to plan and be ready for every possible emergency. Using the law of large numbers, insurance companies can predict how many people in a particular group will experience a loss. No one knows who those people are, but everyone can share the risk by paying premiums to a pool that covers the loss of those few who have one.

4

Life Insurance: Something for Everyone

Life insurance replaces the financial contribution made by a person who has died unexpectedly. Life insurance is not meant to be a lottery windfall to your family; it's meant to let your beneficiaries carry on with their lives once you're gone. That means you should carry coverage on yourself if others rely on you, and carry coverage on anyone you rely on. Important people to consider could be your partner, spouse, parent, child, or business associate. Their financial contribution can come in a variety of forms: their salary contributed to your joint family income, their time contributed to raising your kids or caring for your parents, or their efforts were important to the success of your business, which could suffer from their loss.

ALERT!

Many employers offer group life insurance, but you need to buy your own policy as well. Employer-provided coverage ends when your job ends, but your need for life insurance might not. Don't take a chance of dying between jobs, leaving your beneficiaries unprotected. Carry your own policy in addition to your group coverage.

Basic Types

Life insurance comes in the form of either term or permanent insurance. Term insurance offers coverage for a limited period of time. Permanent insurance has an extra internal investment component that potentially builds value to support the policy for an indefinite length of time.

Term insurance is commonly named for the length of time it will be in force. Annual renewable term, or ART, has a premium that starts low but increases as it renews every year. Ten-, twenty-, or twenty-five-year level term policies have premiums that start higher than ART, but then stay level for ten, twenty, or twenty-five years, at which point the policy ends. If you die beyond the coverage period, no payment will be made. Group term insurance is provided by many employers and has a premium that increases every year.

Permanent insurance policies feature an extra savings component that is invested and whose value can be called upon to cover the cost of the policy as you age. Whole life insurance is invested with the insurance company, which makes guarantees about the policy's performance. Universal life insurance policies invest the premiums, and returns on those investments help offset future premiums. Variable life policies invest premiums in stocks and bonds and, as with universal life policies, the returns help offset premium costs.

QUESTION?

My parents bought a whole life policy for me when I was young. Should I cancel the policy and just carry term insurance now?
If the policy is old enough and written by a strongly rated company, it may be supporting itself on dividends and you may not need to even pay premiums to keep it active. Keep the policy and reduce the amount of other term policies by the amount this policy would pay.

Who Needs It?

The death benefit, of course, is the most important feature of a life insurance policy, especially in your 40s and 50s. Life insurance costs more as you get older; focus on purchasing the death benefit you need in a good, inexpensive term life policy, and don't get wrapped up in an expensive and difficult-to-change permanent policy.

Because life insurance premiums are based on your age when you apply, minimize the chance you'll need to apply again by planning ahead. Make sure the term you buy is long enough to cover your needs. For example, the term must include the time it will take your kids to grow to independence, the time it will take to pay off your mortgage or accumulate the retirement nest egg, or the time you'll be relied upon by an aging parent.

FACT

Permanent life insurance is called for in some complex estate or business applications. Your estate or business attorney can help you decide if your situation warrants using this product. Be sure you understand what you're buying by having an independent insurance advisor review your plan.

Make sure you buy enough death benefit by adding up the financial contribution—salary and expenses they're paying—of the person you're insuring. In most cases, you'll need four or five times her annual earnings.

What to Look For

Make sure you pay for enough death benefit, but don't overspend. Compare the total cost of annual renewable and level term over the time you'll need the policy. If you're unsure, buy a longer term and plan to cancel it if the need ends early.

Buy from a strong insurance company. Your death benefit is only as safe as the strength of the insurance company. Stay with companies who are rated "superior" or "excellent" by Moody's, A.M. Best, Weiss, or Standard & Poor's.

Life insurance should be a very straightforward financial product. It pays a death benefit if you die during the time the policy exists. Don't buy a product you don't understand.

The death benefit of life insurance isn't taxable to your beneficiaries, but if you own your policy yourself it may be taxable to your estate. Avoid this costly penalty by having your estate planning attorney guide you on how to structure ownership of your policy. You may need to assign ownership to another individual or a trust.

Estate Planning and Beneficiaries

Life insurance benefits pass to the beneficiaries listed in the policy, regardless of what your will says. Ask your estate attorney for language to use in the policy if your young children will be the beneficiaries. Review your beneficiary designation if your life changes, especially if you get married or are divorced or widowed.

Health Coverage: Don't Leave Home Without It

Unexpected medical expenses can destroy your financial security. People who are between jobs or working for a small company often go without coverage. But medical costs are not something you can delay until you can afford them. It's critical to have good coverage that fits into your plan, but doesn't break the bank.

How to Compare Plans

Medical insurance manages health care expenses by capping the amount you'll pay per year. Instead of facing unknown and potentially catastrophic medical costs, your expenses are limited to your policy premiums, copayments, deductible, and annual out-of-pocket cost. You pay copayments for each doctor visit or service. Your deductible and annual out-of-pocket cost limits the amount you'll pay beyond the copays. Some policies exclude some expenses or have a gap in coverage at certain expense levels that add to your cost. Be sure your policy has an unlimited lifetime benefit to protect against the cost of a long, expensive illness.

Make a comparison chart by listing last year's medical costs and activities and the total amount you spent. Compare new policies by making a hypothetical chart of what your costs would have been under that policy. Don't just look for the lowest premium.

As with any insurance coverage, health insurance is only as reliable as the company that issues it. Look for strong ratings from A.M. Best and the other rating companies, and check with your state insurance commissioner's office to be sure your company is in good standing.

With Employer Plans and Without

If your employer offers health insurance coverage, you'll be able to enroll during their annual enrollment period or when you have a life-changing event such as divorce, marriage, or a new child. Employers without plans will often contribute toward the coverage you buy on your own. Be sure to check with your state to see if you're eligible for premium assistance in this case.

Many insurers have dropped their plans for couples with no children, called 1+1 plans, in favor of individual and family plans. In this case, it's often cheaper for two-person families to buy two separate individual policies rather than paying extra for a family plan, which has been priced to include medical care for children.

In Retirement

Some companies and many states offer health coverage to their retirees, but most people rely on purchasing federally funded Medicare insurance directly. Workers who worked under the federal system for ten years and their spouses, widows, or widowers are eligible for Medicare starting at age 65. Medicare has three parts. Part A covers hospital expenses, and the premiums are part of your social security benefit. Part B covers regular medical expenses. Part C covers prescriptions. If you're enrolled in parts B and C, the premiums are deducted from your social security benefit check.

To minimize coverage gaps and make management easier, retirees often favor plans that include all three coverages in one policy. Senior health management plans are offered by most of the nationwide carriers and offer coordinated benefits through one premium payment.

For Kids in College

Children in college and under the age of 23 can often be carried on their parents' health plan. Many colleges also offer coverage, and if your student is working, his employer may provide plans as well. If your student doesn't start working immediately after graduation, he may lose coverage. Check with your state for young adult plans. And check with your human resources department; your child may also be eligible for COBRA under your employer's plan because of his loss of dependent status.

Self-Employed and Recently Unemployed

COBRA (the federal Consolidated Omnibus Budget Reconciliation Act of 1985) coverage is required if your employer has twenty or more employees. If you're laid off or voluntarily leave your employer, you can continue health coverage under COBRA at your own expense for up to eighteen months.

If you're self-employed, you have access to discounted group coverage through industry associations and chambers of commerce. You don't need to be running a company to be self-employed. As soon as someone has paid you for services outside of your employer, often called "being paid on a 1099" after the tax form used to report this income, you're self-employed and eligible for benefits through the associations.

States are beginning to require residents to carry health insurance coverage and some forbid insurers from denying coverage to people with pre-existing conditions. In this case, the state will have information on coverages available to individuals.

Long-Term Care Insurance: Should You Self-Insure?

Long-term care insurance is meant to cover the cost of care that Medicare doesn't cover. Medicare covers hospitalization, medical costs related to making you well again, and prescriptions. But what if you become chronically ill and need quality-of-life care? Many 40- and 50-somethings find themselves considering long-term care insurance policies—often called "nursing home insurance"—for themselves and their parents.

Should You Buy?

The cost of long-term care, or LTC, at home or in a nursing care facility can easily run into the tens of thousands of dollars a year. LTC insurance gives you a pool of money beyond your own assets to pay for this care. If you have minimal assets, your state has a program under Medicaid to pay for your care.

With policies costing thousands of dollars per year, LTC insurance is not cheap and there's no guarantee you'll ever be ill enough to use the coverage. Consider a policy if you're concerned about supplementing your care budget and you're sure you can afford the premiums, and any premium increases, for the rest of your life. LTC insurance is like auto or home insurance; you pay annually for the coverage you'll receive the next year, whether or not you have a claim. If you don't think you can afford the premiums, it may be better to plan on using your own assets for care. Buying a policy you keep only a few years could be a waste of money.

What to Look For

Shopping for LTC insurance in your 40s or 50s is ideal because insurability and premiums are based on health and age. Policies pay benefits when you can't perform a number of specific "activities of daily living," or ADLs, such as getting out of bed, bathing, and eating. Look for policies that provide benefits after the loss of only two out of six ADLs and define loss as needing standby or hands-on assistance because of cognitive or physical disability.

It's important to apply for LTC insurance before you've had a health problem. Insurance companies have very strict underwriting guidelines for LTC coverage. If you want coverage, apply while you're healthy to ensure lower premiums and increase your chances of being accepted.

Other important features are:

- Inflation protection so that policy benefits grow over time.
- A ninety- or 180-day waiting period. You pay for care during that time, but the longer waiting period keeps the premium down.
- Underwritten by a large, well-known company with excellent ratings. The number of insurers offering LTC insurance has reduced dramatically. Don't risk being with a lesser company and having your policy sold or premium increased.
- Policy qualified under the 1996 Health Insurance Portability and Accountability Act (HIPAA) to reap the full potential tax benefits on premiums and benefits.

Special Circumstances

If you're concerned about your parents having money to pay for their choice of care, consider purchasing LTC insurance for them. This extra coverage may give you peace of mind if you don't live nearby and you're anticipating home health care or assisted living expenses. Remember, LTC insurance has tough underwriting standards; don't delay discussing coverage with your parents until after someone has already become ill.

Many companies offer group LTC insurance policies to employees. The policies aren't endorsed by the employer and, although they may seem less expensive, they often have more restrictive benefits. Still, group policies often have lighter underwriting standards and may be a good option if your health will make it difficult to get a policy privately.

Disability Insurance

Your ability to show up for work and earn a paycheck is easily your biggest asset. Disability insurance makes sure you have money available to cover expenses if that asset suddenly goes away when you become injured or sick enough that you can't work.

What to Look For

Disability insurance comes in two varieties, short term and long term. Short-term disability insurance kicks in as soon as you're disabled and continues for up to sixty or ninety days, depending on the terms of the policy. This coverage provides a percentage of your income for the length dictated in the policy. You can save paying premiums on a short-term disability policy by using your savings to self-insure. Be sure you always have enough emergency cash to cover expenses between the end of short-term disability benefits and the beginning of your long-term disability benefits, usually ninety or 180 days. You'll save premium expenses on your long-term disability if you can self-insure to cover a 180-day waiting period.

Long-term disability can pay benefits for three or five years, or even until you are age 65. Be sure the insurer has high ratings and is a well-known company. Don't cut corners to save on premiums; your benefit is only as good as the strength of the insurance company.

Employer Plans or Private

Most large, and some smaller, employers offer disability coverage as an employee benefit. Premiums are generally reasonable, and in many cases short-term disability coverage is free to the employee. Some employers will give you the option to pay your long-term disability premiums yourself. Taking advantage of this will make your benefits tax-free. If your employer pays the premiums, your disability benefits will be taxable.

If your employer doesn't offer a plan or if your current employer has a plan but many employers in your industry do not, consider buying a plan yourself privately. Premiums are based on age, so doing this now rather than waiting could be smart. You don't need to buy coverage for your whole income. If you can live on less than you make, but don't quite have the assets to retire today, consider buying enough coverage to keep you afloat if the worst happens. You can save on premium costs by limiting the benefit period to five years, extending the waiting period to 180 days, and forgoing the inflation rider.

FACT

Workers' Compensation is a government disability benefit that replaces a part of your income if you're hurt on the job. Disability insurance pays whether or not your injury is job related. Many self-employed people are eligible to opt out of the Workers' Compensation pool. If you have done this, it's even more important to carry private disability insurance.

Self-Employed

Once you've been self-employed for two years, with consistent income on your tax return, insurance companies will consider you for disability coverage. You don't need to buy the maximum benefit they offer. Consider saving on premiums with a policy that covers the minimum you need for personal expenses. Think about whether your business would continue if you were disabled. Do you have an employee who could take over? Would you instead change industries and work at something different if you were disabled? A policy with a high benefit for just five years might help make a transition to a new vocation while saving on premium expenses. If you have an employee who could help with your business, buying a policy that pays to age 65 but that has a longer waiting period may be a better choice.

Protect Your Hearth and Home

Too many people take their homeowner's insurance too lightly. They started the policy a few years ago when they bought their house. They reviewed it two years ago when they refinanced, and they haven't thought about it since. Housing replacement values grow over time, and you accumulate things that need to be insured. An annual review of your homeowner's policy—or renter's policy if you're renting—is very important.

Important Features

Your homeowner's coverage is meant to reimburse for the value of or make repairs to your home if something happens. This may mean reimbursing you for the cost of repairing damage after a fire or other disaster. It also may mean paying to replace articles that were lost from inside your home. Imagine the replacement cost of the things you cherish in your home. Insurance brings you back to where you were before the disaster.

If you live in a home with special construction or that has appreciated significantly in value, ask about replacement cost coverage. If you have special electronics, jewelry, or other expensive luxury items that you would want to replace if they were stolen or destroyed, schedule them with special coverage on the policy. Ask for identity theft resolution insurance—a small rider that is usually provided for free and that covers the costs of working through an identity theft situation.

QUESTION?

I'm living in an apartment while I'm separated from my spouse. All my valuable belongings are still back at my house. Do I need renter's insurance, too?
Yes, you do. Be sure to coordinate with your homeowner's insurance agent. You may be eligible for a multiple policy discount.

Be sure your policy covers your kids' things at the dorm or in the apartment they're renting. Depending on the circumstances, you many need an additional policy for them. Make sure your parents are covered in the in-law apartment, too. If they aren't, they'll need separate coverage as well.

Be sure that you can talk to your agent, and that she is available and offers a high level of service, before you need her for a claim. Many agents specialize in several lines of coverage. Work with an agent that focuses on home, auto, and business to be sure you get the best service on your home coverage.

Money-Saving Tips

Making a home insurance claim for under $1,000 can cost you increased premiums in the future. Your emergency fund, not your homeowner's or renter's coverage, should be used for emergencies that cost $1,000 or less. Increase your deductible to $1,000 so that you're not paying for this coverage that you won't use.

Ask about discounts for having multiple policies through the same agent. Also ask for smoke alarm, burglar alarm, and nonsmoking household discounts, and upgraded utilities discounts, if they apply. Homeowner's coverage includes liability protection if someone is hurt on your property.

Home Office Considerations

Homeowner's insurance only covers personal activities. If your friend comes over for dinner and trips and hurts himself on the stairs, your homeowner's liability coverage will cover the damages. If the same friend comes over for a purpose related to your business and falls on the same stairs, your homeowner's policy may not cover it. If you have an office in your home, be sure you ask about special business-purpose coverage for liability and the loss of business-related items in your office.

Auto Coverage

In many states, auto insurance is mandatory and is a condition of your auto registration—if you don't have insurance coverage, you're not registered, and if you're not registered, you don't have insurance coverage. Few people forget to insure their cars, but many people spend too much or carry too little insurance.

Important Features

Auto policies have a collision component that pays for damage to your car. Collision isn't required unless you're financing the car and coverage is required by your lender, but it is a good idea if your car is new or expensive. Most states require a minimum amount of liability insurance to pay for repairs to the other car involved in an accident. Comprehensive coverage pays for damage caused by things other than a vehicle accident, such as fallen tree limbs, fire, and theft. Even if auto insurance is required in your state, you may still be involved in an accident with an uninsured or underinsured driver. Carrying uninsured and underinsured motorist coverage will protect you in this case. Your agent will guide you on the minimum coverages required or recommended in your area, based on your circumstances.

Your insurance company is only required to pay up to the book value—the value on the used-car market—of your car in a loss or damage situation. If you're leasing or financing, consider buying gap insurance to cover the difference between the lease or loan amount and the car's value. Your car might be losing value due to age or wear faster than you are paying down the loan or lease.

Money-Saving Tips

If your car is older than seven years, you may be paying for collision coverage when you don't need it. Increase your deductible to $1,000 and you'll save, especially if you live in a city or drive a car that's easily damaged or a popular theft target.

Make sure you're getting your multiple policy, good driver, and alarm/antitheft discounts if they apply.

Talk to your agent if you have teenagers driving your car. It may be less expensive to list them as primary drivers on a lower-value car and to carry less coverage on that car than you do on yours.

Small-Business Tips

If you drive a lot for your business, be sure your agent knows it. If your accident occurs on your way to a sales presentation or to meet a client, your auto policy might not cover damages. Tell your agent if you lend your car to employees for errands or deliveries. Depending on the frequency of these trips, you may need to reregister your vehicle as commercial in order to have proper coverage.

Umbrella Liability

Your auto and homeowner's or renter's policies will have a base amount of liability insurance included. Umbrella liability adds to that basic coverage with an additional pure liability amount.

You may need to increase the liability on your auto and homeowner's policies so they coordinate with your umbrella coverage. This will increase the cost of adding umbrella liability to your policies but can be necessary to ensure adequate coverage.

Why Bother?

Most home or auto policies have $300,000 or even $500,000 of liability coverage. If you're sued for an amount beyond that, your assets and future income could be fair game in a damages award. The chances of this happening are slim, but the result would be devastating. This is exactly the kind of risk you should transfer to an insurance company in the form of an umbrella liability policy. Why not pay a little money—$200 per year or so in most cases—for an additional $1 million of coverage?

How Much to Buy

Most people are fine with $1 million in umbrella liability coverage. But if your income is upward of $200,000 a year and you have assets over $1 million, you should consider $2 million in coverage or more.

Be sure the coverage includes your children's cars and apartments or make sure that they have coverage of their own. And double check your parents' coverage if they are still driving.

Do You Need Other Liability Coverage?

If you run a business or invest as a partner, sit on a board, participate in sports, or let your employees or household help use your car as part of their job, you should be aware of your liability. Check with your agent annually and outline with them all the areas you are involved in. There is often liability exposure you're unaware of.

CHAPTER 5

Retirement Income to Fulfill Your Dreams

It's never too late to start planning for life after work. In fact, your ideas of retirement are probably much clearer now than they were when you were in your 20s and 30s. You may want to retire early and volunteer or work part time, you may want to change careers and work longer, or you may want to build your nest egg so you can decide later when you'll quit working. Use this clarity to your advantage, and no matter how far behind in your planning you may feel, you'll be caught up in no time.

Career Versus Retirement Lifestyles

As you work toward your peak career years, your job offers structure to your life. An important part of retirement planning is deciding what you want your days to look like once that structure changes. Creating an achievable goal is about building a nest egg to support you, but also about planning hobbies and building interests around what you would like to do after you retire.

Does Your Current Career Support Your Retirement Goal?

Too many people don't spend enough time thinking about what they would like their retirement lifestyle to look like. Start developing your retirement goal by making a list of your priorities.

Answer questions such as:

- What sort of activities and interests do you want to spend your days involved in?
- What region and kind of home do you want to live in?
- What additional hobbies or activities would you like to cultivate that you don't have time for now?
- What transitions or changes do you foresee during your retirement years? After all, your retirement could last twenty to thirty years or more. How do you see your life changing over that time?

Write your answers down and read through them periodically. Allow your ideas to change over time.

Plan to leave yourself options when you retire from your current job. Be sure the skills you'll have will keep you busy with part-time work, volunteering, or hobbies. Plan for a tax-efficient nest egg that includes investments in retirement accounts such as IRAs and 401(k)s, as well as investments outside of these plans. Spend money on your health now to improve your quality of life and reduce the cost of health care later.

QUESTION?

Thinking of life after work really stresses me out. I'm sure I'm behind in my savings. How can I catch up?
First, don't stress. You start getting on track the minute you start thinking and planning. Set up your accounts. Let yourself dream. Define your goals and you'll be surprised how quickly you feel more in control.

Planning to Work into Your 70s

Many people plan to work into their 70s at their current job or at a different one. This may be a lifestyle choice for some, and for others it's a way to avoid the pain of saving now for retirement. After all, if you earn money into your 70s your nest egg can be smaller because it won't have to support you as long.

Be realistic about your health and the industry you're working in if you're planning to work into your 70s. Realize that you may want to work, but your health or age discrimination in your industry might prevent you. Whether or not you're planning to work into your 70s, it's better to plan your savings so that you don't absolutely need to work much past age 65 or 67.

FACT

Retirement accounts are accounts with tax law restrictions on making withdrawals before age 59½. Examples are IRAs, 401(k)s, and 403(b)s. Nonretirement accounts don't have these tax law restrictions; money can be withdrawn from them at any time. Examples of these are your individual, joint, and trust accounts.

Tapping Home Equity

For many people, their home is their biggest asset. This can present problems in retirement because home equity can only be tapped by borrowing against that equity—and incurring additional interest expenses— or by selling the house. Planning to sell is fine if you've set that goal and psychologically have come to grips with it, but don't paint yourself into a corner by building home equity at the exclusion of all else.

Set up your plan so that you're paying down the mortgage as well as building investments in retirement accounts and nonretirement accounts.

Retiring Early into Part-Time Employment

Retiring early is an option if you pay close attention to your budget and investments. Retiring gives you fewer years to build your nest egg and increases the number of years you'll spend in retirement. Tax laws, pensions, and social security also need a closer look if early retirement is in your future.

Investment Considerations

Retirement is a transition, not a finish line. Life after retirement is very similar to life before it; you'll have monthly bills, car payments, and other regular expenses. The economy and the stock market will continue to go through the same cycles they do now. Retirees often think differently about these realities because they are relying on their investments to support them, not their job. Consider how economic fluctuations, and the continuing pressure of day-to-day finances, will affect your attitude in retirement, then plan your investments around your concerns.

Early retirement means inflation will have longer to act on your expenses. Be sure your portfolio continues to hold stock investments even after you stop working. A mix of bonds and fixed-income investments that pay interest can reduce the volatility of your accounts. Many investment companies have tools and calculators to help you decide how much of each to hold.

Don't let your feelings about the current economic or political environment color your entire retirement plan. Economics and politics work in cycles. If you are retired for thirty years, you will go through many of these cycles—good and bad. Construct a sound plan, and then stick with it.

Tax Planning

Retirement accounts such as IRAs and 401k(s) have rules that penalize you for withdrawing money before age 59½. If you retire early, you can use a scheme called "substantially equal payments" to withdraw income from the accounts before that age without penalty. The calculations for this are very precise and the penalties high if you make a mistake and withdraw too much or too little. Be sure to consult a tax professional for help if you decide this is a good option for you.

Make your portfolio more tax efficient by concentrating your income-generating investments—such as bonds and fixed-income investments—inside your retirement plans and your stock investments in taxable accounts outside retirement plans. Stock dividends and capital gains are taxed at a lower rate than interest income. Stock investments are also more volatile than bond investments, and if they are in taxable accounts you can take advantage of this using a strategy called "harvesting gains." By selling equal amounts of investments that have gained and lost value, tax can be reduced because capital gains and losses cancel each other out.

FACT

Take advantage of tax laws that let you cancel out taxes on investments sold at a profit by also selling investments that have lost money. This strategy is called harvesting gains. Realize gains or losses by selling an investment; capital gains can be reduced by the amount of capital losses you realize in the same year.

Pensions and Social Security

Many pensions will allow you to start drawing before age 60 if you retire, but the benefit is often reduced. Pay close attention to how early retirement affects your pension benefit. Most pensions increase significantly in the last few years you work. Be sure you calculate the benefits you're losing if you retire early.

ALERT!

If you're eligible for a state pension, your social security may be reduced under a rule called the "windfall" provision. Check with your retirement benefits coordinator at work, or online at *www.ssa.gov* for details. If you worked under social security for a long time before moving to the state job, you might be eligible to collect from both.

Federal social security benefits are not available to you until age 62. If you retire before then, plan on making extra withdrawals from your nest egg to cover expenses until then. In most cases, it's best to start drawing social security as soon as you're eligible, unless you're working part time. Social security benefits are reduced if you are under age 65 and earning an income. Once you're age 65, you can collect social security and still work without reducing the benefit.

Domestic Relations

Many couples experience stress when one or both retire and the familiar habits are disrupted. Start thinking now about how your retirement lifestyle will affect your partner. Talk about how your lifestyles will stay the same or alter. Decide whether you'll both retire at the same time or at different times.

How Will Your Work Lifestyles Mesh?

Whether your partner has been home while you've worked or whether you're both working, you've created certain territorial feelings and habits related to your current lifestyle. As part of your retirement planning, talk together about how you both expect your lifestyle to change. The more you can talk together about your feelings about retirement, the better. Minimize surprises by frankly sharing your goals, and plan together for shared time and time apart.

The Age Differential

Being twelve or more years apart in age can add a few challenges to your retirement plan. People often prefer to retire together, and if this is the case with you, the younger partner may need to plan for an early retirement. This dramatically increases the necessary nest egg. If you're the younger partner and you want to keep working after your partner retires, this may affect where you live during that time and might limit access to home equity as an income source.

Retirement planning can be stressful, especially if you and your partner have different ideas of what you'd like to do or how much you'd like to spend. A disinterested third party such as a financial planner, marriage counselor, or life coach can help mediate your discussions.

Pay close attention to medical insurance and estate planning. The younger partner may need to accept the fact that he may live the last years of their retirement alone. Be sure you've planned for long-term care expenses so that you're not left with a nest egg decimated by the medical bills of the older partner. If you're not married, check your will and estate plan to be sure assets pass to support the younger partner.

Easy Budget Advice

Deciding how much you might want to spend in retirement can be difficult. Establish a baseline now so you can plan your savings targets and then refine the budget as you go along.

Start your plan with the budget you need now to support your current lifestyle. Look through the list and decide which items will definitely not be there in retirement. These might include children's expenses, such as day care, clothing, school and sports fees, and college tuition. Also probably gone by retirement will be college savings, and of course your investments toward retirement itself.

Only delete the expenses that are clearly not going to be there in retirement. Don't try to estimate how much the grocery bill will go down without the kids, how much you'll save on gas by not commuting, or what you'll save on clothing or dry cleaning by not having to go to the office. These smaller expenses will be replaced by other, similar expenses in retirement. Remember, the reason you're projecting your budget now is to know how to prepare for retirement. If you shortchange yourself by shooting for too low a goal, you'll be disappointed by how much you can spend when you retire.

The Cost of Fun

Now that you have the basics considered, add in the extra costs of things you'd like to have money for. This might include additional travel and hobby costs that you don't pay now. If your hobby could make you money, avoid the temptation to overestimate what you could earn. It's better for planning purposes to be conservative and figure that the hobby will cost more than it earns.

Self-Employment Income

Self-employment income is a great way to supplement your retirement savings. But if you have never worked for yourself, be careful of being overly optimistic about what you'll earn. Unless you're a seasoned self-employed person and can use past experience as a guide to what you can earn, it's better to plan for no income and then use any income you might earn to enjoy a little extra spending in retirement.

Self-employment income is taxed more highly than regular job income because you are both employer and employee. As such, you have to pay both sides' share of the payroll taxes. A good rule of thumb is to set aside 30 percent of whatever you make for income taxes.

Expenses Change with Time

Some people expect to have higher expenses in the beginning of retirement and lower expenses later on. They reason that there will be more things they want to do and places they want to explore while they're younger. Other people look ahead to how their retirement will look and decide their expenses will stay pretty level. Deciding how you might want to live in retirement and then accounting for health costs, moving to another home, and the finances of your family are important considerations.

Level Versus Front-Loaded Retirement

Instead of planning for high expenses at the beginning of retirement to cover those things you always wanted to do, plan your living expenses without those extra expenses and then use a separate savings plan for the extras. It's hard to reduce your lifestyle once you've grown accustomed to a certain way of living. By planning your base level of spending and then creating savings baskets for the extras—such as big trips or sizable purchases such as a boat or RV—you'll avoid the temptation to overspend.

Map out the extra things you'd like to do. Calculate the savings needed to accomplish them using one of the calculators listed in the resources section of the book, and start saving using your money baskets.

Planning for Increasing Health-Related Spending

One of the reasons to be careful about underestimating your income need in retirement is the vast unknown cost of health care. Right now your employer may be paying your premiums, but in retirement you'll be paying them. Medicare is available at age 65, and many people currently have access to retiree health benefits through their employer. Right now, retirees covered by Medicare can pay from $150 to $400 each in premiums for various all-inclusive HMO-style plans. Budget at least that much into your retirement plan.

Where You'll Live

You might be among the many people who prefer to retire in the same place you're living and working now. Being close to family, friends, and familiar support systems are important, after all. Or you might be among those looking forward to a warmer climate or the opportunity to move either into a city or out into the suburbs or the country. It's important to allow some flexibility in your thinking about where you plan to live. If you've moved a lot while you've been working, don't expect that you'll change in retirement and want to stay in one place. If you've lived a long time in the same place, allow for the desire to move either for a change of climate and lifestyle or to be closer to children and grandchildren.

Now is not the time to overinvest in your housing. If you're now in your highest-earning years and your kids have left home, avoid the temptation to demonstrate your new wealth by going overboard by redoing your home. Be careful to calculate whether you'll be able to recoup your investment in a home project before you retire and how the added maintenance expense and real estate taxes will affect your budget. If the kids are grown, now is the time to be sure you've completed any deferred home-maintenance projects and that your house is reasonably up to date with current styles.

ALERT!

Your kids will want to visit, but they don't have to stay with you. Don't jeopardize your retirement nest egg by planning a big addition so you have room to have the kids back home. Pay for a hotel when they come. You all need your privacy and you need to save on the added taxes and maintenance of a bigger house.

If you think you might want to live in another city, region, or even country, start visiting now. Plan vacations in the areas you might want to live in. Make these trips off-season—both to save money and to see what they're like in their least desirable seasons. Pay close attention to costs of living while you're there so you can refine your retirement income goals.

Making Reasonable Assumptions

Most retirement calculators will suggest assumptions to use in your plan. These usually cover social security income, investment returns, inflation, and how long you'll live. It's not always best to take the default value they suggest without considering how it fits your personal situation.

Social Security and Longevity

Social security is not going away any time soon. Just think of how the economy would suffer if social security benefits suddenly stopped. Social security won't disappear, but it will change. These changes might be reflected as reduced cost-of-living increases on benefits, higher income taxes on benefits, or older eligibility ages. It's impossible to project how this will affect your plan, as shifting political winds can't be predicted. That's all the more reason to be sure you don't underestimate your need for retirement income.

Once a year, three months before your birth month, you should receive a social security statement in the mail. If you don't, go to *www.ssa.gov* and order a statement. Be sure the statement accurately reflects your past wages and that your personal information is correct. There's help on how to make corrections included in the statement.

Projecting that you'll live at least until age 95 in your retirement plan will protect your plan against low social security cost-of-living increases and higher tax rates. Assuming longer life will also reduce the chance that you'll outlive your money or be worried that you will.

Investment Growth and Inflation

At the time this book was being written stock investments have done very well and inflation has been low. Some calculators will suggest using a 9 percent or 10 percent annual rate of return on your stock investment accounts and factor in 3 percent inflation. Here's a case where being conservative is the wisest course. It's better to project a lower investment return of 6 percent or 7 percent, and slightly higher inflation, about 4 percent to 4.5 percent. Remember that individual investors don't always do as well as the market averages. Being careful not to over-rely on portfolio growth will help make sure that you are saving enough toward your plan now.

Planning with Younger Children

If your kids are still young, you have the added challenge of trying to provide for them while still saving for your own secure retirement. Balance your care for your children with the importance of your retirement, and don't overprovide for them at the expense of exposing yourself to decades of underfunded and insecure retirement.

Savings Plan and Budget Adjustments

If your kids are still young, you'll need to stretch your plan a little to make sure they have security until they're adults. Beyond ensuring that your life and disability insurance will protect them until they're through college, avoid the temptation to overspend for their benefit. If these are your high earning years, the temptation can be to indulge your kids with this extra income. If you're close to retirement, this can be particularly dangerous because it sets up expectations in them that the spending will continue. Err on the safe side and keep their lifestyles modest, even if you could afford to spoil them. Invest the money, and if it turns out you don't need it, you can help them out later.

Are your kids independent or at least well on their way? Helping to make sure they're self-supporting well before you retire will minimize the number of emergencies you could have to help them with after you're retired and are on a fixed income.

Planning College and Retirement Concurrently

The biggest adjustment you can make to your plan if your kids are young is to plan to retire after they've finished college. Getting them through school can help minimize the unexpected financial surprises that can happen when they are younger. Minimize the amount of debt you take in your name for their college. They are young—they have more time than you to deal with debt, and better earning potential than you do if you're getting ready to retire. Remember the risk you face of age discrimination; avoid the temptation to plan extra work years to make up for missed retirement savings. That option may not be one for which your employer can be relied upon.

Finding Real-World and Online Advice

Finding a professional to review your retirement plan is important. You don't need to spend a lot or even enter into a long-term relationship with an advisor. This relationship could be pivotal; you can't exactly go back and redo your plan once you've reached retirement and discover that you don't have enough money to make your plan work. Talk to your friends or check with the associations in Appendix B for lists of professionals.

How Different Advisors Work

Advisors can be categorized by how they are compensated: commissioned, fee based, and fee only. Commissioned advisors won't bill you directly for services. They receive commissions from the financial products you buy. This might be helpful if you need to buy insurance or another product, but it would be difficult for a commissioned advisor to spend time giving you an independent opinion of your retirement plan if you needed only advice, not their product.

Fee-based advisors typically focus on investments. They manage your accounts and charge you an assets-under-management, or AUM, fee. The AUM fee is a percentage of the assets they are managing, usually 0.5 percent to 2 percent. Like the commission advisor, this AUM arrangement can be helpful if you have a large portfolio to manage and don't want to do it yourself. A fee-based advisor may be able to offer retirement planning if you have a minimum amount of assets invested through her.

ALERT!

Financial advisors have a variety of credentials indicated by the acronyms after their names. Certified Financial Planners carry the CFP acronym and have broad-based educations, and often have practices focused on holistic financial planning. Check *www.cfp.net* for more information.

Fee-only advisors work directly for you and are paid only by you. This is the best choice if you're a do-it-yourself investor or if you need an independent professional review of your retirement plan. Fee-only advisors typically charge between $150 and $300 per hour depending on their experience and location. If you've done your homework ahead of time they can be especially helpful in making sure you've considered all the necessary aspects of your plan.

Online Resources

New online resources to help with retirement planning are being created every day. A list of current ones can be found in Appendix B. Be sure you use a variety of different online tools and calculators, even if you find one you particularly like. Depending on your inputs, each tool could yield different recommendations. Look for tools that are independent of a brokerage or insurance sales relationship.

Look for tools with Monte Carlo modeling capability that let you enter your own assumptions for inflation, asset growth, and longevity to enable you to draw comparisons with their default variables. Monte Carlo results present the statistical likelihood that your plan will work as you expect. Planning for at least 70 percent likelihood or higher probability of success is important.

CHAPTER 6

Retirement Accounts

The types of accounts you choose are critically important to maximizing your retirement resources. Unfortunately, by their 40s and 50s, many people have accumulated a jumble of random accounts from previous employers or past financial advisors. Ignoring these accounts can cost money through fees or the "opportunity cost" of staying with a bad choice. Whether you're organizing a glut of scattered accounts or starting from scratch, understanding the features, advantages, and disadvantages of each type of account will help make sure your nest egg benefits you now as well as in retirement.

Catching Up if You're Over 50

It's never too late to start saving. Careful planning and aggressive budgeting can help create a strong retirement nest egg even if you've only got ten or fifteen years before you want to retire. Adjusting your current spending budget down to the income you're likely to have in retirement—and then investing the difference to increase your annual savings—will build your nest egg faster, as well as maximize tax savings and employer matches. Choosing the right type of investments for each account will help grow your nest egg by saving on fees and taxes on withdrawals in retirement.

FACT

The term "opportunity cost" is one that you'll hear often when discussing investing. Simply put, it means the lost ability to do something else with money that's locked up in some sort of investment. If an investment is underperforming another investment opportunity, the opportunity cost is the difference between the returns on the two alternatives.

Expectations about Future Contribution Limit Increases

Tax laws are often written to encourage a specific behavior. The laws governing retirement accounts are no different. Recent tax law changes that allow greater contributions to retirement savings provide a clear message that individuals need to be saving for their own retirement and not betting on social security.

Because of their tax benefits, retirement plans are usually restricted by limiting the amount you can contribute annually and by capping your eligibility to contribute based on your income. These limits will change as the laws are updated; it's important to check *www.irs.gov* each year to make sure that you're eligible to make contributions to your plans that year.

Using the Employer Match

Employers encourage employees to save for retirement by offering to match their contributions to the employer's retirement plan. This match is often expressed as a percentage of what the employee deposits. For example, your employer will match 50 percent of your contributions until your contributions reach 6 percent of your pay. In this case, you want to contribute at least 6 percent of your pay in order to get the match. This match amounts to free money to you, money that you won't get as salary if you don't contribute to the plan.

Don't forgo emergency-fund saving in order to contribute to a retirement plan. Retirement plan withdrawals are often taxable and can carry penalties, so you shouldn't rely on them for short-term expenses or emergencies. Be sure you have emergency money in a savings account as well as money invested toward your retirement.

Your personal contributions to a retirement plan are always your own, but your employer's match will be limited by a vesting schedule. This means that you don't own the employer's contribution until you have worked at the company for a specified number of years. The employer contribution will appear on your statement, along with information about how much of that contribution is vested. Schedules vary, but are often spread over three, five, or seven years. If you're planning to leave your job, make sure you understand the employer's vesting schedule.

Choosing the Investments

Plan providers such as your employer, bank, mutual fund, or insurance company will post asset allocation tools on their websites to help you choose the mix, or allocation, of various stock, bond, and cash investments you want in your account. Chapter 10 will teach you how to use these tools, but it's important to note that they're especially critical when it comes to your retirement funds. Investors too often pick the accounts in their plans without regard to their risk or how their balances will fluctuate from month to month. This can hurt you in any account, but especially in a long-term account such as a retirement plan.

ALERT!

Ask your employer about the fees in their plan. Many employers have negotiated special agreements with plan providers that save their employees money, but some companies are too small to do this. If your employer's plan is expensive and doesn't offer a match, you may decide that investing in a personal plan instead will make better sense.

Fees within the investments are not paid by you directly, but are subtracted from the investment account itself, directly reducing the fund's performance and invisibly degrading your account value. A report from the investment provider called a prospectus will detail these fees, and you should look closely for them.

Juggling Your Plans

Fortify your retirement nest egg and save money on interest, fees, and taxes by using different types of investments and accounts and balancing debt reduction with retirement savings.

The Three-Legged Stool of Retirement Income

Plan your retirement savings now to maximize the three basic sources of income in retirement: social security or pension benefits, retirement accounts, and taxable accounts. Chapter 5 looked at how social security works. In addition to that income stream, investing now in both retirement accounts and nonretirement—or taxable—accounts will help you manage your taxes, cash flow, and interest costs once you're retired.

With a few exceptions, income or earnings in retirement accounts are not taxed until they're withdrawn. When withdrawals are made, the amount is taxed as income. Penalties are assessed on withdrawals made before reaching age 59½. Withdrawals, which are taxable, are required to start after you turn 70½.

The same transactions that are sheltered from current tax when in retirement plans are taxable immediately when in taxable accounts. Taxable accounts—for example, an individual investment account or a joint investment account—don't have the tax shelter that delays taxes until withdrawal that retirement accounts enjoy. The deposited funds have already been taxed as income, but their advantage is that some of their earnings—the increased value of the investment, called capital gains—are taxed at a capital gains rate that is lower than the income rate, and withdrawals can be made at any age.

Make it your goal to retire with a regular income stream that you don't have to manage—such as social security or pension benefits—and a combination of retirement and taxable accounts from which you can make withdrawals based on the best tax strategy.

Saving While Paying Down Debt

Don't delay saving for retirement because you're focused on paying down your debt. If you do, you'll miss the tax advantages of retirement plans and the compound interest advantages of long-term investing. Instead, if you're buried in high-interest debt, put 80 percent of your available monthly investment toward debt principal, 10 percent toward emergency savings, and 10 percent toward retirement savings. As your debt is paid down increase the amount you invest toward savings and retirement.

Retirement plans at work are often named for the tax law paragraph that defines them. Your work plan may have a name easy to recognize, such as "employee savings plan," or something more arcane, such as 401(k), 403(b), or 457 plan. For-profit employers typically have a 401(k) plan. The nonprofit equivalent is the 403(b) plan. Government employers often have 457 plans.

Plan Safety

Many, but not all, retirement plans are protected from the failure of the employer or the vendor providing the plan. Protected plans, such as 401(k)s or 403(b)s, are not considered assets of the employer and are not at risk if the employer goes out of business. Other plans, such as pensions and deferred-compensation accounts, don't have the same guarantees.

With some restrictions, pensions can be modified at the discretion of the employer. For example, employers can cut promised benefits if they run into financial difficulty. Deferred-compensation plans are susceptible to the financial health of the employer as well.

FACT

There are many variations of retirement plans. The plan will have a report called a Plan Document with all the details you need to understand. Ask the plan sponsor—the investment company or your employer—for a copy before you invest. Talk to an advisor who is independent of the plan or the company for advice if you're not sure of the plan's risks.

Many companies match employee retirement plan contributions using company stock. This increases your risk, because both your job and part of your retirement account are tied to the fortunes of one company. Recently enacted rules have increased employees' ability to diversify out of their company's stock in their retirement plan. This is an important option to take advantage of; never hold more than 10 percent of your investments in one company's stock.

The Bottom Line: Employer Plans

One of the great things about workplace retirement plans is that the employer has already created the plan, minimizing the research you have to do. Understanding the plan—such as whether contributions are made by the employee, the employer, or both—is still your responsibility to be sure you get the most out of it.

Defined Benefit Versus Defined Contribution

Employer retirement plans are either defined-benefit or defined-contribution plans. If your plan has a defined benefit, you'll be told that as long as you work for the company for a certain time, you'll receive a regular defined income—benefit—upon retirement. These are the old-fashioned pensions that some, though increasingly fewer, employers offer. Employees do not contribute to these plans and employers can change them if they need to, even affecting retirees.

In recent decades, defined-contribution plans have become much more popular; they're less expensive to employers and fully portable for employees who change jobs. You have a defined-contribution plan if you're told that you can contribute a specified amount to the plan each year. Your future benefit from the plan is dependent on how much you contribute and how well the investments perform. The employer may or may not contribute to the plan, and some plans allow contributions by employers and not from employees.

Defined-contribution plans—such as the alphabet soup of 401(k)s, 403(b)s, 401(a)s, and 457s—can be transferred into personal retirement plans.

In 2008, the most common employer plan, the 401(k), allowed employees to contribute up to $16,000 per year from their paycheck. Employees over age 50 are allowed an additional $5,000 "catchup" amount, for a total of $21,000.

Auto Enroll—Things to Check in Your Plan

Many defined-contribution plans are "qualified," meaning they must follow certain rules, including making them accessible and fair to all the employees, regardless of compensation. To encourage participation from all employees, many employers have started an automatic enrollment program. Auto-enrollment means that instead of having to remember to enroll in the plan, you are already enrolled and have to remember to unenroll. Inertia keeps most people in the plan.

If you have been auto-enrolled, you still need to make sure that the amount you're contributing is enough to meet your retirement goals and that the investment choice in the plan is appropriate. The default for many auto-enroll plans is too low for most employees' retirement savings needs. Some plans are set to start at 3 percent or 5 percent of pay when the employee should be saving 10 percent or more. Some plans set the auto-enroll investment default to a type of account that is too conservative.

Early Access Options

Check your plan document to see what your options are if you need to withdraw money before age 59½, or while you're still working for the employer. Some employers will allow loans against the plan balance or hardship withdrawals. Loans are not taxable unless you take longer than five years to repay the balance or if you leave the employer. Hardship withdrawals are taxable as income and have a 10 percent penalty if you're under age 59½.

The Bottom Line: Personal Plans

Personal retirement plans have lower contribution allowances than 401(k)s and other employer plans, but since you pick the investments yourself you have great control and can choose accounts with better investments and lower expenses. Individual Retirement Accounts, or IRAs, are great for people without employer plans or with employer plans that offer investments with excessively high expenses. If you have an expensive employer plan, you might choose to divide your contribution budget between the employer's 401(k) and your own IRA.

Traditional IRAs

The amount you can contribute annually to an IRA—also called a traditional IRA—is 100 percent of your taxable income up to a specified limit. In 2008, the federally established IRA cap was $5,000. If you're over 50, you can add another $1,000 per year, for a total of $6,000. Your spouse, whether or not he is working, can contribute up to the same limits. In most cases, contributions need to be made by the following year's April 15 tax deadline. These limits regularly change; check *www.irs.gov* for updates.

QUESTION?

I have several small 401(k) accounts from previous jobs. Can I combine them into my IRA account?
You certainly can. Don't mix pretax assets like your 401(k) accounts with assets that don't permit the tax deduction, like some IRAs. If you're unsure, open a new IRA to hold the money from all your old 401(k) accounts.

Deductible Versus Nondeductible

Unlike employer retirement plans, IRA contributions are not always tax deductible. If you or your spouse has an employer plan available—whether or not you contribute to it—part or all of your IRA contribution may not be deductible based on your income.

Don't avoid IRA contributions just because you can't deduct them now. Remember, the accounts are tax-deferred until you withdraw the money. If you are in a high tax bracket, this could be a great way to grow your investments without having to pay income tax until later, when the rate might be lower.

Stretch IRAs

Retirement accounts are not controlled by your will or the probate court when you die because you can list an individual beneficiary for each account. IRA beneficiaries have the option to delay withdrawals when they inherit an account, thus stretching the tax deferral. It's important that the beneficiary designations on your family's retirement accounts are kept up to date. Be sure the beneficiary is a person, not a trust or the owner's estate.

If you inherit an IRA and the owner was over age 70½ and taking required withdrawals—called minimum required distributions—you need to continue taking distributions. If the owner was younger, then you may have the option of delaying withdrawals—or of taking very small withdrawals—over your lifetime. Talk to the company holding the retirement account about what the beneficiary's options would be.

Special IRAs

IRA accounts are useful for purposes other than making annual contributions. In addition to your traditional IRA, you may also need a "rollover" IRA to receive the balance from your previous employer's retirement plan. If you inherit an IRA, the proceeds may be deposited into a "beneficiary" IRA so that you can continue deferring taxes until you make withdrawals.

There are two allowances for transferring money between retirement accounts: the sixty-day rollover and the direct transfer. You may decide to make a transfer between IRAs because you prefer the investment options of one over the other, or because you've left your job and want to transfer the balance of your 401(k) or other employer plan to your personal IRA account. You can make as many direct transfers as you want. A direct transfer takes place between the two IRA accounts exclusively. Although you might receive a check made out to the receiving IRA that you then forward to the IRA trustee, you don't ever have access to the cash.

In a sixty-day rollover, you receive the balance from the account and can use it as long as you redeposit it back into an IRA within sixty days. You can make one sixty-day rollover per year. The tax rules on sixty-day rollovers are sticky. In most cases, a direct transfer is a more desirable way to move money between accounts.

Be careful when contributing to, moving, or making withdrawals from your IRA accounts. Tax penalties can be steep if you make a mistake. Get advice in writing from your accountant, CPA, or financial planner.

Early Access Options

Like other retirement accounts, IRA withdrawals are taxable when you make them and they carry a 10 percent penalty if you're under age 59½. If part of your IRA includes nondeductible contributions—meaning that some or all of the deposits you made were not deductible—then your IRA has a so-called basis. This basis amount represents your nondeductible contributions and is not taxable when you withdraw it. Form 8606 in your tax return lets you track the basis in your nondeductible IRAs.

If your IRA deposits are at least five years old, early withdrawals without the 10 percent penalty are allowed if:

- The IRA owner is permanently disabled.
- The IRA owner has died.
- Withdrawals are used to pay nonreimbursed medical expenses.
- Withdrawals are used toward first-time home purchase.
- Withdrawals are used toward higher-education costs.

- Withdrawals are used to pay back taxes after the IRS has put a levy against the IRA.

The bottom line is that while IRA withdrawals are allowed under certain circumstances, you should avoid them when you can.

The Bottom Line: Roth Plans

Roth IRAs carry many of the same rules as traditional IRAs, except that contributions are never deductible and withdrawals after age 59½ are never taxable. Also, you don't have to start making withdrawals from your Roth when you reach age 70½.

The Tax Advantage

The tax-free growth in Roth accounts makes them very appealing to anyone who qualifies for them. You can contribute to a Roth IRA only if your income falls below a certain threshold. For example, in 2008 your income must fall below $95,000 if you're single or $150,000 if you're married to be allowed the full Roth contribution. Check *www.irs.gov* for updates on these limitations.

Roth IRA Conversions

Since Roth IRA withdrawals in retirement aren't taxable, they are a great tax planning tool. If your income is less than $100,000, then you can convert all or part of your traditional IRA to a Roth account. You'll pay income taxes on the amount you convert, but if you're in your 40s and have twenty or more years until you want to retire, the future tax-free growth of the account could be very beneficial.

Roth Employer Plans

Many companies now have Roth options added to their employer retirement plans. These Roth 401(k) or Roth 403(b) accounts don't carry the income limitations that personal Roth IRAs do, so any employee can contribute through her paycheck. The same contribution limits of employer accounts apply to the Roth and non-Roth part of the plan, combined. For example, if you're eligible to contribute up to $21,000 to your employer plan, you can contribute all or part to the Roth part of the plan. If you contribute $15,000 to the Roth part of the plan, that amount isn't deductible. The remaining $6,000 that you contribute to the regular retirement plan will be deductible—or you may hear the deposit referred to as pretax.

QUESTION?

I'm overwhelmed by the number of options and exceptions involved with personal retirement accounts. Who should I turn to for advice? Talk to an independent financial planner who specializes in helping people choose investments for themselves, rather than an adviser who sells or manages investments. Check *www.napfa.org* for a fee-only advisor in your area.

The Bottom Line: Special IRAs for the Self-Employed

Complex employer retirement plans such as 401(k)s and 403(b)s are too expensive for self-employed individuals or small employers to create. Special IRAs with higher contribution limits are available to this group. They all follow the same rules as traditional IRAs, except their contribution limits are higher and they must be established by the small business or can only accept contributions from your self-employment income.

SEP IRA

The Simplified Employee Pension, or SEP, IRA receives contributions from the employer, not the employee. This will work fine if you are self-employed without employees because you're making contributions for yourself. All the same traditional IRA rules apply, but you can contribute up to 25 percent of your self-employment compensation up to a specified limit, which adjusts annually. Check *www.irs.gov* for the current limits.

Your SEP IRA account can be established up to the time you file your taxes.

SIMPLE IRA

A Savings Incentive Match Plan for Employees, or SIMPLE, IRA plan might be a better option if you have a small business with employees. Employees contribute to SIMPLE plans themselves, and then the employer makes a matching contribution. SIMPLE plans need to be established by October 1st of the year before you want to contribute. Employees can contribute 100 percent of their pay, up to a maximum of $10,500 annually if they are less than 50 years old, or $13,000 if they are over 50. This limit increases with inflation; check *www.irs.gov* for the limits in the year you want to contribute.

Single-Person 401(k)

If you are self-employed without employees and you're anxious to contribute as much as you can to a tax-deductible retirement plan, a single-person 401(k) might be your best option. Single-person 401(k)s have higher contribution limits than SIMPLE and SEP IRAs. All the same rules apply as to a regular 401(k), but since you're the only one using the plan, the reporting and administrative costs are reduced. If you're planning to stay on your own and not hire employees, this may be the best option.

CHAPTER 7

Employer Benefits

Being in your 40s and 50s can mean that your career is just hitting its stride—or that you're dealing with major job disruption. This is the stage in your life when your job is particularly important to providing savings for approaching retirement and the stage when divorce or widowhood can start to make earning and investing more difficult. Your employee benefits can easily add up to 30 percent of your total compensation; understanding them and how to maximize their value to you is an important part of building security during these years.

Pensions: An Endangered Species

Many companies are abandoning their traditional defined benefit pension plan—in which a specified future benefit is promised and the employee doesn't contribute savings to the plan—in favor of less-expensive defined contribution plans such as 401(k)s in for-profit companies and 403(b)s in nonprofit organizations. If you're lucky enough to still work under a pension, it's important to understand how the benefit works and how it should fit in with the rest of your retirement planning.

Remember, pensions are only as strong as the promise of the company or government offering them. Pensions can be closed or frozen. Benefit amounts can be changed or inflation adjustments reduced if the employer decides to cut costs.

Calculating the Real Value

Your pension plan will promise a series of payments for the rest of your life. The current value of the pension is roughly equal to the amount you would need to have invested to pay yourself the same benefit. (Check Appendix B for a list of calculators to help you arrive at that figure.) Knowing the equivalent value of your pension is necessary to help you decide whether it makes sense for you to work extra years in the job.

QUESTION?

My employer closed the pension plan and started a Cash Balance plan. Is the new plan as good as a pension?
The Cash Balance plan is not as good as a pension for workers in their 40s and 50s. In Cash Balance plans assets are invested conservatively by the employer, making these plans more beneficial for workers with more years before retirement.

Don't forget to factor in the pension when you're tallying assets for a divorce. Calculate the present pension value and include it as an asset. Decide, based on the value of the asset and the strength of the company offering the pension, whether you want to include the pension in the list of assets you request. Since companies can alter pension benefits, if there are other assets equal in value, they might be a better choice. The old adage is right: a bird in the hand is worth two in the bush.

Pension benefits often ramp up quickly in the last few years of the worker's career. Consider this if you're deciding to retire early. One or two extra years on the job could mean a lot of extra money in your retirement.

Lump Sum Versus Annuity

Many pensions offer a choice between taking a lump sum or a regular payment called an annuity payment. The annuity option will also include choices that provide a lower current benefit and then continue making payments to the pensioner's spouse when the pensioner dies. Most pensions currently revert back to the higher benefit if the spousal option was chosen and then the spouse dies first.

Carefully compare the current value of the pension payments versus the lump sum the employer is offering. Often, the employer is able to offer annuity payments higher than you could achieve on your own after taking a lump sum payout. That said, if you're concerned about the financial health of the employer, taking the lump sum may afford greater peace of mind.

Maxing Your Benefit

Working extra years is often the best way to increase your pension benefit, but it may not be an option for you. Carefully planning which spousal benefit to pick and deciding whether to buy back years are other ways to be sure you get as much as you can from the pension. Planning for windfall provisions that affect state pensions and social security benefits is also important.

The annuity options of your pension will offer several choices that pay your spouse if you die first. Each reduces your monthly pension payments by a certain amount, and then pays your spouse a corresponding amount. Think about how your other assets and your spouse's pension income work into this choice.

Government pensions typically offer buy-back provisions. That means if you worked for the government then left the job, taking your pension as a lump-sum rollover to an IRA, and later returned to the government, you can buy back the years you missed at interest. Use the present-value pension calculators to determine if the investment will be worth it in your case.

Employees covered by government pensions often fall under the windfall provision. This provision reduces your social security benefit in an amount related to your other government pension. Check the Social Security website for a tool that will help calculate how the provision affects you.

Employee Stock Options: The Hot Incentive

Many large, publicly traded companies started using employee stock options as a benefit a few years ago. Employee stock options give the employee the ability—the option—to purchase the company stock at some point in the future at a certain pre-fixed price, called the strike price. The vesting schedule that is provided to employees when the options are awarded specifies when the purchase can take place. Purchasing the stock is called exercising the option. Options are issued in groups called grants. Parts of each grant vests over a particular schedule, the vesting schedule.

There are two types of employee stock options, incentive and nonqualified stock options. You can differentiate between the two by the way you are taxed on them.

Incentive Stock Options

Incentive stock options (ISOs) qualify for special tax treatment. They are not taxable when issued to you or, in most cases, when you exercise them to buy your company stock. If you keep the stock for at least one year from your exercise date before selling it, and two years from the date your employer granted the ISO to you, you will only pay capital gains tax on your profit. In most cases, the capital gains tax rate is lower than the tax on your income. Remember, this special treatment only really matters if the stock increases in value after you purchase it.

ISOs are tricky because their special tax exclusion at exercise can generate something called an alternative minimum tax, or AMT. This alternate income tax calculation disallows many common tax deductions and benefits that you claim on your regular tax return and assigns a minimum tax amount that the taxpayer must pay. This AMT could be due when you exercise your ISO options when regular income tax normally wouldn't be, making ISOs less appealing if the stock then loses value while you're waiting for the one-year anniversary to sell.

Expert advice is very important when working with stock options. Be careful not to let the tax tail wag the option dog. While waiting a mandatory twelve months to get a lower tax rate on your stock sale, you might lose more in lost stock value than you would have saved in taxes. Your CPA or financial advisor will help you decide whether exercising and selling ISO stock immediately is a better idea than holding the stock and taking the risk that it loses value.

Nonqualified Stock Options

Nonqualified stock options are not eligible for the special tax treatment of incentive stock options—hence their name. When you exercise "nonquals," as they are called, the difference between the strike price and the value of the stock is immediately taxable as income. Check your pay stub and your W-2 form and you'll see this value represented as income.

Companies anxious to avoid recent controversies surrounding stock option accounting and backdating have reduced or stopped issuing new stock option grants in favor of issuing restricted stock. Employees own the stock right away, but are limited by a vesting schedule that dictates when they can sell.

Strategies and Mistakes

Deciding whether to hold your company stock after exercising a stock option can be a difficult choice. Many people make the mistake of letting their fear of taxes drive their decision. The fact is that the employee stock option is a benefit that encourages you to own company stock. The argument goes that owning company stock gives employees some "skin in the game" and makes them more interested and invested in the overall performance of their company. It's also cheaper for the company to give you options than to give you a straight cash bonus. Think about whether you are better off with the cash than with the stock. If you have few other assets to diversify against your company stock, it may be better for you to sell the stock and invest the gains in a mutual fund or other investment less concentrated in the fortunes of your employer.

Restricted Stock: Golden Handcuffs

Restricted stock, initially created as a "golden handcuff" to offer executives enough of a compensation sweetener to keep them attached to the company, has recently become a more popular benefit for rank-and-file employees. Restricted stock shares have a vesting schedule that limits the number of shares you can sell each year. As with employee stock options, they are usually issued to employees in grants, and each grant has a particular vesting schedule. You lose any unvested restricted stock when you leave the company.

What They Are

Restricted stock shares are a little nicer benefit than employee stock options when your company stock is not increasing rapidly in value. Stock options are issued with a strike price equal to the price at which the stock is currently trading, but with a strike date set in the future. If the share price doesn't increase, your option may never gain value—a situation called "being under water"—because if you were to exercise the options, you would find yourself holding shares worth less than what you paid. Restricted stock shares—or units—represent real shares in the company. Regardless of what happens to their price after you receive them, as long as you're on the job when they vest, restricted stocks still have value to you.

Don't Overdo It

Restricted shares are taxed as income in the year they vest and are available to sell. Consider this, and whether you also own employee stock options, when deciding to sell your stock. If your job and much of your net worth is connected to the fortunes of the same company, you may be taking more risk than you realize.

Employee Stock Purchase Plans: Getting Your Share

Under an employee stock purchase plan (ESPP), employees can buy company stock at a price below market value. This price discount can be a great way to add value to your portfolio as long as you understand how to use the program.

What They Are

Under a typical ESPP, employees deposit 10 percent or 15 percent (depending on the individual plan rules) of their pay into a pool to buy company stock. The stock is sold to the employee at three- or six-month intervals at a price discount of 15 percent. Since the employee's discount is calculated on the price at the beginning or the end of the interval, depending on which is better for the employee, the employee may realize more than a 15 percent profit. There isn't a vesting period for ESPP stock, so the employee can sell right away—called a same-day sale—to lock in his profits.

Tax laws are always changing. Be sure to check with your employer and your tax advisor to be sure you understand the details of your benefit plan before participating. Pay extra attention to the cost of plans such as ESPPs that can increase your taxable income. Higher income may reduce the value of tax deductions such as mortgage interest.

If your company's plan is a qualified ESPP—ask the plan manager if your plan is qualified under section 423—you won't owe any tax when you buy the stock. When you sell, your price discount is taxed to you as wages and any gain in the price of the stock from when you purchased it is taxed at capital gains tax rates. Capital gains rates are lower than wage rates. If your plan is nonqualified, then you'll owe income tax on the amount by which the price was discounted.

Strategies

Many employers allow employees to sell shares they bought through their ESPP immediately after they receive them—the same-day sale mentioned in the preceding section. Selling quickly can guarantee that you don't lose your profit if the shares were sold to you at a discount. Same-day-sale profits are taxed at higher income tax rates, but the higher taxes might be worth it if you use your cash to buy more diversified investments.

Is stock flipping okay? Selling your ESPP shares on the same day you bought them in order to get the guaranteed profit of the discount your employer offers is called flipping. Many people frown on this practice because they feel the ESPP should be used to encourage stock ownership, not quick profits. But it's your money, and that's what's most important to your financial plan. Go ahead and flip!

Some employers' ESPPs don't offer a price discount and some have blackout periods that restrict how quickly you can sell your ESPP shares. If this is the case with your plan, you might decide that the risk of being in the plan and not being able to sell quickly, or not getting a guaranteed profit, makes it a bad idea to participate.

Comparing Job Offers

Employee benefits are a big part of comparing job offers. Often a lower salary is worth it if other lifestyle or financial benefits make up for the difference. Measuring and comparing the differences is especially important in your 40s and 50s, because you're probably at your career peak and age discrimination could soon start to affect you.

Lifestyle Factors in Your 40s and 50s

Age discrimination is an unfortunate fact of life in many industries. Thinking about how your job at this age could be affected by age discrimination is an important part of career and financial planning at your age. Some jobs, like airline pilot, require you to retire at age 60. Others don't require retirement, but have a culture that promotes youth or a work environment that is physically strenuous. Consider whether your current job, or the jobs you are considering and comparing with each other, set you up to be successfully working up until your planned retirement age. If they don't, this might be the best age—and maybe your last chance—to make a change to something that will support you.

If the job you're in, or the job you're considering, isn't going to be doable until retirement, is it a path to part-time work? The job may still be a good one for you if it puts you in a position to transition to part-time work at a point that fits your retirement goal. Even if the job itself can't be continued part time, it may develop skills for you that can be used in another position.

ALERT!

If you're lucky enough to have a career that will let you work as long as you want to, target your savings so you're finished saving by age 62 or 65. That will assure that you won't feel pressed to keep saving after that age and can work without the stress of having to save while also investing.

Financial Factors

Compare the value of employment benefits at your job by pricing what the benefits would cost if purchased directly, and the value of any nonsalary employer perks. Check with your insurance agent for the direct-purchase cost of health, disability, or life insurance. Calculate the value of paid vacation days, holidays, and the employer match into the retirement plan. Check the retirement plan itself, and decide whether one employer's plan is more expensive than the other's. Talk to people who work for the employer and compare the hours you're expected to be on the job. Compensation may be comparable, and the work environment could be your deciding factor.

Don't forget the cost of commuting when comparing jobs. The time you spend commuting in addition to the cost of travel and parking is an important consideration.

Negotiating a salary when you're older is different than negotiating when you're younger. Focus on your experience in the field, but be aware of whether the organization values that experience. Reach out to your network of friends and past business associates to learn as much about the company as you can. Above all, don't try to hide your age or behave younger than you are. And be ready for the person interviewing you, and the one eventually supervising you, to be younger than you are.

Where to Find the Best Advice

Information resources for your employee benefits often have conflicts of interest. In many cases, the people most familiar with the plan are financially linked to it. Be sure to ask about conflicts and use the list at the back of the book to find independent advice when you need it.

QUESTION?

Should I invest in a life insurance policy after maxing out the amount I can put in my 401(k)?
Probably not. Life insurance fees are higher than for other investments, and profits are taxed at higher income tax rates on withdrawal. Look at lower-fee mutual funds and take advantage of the lower capital gains tax treatment instead.

Retirement Plan Providers

The insurance, brokerage, or investment advisory company that provides your retirement plan gets paid by both the employer and the plan participants. Most providers target a total fee they want to generate from the plan and then the employer decides how the fee is paid. This can be confusing to figure out. Your employer probably won't tell you what they are paying, but you can usually figure your costs to participate by researching the investments at Morningstar.com, in the investment prospectus, or in your plan's information online.

Most providers send a representative to the workplace to explain the plan to the employees and to help them sign up. Keep in mind that the expenses, and therefore the commissions paid to the plan provider, can vary from one investment choice to another. Ask the provider whether they have this conflict of interest. Some provider representatives are paid a salary, so they won't be conflicted, but others are paid based on the investment fees generated.

FACT

Investment advice is regulated by your state securities department, the federal Securities and Exchange Commission, and the National Association of Securities Dealers, depending on how the advisor is compensated and the amount of money clients invest with them. Ask your advisor which agency regulates his firm and check that agency's website to see if any complaints have been filed against the advisor.

Employee Assistance Programs

Many employers offer employee assistance programs (EAPs) as a benefit. The advisors in the EAP are independent and your conversations with them are confidential. EAPs can be tapped for a variety of life-balance advice ranging from psychological counseling and addiction issues to general health and wellness and financial and legal advice. Services through the EAP are paid by the employer and often have restrictions that limit the number of hours each employee is eligible for.

In many cases the employee can choose to directly contract with the advisor or a referral from the EAP advisor after the EAP benefit has been used up. Be sure to compare the advisor's fees to others before contracting with her—just as you would if you were researching your advisor from scratch. Keep in mind that her fees may be higher than others'. Assess whether the higher fee is worth it based on the work you have already done through the employer program.

The advisors available through your EAP benefit will have a wide range of training. Your employer has vetted the program, but won't have the resources to make sure the advisor you're using is the best for you. Ask the advisor about her background and experience with the EAP. Find out what her success has been with cases and questions like yours.

CHAPTER 8

Investing 101: Bonds

The maze of investment choices is full of details that seem to be designed for maximum confusion. Can't you just keep your money in a passbook savings account? Not if you want to squeeze the most value out of your money and keep up with inflation. Good investing means picking a diverse array of investments to help grow your money while managing the variety of risks your portfolio faces. Even if you decide hiring an investment advisor is the best option, it's still vital that you understand the basics yourself.

Investing Your Cash

Cash is truly money in the bank. Cash needs to earn interest, but at the same time be safe and available to withdraw quickly. Banks and investment companies provide accounts to hold your cash and pay you interest. They loan your money out to borrowers and in turn pay interest back to you for letting them use your money. It's pleasing to see the balance increase with each statement—if even just a small amount. And it's comforting to know that the balance isn't at risk . . . that the statement will always show an increase no matter what and your money is available, in full, anytime you may want it.

Understanding the terminology is key to being an informed, alert investor. When you hear someone use the words "fixed-income security," in most cases they're saying the same thing as if they're saying "bond." The words "interest" and "yield" aren't technically the same, but they're often used interchangeably.

What's Guaranteed Safe and What Isn't

There are two ways to invest your cash: savings accounts and money market accounts. Savings accounts are available at your bank or credit union and are usually insured by the Federal Deposit Insurance Corporation, or FDIC. Your financial institution will advertise that your deposits up to $100,000 per depositor are FDIC insured. This means that your money is safe regardless of what happens to the bank itself. There's a cost for this insurance, of course, and it's passed down to you in the form of slightly lower interest rates on insured deposits compared to uninsured, but still very safe, money market accounts.

Money Market Accounts

Money market accounts are offered by investment companies and banks as a way to invest money at better interest rates than plain vanilla savings accounts, with very low—but not zero—risk and with high liquidity.

Money market interest is higher than savings account interest because the money manager hasn't paid for FDIC insurance. Your deposits in a money market account are only as secure as the financial company itself, however. Technically, if the company runs into trouble, you could lose some or all of the principal you invested. In practice, though, large financial entities have staked their reputations on their money market accounts. When the economy gets difficult, companies have been known to reduce their fees or even deposit some of their own money into their money market accounts to help them maintain value.

The money market accounts of large financial institutions are a great way to invest cash at a decent interest rate while maintaining quick access to your money.

Liquidity refers to how easily an investment can be converted into cash. To say a bank account is liquid means that you can withdraw the balance quickly and without losing value. Real estate, however, is generally considered illiquid because it may take a long time to sell and could sell for less than its purchase price.

Trading Liquidity for Interest

Investors are sometimes willing to sacrifice liquidity for higher interest. Certificates of Deposit, or CDs, are a safe, higher-interest alternative to money markets for cash you don't think you'll need for a while. The longer the maturity, the higher the interest you should expect to collect. Typical CDs mature in three months, six months, twelve months, or even two years. Earning higher interest is only fair to you, for letting a financial institution use your money and for risking the likelihood that inflation would have eroded some of your cash's value in the meantime.

Understanding the Mechanics—and the Risks

Fixed-income investments, or bonds, have two important components: the principal component—the amount of money you deposited, also called the face value—and the interest payments—the regular income you receive in return for investing in the bond. Bond investments also involve two basic types of risk: inflation risk and default risk.

Inflation Risk

Inflation risk is the risk that your money won't buy as much when you get it back at maturity as it did when you invested. For example, if you bought a bond that returned 5 percent in an economy in which inflation averaged 6 percent over the life of your bond, the buying power of the money you received at the bond's maturity would have shrunk. Goods and service prices rose faster than your investment value.

Default Risk

Default risk is the risk that you don't get your money back at all. Your principal is only as safe as the entity that issued the bond. If the company or the government agency issuer becomes insolvent and can't return your money when the bond matures, then they have defaulted. Default risk is an important consideration when buying bonds and when looking for higher interest. During the 1980s, many investors bought high-paying, very-high-risk "junk bonds" without realizing that their principal could be lost.

QUESTION?

How can I use the Internet as a more effective financial planning tool?
Try to do business with companies that broaden their services to include high-interest checking accounts as well. And if you find you're comfortable managing your money market account via the Internet, expand your online horizon by exploring online bill-paying and other web-enabled transactions.

Assessing the Risk

Bonds are assigned credit ratings—professional assessments of the likelihood a borrower will be able to pay on their bonds as promised—to help investors gauge their default risk. Two independent agencies, Standard & Poor's and Moody's, each rate bond issuers based on their financial health. Issuers with strong credit ratings can offer bonds with the highest ratings and pay lower interest. On the Standard & Poor's scale, bonds with AAA, AA, A, and BBB are considered investment grade, while BB, B, CCC, and CC rated bonds are considered speculative. Issuers offer higher interest on riskier bonds to overcome investors' reluctance to take on higher default risk. Be sure you understand this risk before you invest.

Lending to Uncle Sam

Bonds issued by the U.S. government are called Treasuries, and although they're not officially rated, they carry an implied AAA rating. Treasury "bills" have maturities from a few days to as long as twenty-six weeks. Treasury "notes" are issued with two-, five-, and ten-year maturities. And Treasury "bonds" have thirty-year maturities. Notes and bonds pay interest every six months, a real benefit if you need regular income or if you'd like to reinvest the interest in something else.

Lending to Lower Government Levels

Municipal governments issue bonds—called muni bonds—to fund projects such as roads, schools, and other public works at the state, county, city, or town level. Municipalities pay close attention to their credit ratings because investors would insist on higher interest for lower rated (meaning riskier) bonds.

Agency bonds offer guarantees from their issuing quasi-governmental agency but are not technically backed by the U.S. Treasury. Therefore, they offer slightly higher interest than Treasuries to compensate for this risk. Most commonly, you'll see bonds called Fannie Maes issued by the Federal National Mortgage Association, Freddie Macs by the Federal Home Loan Mortgage Corporation, Sallie Maes by the Student Loan Marketing Association, and a handful of others.

Corporate Bonds

Ratings are especially important in comparing bonds issued by individual companies, called corporate bonds or "corporates." Corporates pay regular interest and are issued with a variety of maturities. Issuing bonds is only one way a company can raise cash to fund growth or operations. In case of bankruptcy, the company's creditors, including its bond holders, have priority over owners and stock holders and may receive money back when others don't. Many investors consider buying the bonds of even a risky company before they would buy its stock.

Build a Bond Ladder

Deciding on the maturity—or term—for your bond investments involves a bit of skill. All other things being equal, shorter-term bonds carry lower risk than longer-term bonds. Unfortunately, in economics, all things are almost never equal. Even with super-safe Treasuries, there's still a chance your money won't grow with inflation—or if it does, that once your Treasury matures, the next Treasury you invest in with your returned principal won't keep pace with the one that just matured. This is yet another form of risk, called interest rate risk. It happens when rates on new bonds are lower than a bond that just matured.

ALERT!

High-yield, or junk, bonds pay higher interest for a reason: they are risky. In the 1980s, the term "junk bonds" was coined when bond trader Michael Milken fueled a craze for investing in these securities, which are often backed by complex business deals, and many investors lost money. Don't take these special bonds for granted; do your homework.

Rung by Rung

Beginners and veterans alike use "bond ladders" to balance the effects of interest and inflation risk on their fixed-income portfolios. Like adding rungs to a ladder, they buy a bond to mature each year over a course of ten years—when you first create the ladder, you buy a bond to mature in one year, in two years, and so on, up to ten years. Then, after the one-year bond matures, you buy another ten-year bond. The idea is to have a ten-year horizon in which one bond is maturing each year. Each bond has the same principal value and is usually sold by the same or a similar issuer so the credit rating remains the same. This strategy is something like crossing a wide river with only ten steppingstones. You lay the stones down, and then carry the first stone with you to place beyond the tenth one, continuing the process until you're across. With a bond ladder, you will always have a bond maturing.

QUESTION?

How do I buy bonds?
Your broker has bonds in his inventory to sell you. He will offer you a price and calculate the yield for you. The broker will have government as well as corporate and municipal bonds and CDs. You can buy Treasury bonds and other government bonds directly at *www.treasurydirect.gov.*

Bond Yields and Taxes

So far, you've learned about interest paid by bonds under the simplest scenario, which is that you bought your bond at face value. And you've been thinking only about the interest paid by bonds, while assuming that your invested principal was exactly the same as the face value—the amount you get back when the bond matures. Because this face value is the same amount you initially paid for the bond, the only income you receive are the interest payments.

Yield Versus Interest

Buying a bond at a time other than at issue, and at a value other than face value, brings into play another bond term: the yield. Thinking of bonds as they were treated a hundred years ago will help make this concept clearer.

Before computers ruled the financial world, bonds were printed on paper. The front of the bond—its "face"—indicated how much the bond was worth. A bond with $1,000 printed across the front had a face value of

$1,000. Printed across the bottom were the bond's coupons, literally clippable tabs that each represented one interest payment on the bond. The investor would clip the coupon off the bottom and present it to the issuer in return for the interest payment.

Since bonds were unchangeably printed on paper, their face value could not be altered, but changes in the market would still affect their value. Different interest rates on new bonds or the credit rating of the issuer could affect how much an investor was willing to pay for an old bond that someone was trying to sell her. The new investor would have a profit at maturity if she paid less than face value, or a loss if she paid more. This total value received—the bond's interest payments, plus or minus their market value—is called their yield.

The Old-Fashioned Way

Think about it this way. You buy a $1,000 bond with a 5 percent coupon rate. At the first six months, you clip the coupon, take it to the issuer, and they give you your coupon payment based on that face value and interest rate. Now let's suppose that you decide you want your money out of the bond right now and can't wait until it matures. You go to a friend and ask him to buy the bond from you. Your friend would like to help, but comparable bonds are now offering higher interest. It wouldn't be fair to your friend to pay you the full $1,000 face value for the bond and then only collect the lower interest than he could earn with a newer bond. So you offer to drop the price of the bond and take less than $1,000 for it. He pays you the lower price, he still collects his 5 percent interest payments, and when the bond matures he collects the $1,000 face value. Since he paid less than $1,000 for the bond, his total yield is his profit, plus the interest payments. This yield would be equal to the higher-interest new bonds we're paying other investors.

What if Rates Rise?

Of course, in this example, as interest rates increased, the price of your bond dropped in order to balance with the higher market-rate yield. If interest rates were falling, the situation would be reversed. Your 5 percent interest rate would be mighty attractive to someone who was looking at new issues at a lower rate. She would be willing to pay you more than face value to get her hands on the comparatively high coupons you own. At maturity, paying more than face value would bring their final yield down to the market rate.

Interpreting Your Account Statement

This dynamic—rising interest rates bringing bond prices down and falling rates sending bond prices higher—is important to remember when looking at your account statements. If interest rates have gone up since you bought your bond, the value of the bond will show lower on the statement. Don't despair; the nice thing about high-quality bonds is that you get your principal back if you hold it to maturity . . . no matter what happens with rates in the meantime.

FACT

Buying or selling the bond sometime between the initial offering and maturity is called trading in the secondary market. Secondary markets exist for just about any security that others want to buy after it's been initially offered. Stocks, for example, are "new" only when a company goes public. All sales of those stocks later are technically on the secondary market.

Factoring the Tax Impact

Bond investors must consider two types of tax. Profit generated because you paid below face value creates capital gains tax when the bond matures. Interest paid by bond investments, with a couple of exceptions, is taxed as income.

Interest from Treasuries is exempt from state and local taxes, and interest on muni bonds is exempt from federal income taxes. If the muni you bought was issued by the state where you pay your taxes, the interest is state and local tax free. This is a great deal for investors in higher income tax brackets. But beware: if you're paying alternative minimum tax, you need to rethink your investment. Taxable bonds might be better in your case. You'll learn all about the alternative minimum tax in Chapter 16.

Could Taxable Bonds Be Better?

Munis and Treasuries have lower coupon rates than fully taxable bonds such as corporates and CDs. If you're not in the highest income brackets, don't be fooled by their tax-free status. It may be wiser to take the higher interest and pay the tax than to take the lower tax-free rate. Check the Resource section (Appendix B) for online calculators to help you figure the difference.

Bond Mutual Funds: Putting a Pro to Work

Researching, tracking, and buying individual bonds can be a full-time job. Many investors choose mutual funds to make investing easier. Bond mutual funds are run by a professional manager who selects, buys, and sells the bonds in the fund. Individual investors can deposit or withdraw money at any time.

Where They Fit Best

Bond mutual funds fit especially well in accounts where there's a limited amount of money to invest or when you're making smaller regular deposits—such as through a payroll deduction as a monthly investment. Individual bonds are often priced to discourage purchases below a full $1,000 bond, making small deposits expensive. In fact, bonds are often not even available in increments smaller than $100 or $1,000. Mutual funds are sold in dollar-and-cent increments so it's easy to buy an odd amount or to make a smaller regular contribution.

Mutual funds don't pay their own taxes. Income earned by the fund is passed through—after expenses—to the investors, who must pay the required tax. The same applies for capital gains earnings. Funds are great for liquidity, but their pass-through taxation takes a little planning. Get in the habit of keeping accurate records and considering whether you want to own your fixed-income mutual fund in your retirement accounts to shelter the tax.

Passive Versus Active Management

There are two schools of thought when it comes to investment management. One, the passive school, believes that the market is the market and there's no way for an investment manager to consistently beat it. The other argues that a smart manager following an active management approach can figure a way to top competing managers and even the market itself. In fact, looking back over the years, many managers have topped the market fairly consistently. Unfortunately, only in hindsight is the view 20/20. Investors looking to buy bond mutual funds are faced with deciding which managers will be successful *in the future*, far harder than identifying the winners in years past. What's the best solution? Hedge your bets: do a little of both.

Sometimes Advice Pays

Any time you have an inefficient market—a market in which all the players don't necessarily have all the information at exactly the same time—there are opportunities for a good manager to add value to the investment by being clever enough to get good information early. This is the case especially with foreign bonds and high-yield bonds whose complexity rewards good research. If you've decided that you want these in your portfolio, then researching an actively managed mutual fund would be a good approach. For plain-vanilla, efficient-market investing—as with U.S. government bonds and high-quality corporate bonds—lower-cost passive investing will work just fine.

Stay on Top of the Trends

Bond mutual funds are not exactly the set-it-and-forget-it investment that many people think. Mutual fund managers must invest according to narrow rules established by their particular fund. For example, a short-term bond mutual fund must continue investing within its short-term bond limitation even when the economy is rewarding intermediate- or long-term bonds. Later, you'll hear more about selecting investments to achieve the right asset allocation, but for now just remember the importance of diversified bond mutual funds, including short-, intermediate- and long-term funds.

Index Shares: The Copycat Approach to Investing

Index shares, or as they're sometimes called, exchange-traded funds (ETFs), are a comparatively recent approach to investing in bonds. ETFs follow a passive investment strategy; they hold a basket of bonds meant merely to mirror the market, not beat it. They are traded in shares rather than in dollars like mutual funds, a structure that helps keep costs low and tax efficiency high.

What to Shop For

The exploding popularity of ETFs has given rise to a huge number of new funds, meaning, more than ever, "Investor beware!" You're safest to stay with the older, larger, and more frequently traded ETFs that invest across a broad market; investing in newer, smaller funds can lead to unexpected results.

ETFs and index mutual funds are very competitive. Compare the costs and performance of both before investing. You may find circumstances where the index mutual fund beats the ETF on cost. The Internet has made it easy for you to research these funds, as firms now post all relevant information on their websites.

When Are ETFs a Good Option for You?

Since they are traded in shares, like stocks, ETFs carry a trading commission when they're bought and again when they're sold. That means frequent trades cost you money and hurt overall returns. Their lower annual costs compared to mutual funds make them a more efficient investment for long-term holdings that don't require frequent deposits or withdrawals. Look to ETFs when you're investing a lump cash sum or making a transfer from a previous employer's retirement plan to your own account. Tax-efficient ETFs are also helpful in nonretirement accounts where annual income isn't sheltered from taxation.

Curves Ahead: Yield Curves and Bond Strategies Made Simple

Fixed-income investments are interesting not only as investments but also as a yardstick for the economy. As you learned earlier in the chapter, interest paid on bond investments is different based on the investment's term to maturity, generally moving higher as maturity increases.

The Yield Curve

Check a list of bond investments with different maturities—such as on the CD rate board at your bank or where bond rates are posted online—and you'll notice that the more years into the future the bonds mature compared to today, they generally carry higher interest rates. But that's not always the case. They can have lower interest rates or remain the same years from now as they are today. This pattern over time, if you charted it on a graph, would create what is called a yield curve.

Investing when It's Positive

A normal growing economy would show a positive yield curve, in which interest rates gradually step higher for longer-term investments. The curve drawn out on paper slowly slopes upward toward higher rates as the line moves up the time line. Investors in this case know that in five or ten years the economy will be larger and salaries and prices will be higher, and therefore they need higher interest to maintain their buying power. Investing in this circumstance is easy with a simple bond ladder.

Investing when the Curve Is Flat or Downward

An economy at risk of recession or with other problems will show a flat or downward—negative—yield curve. In these cases, investors aren't insisting on higher interest rates in the years ahead because the economy is pointing toward contraction, with the likelihood of lower or stagnant prices. Investing in this environment is tricky because bond ladders don't work.

Mutual funds or ETFs are far more appealing when the yield curve is flat or turned south, because you can sell and change your strategy when the market rebounds. They are liquid and you're not locked in.

CHAPTER 9

Investing 101: Stocks

Buying a share of stock means you own slice of a company. If the company does well and the price of a share increases, the value of your investment increases, too. If the company stumbles and the price of a share decreases, you lose money. Stocks don't have the interest payment security that bonds do, but corporate shares are an important part of your portfolio. Whether you buy shares directly or in managed baskets called mutual funds or index shares, stocks help make sure your money grows to keep up with inflation.

Advantages and Risks of Stock Investing

Investing in stock is a way for your investment to keep up with inflation. By investing in companies that are growing with the economy, you seek to be sure your portfolio grows with inflation. Stocks hold none of the payment promises of bonds; your investment is only as strong as the companies you're buying. The government encourages investment in shares by giving preferred tax rules to stock owners.

FACT

Watch your terms. The words "equities," "shares," and "stocks" are all used interchangeably. As for fixed-income issues, "bonds" can be issued by governments or commercial interests. "Paper" usually refers to commercial bonds. Notes are short-term Treasury issues. "CDs" are also considered fixed income and are issued by banks.

The Plusses and Minuses of Stock Ownership

Companies sell ownership shares to fund their operations. Stock buyers are rewarded with an investment that is pegged to the fortunes of the company. The goal of a good stock portfolio is to generate growth by creating a diversified mix of stocks, owning many different companies of different sizes and in a variety of industry sectors and countries.

The size of the company makes a difference. Larger companies tend to grow at a slower rate than smaller ones. They have established businesses and are considered safer than smaller companies. As an added perk, some of them pay dividends to stockholders. Dividends are not a guaranteed payment like a bond payment, but they are a nice source of extra income that can offset some of the risk of owning the stock.

Small and midsize companies have historically grown at faster rates than larger ones, but they are riskier. Also called small cap and mid cap, respectively, a number of these companies fail or disappoint investors expecting high returns each year. To diversify against this risk, many investors buy baskets of small and mid-cap companies through mutual funds or index shares rather than picking individual company shares.

Diversification is an important way to protect your investment. By owning investments that are affected by different economic factors, you reduce your risk. As one part of the economy is doing well, another might be struggling. The risk of loss is higher if all your investments are similar and are affected by the same economic factors.

Tax Benefits

Tax laws are often governmental policy tools to encourage a certain behavior, and the taxes on stock gains are no different. Qualified dividends are taxed at a lower rate than interest payments from bonds. When you sell a stock, your profit—or capital gain—is taxed at a lower rate than other income sources such as wages or bond interest. If you've lost value in your stock, you can sell and count the loss against other gains you may have had in the same year, thus reducing your capital gains taxes. If you don't have gains, you can count a limited amount of realized capital losses against your regular income—saving even more tax.

Different Risks

Most people think of market risk when they think about stocks. "Market risk" is the chance that your investment loses value because other potential buyers of your stock are willing to pay less for your shares than you paid. You can protect against market risk by buying stocks that are in different markets. Small companies have different appeal to buyers than mid-cap or large companies. Better yet, adding international companies to your portfolio protects against risks in the U.S. stock market.

"Company risk" is the risk that something damaging happens with the company whose shares you own, eroding their value. You can protect against company risk by buying stock in many companies that are unrelated to each other and having a diversified portfolio.

Own shares of companies in many different industry sectors to protect yourself against "industry risk," or losses related to the economic fortunes affecting one industry. Many people were caught by surprise in 2000 when the technology sector, which had been growing meteorically, collapsed. Be sure your portfolio is balanced among industries that are dependent on different parts of the economy.

Be careful not to put too many eggs in one basket. Make sure you keep your exposure to any one stock below 10 percent of your investment portfolio. If the company is also your employer, try to keep your stock holdings below 5 percent, when you can.

Measuring Tools

Measuring tools called indexes were created so investors could easily see how well a particular market has performed or compare their own investments to the performance of the market. One of the first of these indexes was the Dow Jones Industrial Average. Created in the nineteenth century by the founders of the *Wall Street Journal*, the average price performance of thirty industrial companies was calculated at the end of each day and published in the paper. Readers and investors could use changes in the Dow Jones average to gauge how the market as a whole was doing.

Nowadays, investors are concerned about measuring many more than just one market. There are indexes for practically everything you could imagine. Popular indexes for U.S. stocks are the Standard and Poor's 500—or the S&P 500—that measures large-cap stocks, the S&P 400 for mid-cap stocks, and the Russell 2000 for small-caps.

Foreign Investing

Investments in countries other than the United States make an important component of your diversified portfolio. Historically, investors in the United States have allocated only a small part of their portfolios to international stocks, feeling that economic growth in the United States was a better bet. This is no longer the case. The economies of Europe and Asia are seen as very appealing investments and the availability of professional investment managers through mutual funds have opened overseas markets to U.S. investors.

Types of Foreign Markets

There are basically two types of international markets: developed and emerging. The economies of developed countries are more similar to the U.S. economy than smaller, riskier economies of emerging countries, but they still offer diversification. Owning companies in developed countries gives your portfolio exposure to different currencies and economic cycles than in the United States. When the U.S. economy is slowing, European or Asian economies may be growing. Emerging economies are riskier, but small amounts can be good in your portfolio.

Indexes to Watch

The MSCI EAFE index is calculated by Morgan Stanley Capital International—hence the MSCI—and measures the performance of markets in the developed countries of Europe, Australasia, and the Far East. Morgan Stanley's MSCI Emerging Markets Index tracks emerging economies such as those of Argentina, Brazil, Chile, and South Africa.

Economics of Stocks: Account Considerations

Investors buy stocks so their investments grow in step with the companies that issued the stock. Some investors enjoy betting on individual companies, but most prefer to invest in pools of stocks that either are chosen by a professional manager or track a particular index.

Inflation and Return Expectations

Economic growth has historically helped stocks outpace the performance of bonds over the long term. Investors favor stocks as the growth engine of their portfolio, but returns don't come without risk. Large cap U.S. stocks that have returned, on average, about 10 percent per year over the last century have spent many individual years during that time in the red. It's great to think that U.S. stocks will earn 10 percent every year, but that's an average over a considerable time. You might need your money tomorrow, when a given stock is struggling, and can't wait around for the 10 percent average to develop. Chapter 10 will help you set a mix of investments to help deal with risk.

Active Versus Passive Investing

There are two general schools of thought among investors. One school, the active investor school, believes that, with skill and diligence, an individual investor can find investments that can outperform the overall market. The other, passive school, factors in the time, cost, and complexity of the active approach and concludes that the market is efficient over time and no one individual can beat market performance consistently.

An efficient market is one like the U.S. large-cap stock market, in which all investors have the same information at the same time. It's difficult for any individual to trade on information that no one else has. Inefficient markets are ones where information is scarcer. Small-cap markets in the United States and some international markets are inefficient enough that skilled investors can make a difference.

Many studies have been done proving the relative merits of active and passive investing. Most busy investors prefer to make investing as easy and hassle-free as possible. These investors choose a passive approach in most markets—large and mid cap U.S. and developed international—and an active approach in less efficient markets—small cap U.S. and emerging international. They also choose an active approach when a particular manager offers to buy stocks that fit a particular personal value the investor desires, such as in so-called green or socially conscious investing.

Green and Social Investing

More and more people are interested in investing to match their social and environmental priorities, and investment managers and corporate boards have raced to accommodate them. Companies tout their efforts to protect the environment and boast about their socially friendly policies and values. Investment managers buy the stock of these companies not only to profit from sound technologies or beneficial work force policies, but also to encourage the company's behavior.

Adding green and/or socially conscious investments to your portfolio is a great way to match your investing with your values. The world economy still isn't green or socially conscious enough so that your whole portfolio can be invested this way, but a lot of it can. Buy investments in the countries and industry sectors that fit the green/social model you're looking for, and then fill in the rest of your portfolio with passive investments that follow the market indexes.

Stock Mutual Funds

Few investors, especially busy folks in their 40s and 50s, want to spend the time to choose individual stocks to buy. Even if they did, it's difficult to build a diversified portfolio one stock at a time. Managing market risk, sector risk, and especially company risk is easier through investing in pooled investment accounts called mutual funds. The mutual fund buys the stock so you don't have to.

QUESTION?

Is a large mutual fund better than a small one?
Not if you're looking for an active manager who invests in small- or mid-cap stocks. If the fund is too large, it will be too unwieldy for the manager to quickly take a position in a small company that may have a limited amount of stock available.

Common Fund Types

Mutual funds are run by managers who publish their investment objective in the fund's prospectus. The broad categories of stock mutual funds are large cap, mid cap, and small cap. Each mutual fund then goes an extra step and chooses companies that are considered growth companies—companies reinvesting profits to grow—or value companies—companies that are priced cheaply in the manager's view. Funds that invest in both growth and value are called blend funds.

How to Choose and Compare Funds

Morningstar—available online at *www.morningstar.com*—is a valuable research tool for mutual fund investors. Morningstar publishes research about mutual funds that helps investors pick those that will fit their portfolio. The Morningstar "style box" is divided into nine sections indicating the type of fund being reviewed. Chapter 10 talks more about choosing the mix of funds, but it's helpful to remember that you need to have at least one fund for each of Morningstar's nine boxes.

Mutual funds are run by corporations, of course, meaning that they, too, bear all the same costs of payroll, capital investment, and other operating costs of any other corporation. They pay for marketing, sales and their asset management teams. The mutual fund pays these costs out of investor assets, meaning that a part of each dollar you invest in the fund will be used by the manager to defray operating costs. If the costs are high, they can significantly affect the performance of the fund.

FACT

Morningstar publishes its fund reviews each month and many libraries carry copies. If your access to the web is limited, your local library should have a Morningstar subscription for you to use. The fund company will often mail out tear sheets with the Morningstar data, as well.

Here are some important things to look for when picking a mutual fund:

- A manager who's been in the job at least three years
- A fund with at least five years of performance history
- A Morningstar rating of at least three stars
- An expense ratio below 1 percent for U.S. large cap and below 1.4 percent for U.S. small and mid cap and international stock
- A fund that performs at least as well as its peers

Mutual funds don't pay their own taxes on the investments they hold. Instead, they distribute their interest, dividends, and year-end capital gains from selling stock to their shareholders every year. Capital gain distributions are usually made in the fall each year and represent taxable income—but not actual cash—to the investor. If you're thinking about buying a mutual fund, check to see when this distribution will be made. It represents profits realized by the fund and its shareholders earlier in the year; if you buy the fund just before the distribution you pay tax on gain that you never benefited from.

Sales Loads

Mutual funds are distributed directly to the public by the fund itself or are sold through a commissioned broker. Funds sold through brokers compensate those brokers via sales loads that are applied to the purchase price or sale price, or that are evenly applied each year you own the fund. You won't see the sales load, but it will affect the performance of your fund. "A" shares are funds with front sales loads that are deducted from the amount you pay when you initially buy your shares; "B" shares apply the commission to the amount of shares you sell—so-called back-end loads; and "C" shares apply an annual fee for the length of time you own the fund.

No-load funds are distributed directly by the fund itself or through entities with fee agreements other than commissions. Your fee-only financial planner will recommend no-load funds because you are compensating him separately for his advice. Online brokerages such as Fidelity and Schwab will offer no-load funds because the funds are paying the brokerages through another agreement to be part of their offering.

Be sure your fund keeps at least a three-star rating at Morningstar. Funds with lower ratings can suffer from an excessive number of investors selling out of the fund. When shares are sold, the fund may need to sell some of its profitable stock to pay those defecting investors for their shares. The capital gains tax liability is passed to remaining investors.

Many funds—load and no-load alike—charge investors 12b-1 fees. These fees are meant to cover the ongoing marketing costs of the fund. Like all fees, they affect the performance of the fund. Most load funds and many small or newer funds that don't yet have an asset base large enough that their management fees cover their expenses will charge a 12b-1 fee.

Spiders

Investors who are concerned about mutual fund fees and who are convinced that, in an efficient market, the extra costs of an active manager are wasted, prefer to buy indexes directly. Index mutual funds, and more recently a pooled investment called an index share, give them the vehicle to do just that.

Common Types

Index shares are similar to mutual funds in that they are a basket of stocks that give investors the effect of owning a broad number of companies. Unlike mutual funds, which investors purchase by depositing dollars into the fund, index shares are purchased like stocks. Investors trade the shares on the market among other buyers and sellers. Index shares don't have the added costs associated with managing dollar deposits and withdrawals, so their fees and tax costs—they seldom have taxable gains to distribute to shareholders as mutual funds do—are lower.

The American Stock Exchange created the first index share to track the S&P 500 and gave it the symbol SPY. A nickname took root and investors were able to add Spiders to their portfolios. The American Stock Exchange quickly followed Spiders with new indexes tracking other markets. S&P 400 for mid cap U.S. stocks trades under the symbol MDY. New exchange-traded funds (ETFs), as many of the index shares are formally called, are being created almost daily.

Choosing and Comparing ETFs

ETFs are especially useful when you are making a one-time investment, such as from a previous employer's retirement plan into your own IRA. ETFs are sold like stock, so each trade generates a commission for the broker you're using. This commission is usually lower than what you would pay on a front-end loaded mutual fund and is seldom based on the size of the trade. Most frequently, you might see a $10 or $15 commission charged by your online broker for each ETF trade. The per-transaction cost of ETFs makes monthly investing expensive. If you're planning a monthly contribution to an account, no-load mutual funds offered either directly from the fund itself or through your broker as a no-transaction-fee fund is a better choice.

Trading costs create a huge drag on your investment return. There are plenty of mutual funds that are sold without a transaction fee, so you can find just what you need for your portfolio. Most exchange-traded funds have very low ongoing costs, so they are worth the transaction commission if you're investing a large amount.

Trends

Many investors build their whole portfolio out of ETFs. A selection of the broad market ETFs just mentioned—SPY, MDY, IWM, and EFA—are a great foundation to a portfolio. Recently, more ETFs have been—and continue to be—created that track particular industry sectors or adhere to investing styles such as small-company value investing. These ETFs are often not large enough to truly mirror the index they're targeting. ETFs need to be mature and sizable to be effective. Stick with the ones that have been around for at least five years and check Morningstar to see how well their performance has tracked their target index. Index shares are passively managed investments; if you want to add specific industry sectors or other specialties to your portfolio, an actively managed mutual fund would be a better choice.

Tax Planning with Stocks

Individual stocks, stock funds, and stock index shares are generally more tax efficient than bonds and other income-generating investments because of the preferential tax rates on dividends and capital gains. You should consider this when deciding whether to own stocks in your retirement accounts—which defer taxes until money is withdrawn and then tax withdrawals at higher income tax rates—or taxable accounts that expose transactions to taxes right away but also allow you to take advantage of tax losses and the lower capital gains tax rate.

Many people don't have large enough portfolios to follow this suggestion to the letter, but remember if you keep your riskier stock investments in your taxable account, you'll be more tax efficient. Riskier investments such as small- and mid-cap stock don't usually pay dividends, so they are, in effect, tax deferred. If you lose value you can sell and report the tax losses on your tax return, cutting the amount of tax you must pay.

Statements to Keep and What to Look For

Many people overpay their taxes on investment gains because they forget to keep good records. Keep your statements showing your purchase until you sell the investment. Then store the statement in your tax records for the year of the sale. Keep monthly mutual fund and brokerage statements throughout the year, and then shred them once the year-end statement arrives. If the year-end statement doesn't include a report of all reinvested dividends and interest from your funds, you'll need to keep each of the monthly statements. The idea is to keep all the statements that establish the cost of your investment—your basis.

Calculating Taxes when You Sell

The difference between what you paid for an investment and what you sell it for is your profit, or your capital gain. Keeping track of your total cost is essential to making sure you don't overestimate your profit and pay too much capital gains tax. Your total cost is the total of all your deposits, plus any taxable distributions such as dividends or capital gains, that you have paid tax on and reinvested. Reinvestments are most common in mutual funds, but you may also have your brokerage account set to reinvest dividends from stocks or ETFs. Additionally, your individual stock account might reinvest dividends.

QUESTION?

I have no records to help figure out my investment cost basis. What can I do?

Take your best shot at estimating an accurate basis by checking the newspaper or a historical price website such as Yahoo Finance (*www .finance.yahoo.com*) for the price closest to the day you think you bought the investment.

You might not notice reinvestments because you don't receive any money. The transaction is noted on your account statement and on the year-end Form 1099 that you'll use on your tax return. Many brokerage websites will allow you to keep track of your basis by giving you the chance to enter your cost right on their site. They will usually add additional transactions to your page if the transactions happen through them. Some brokerages will include this info on your Form 1099, making tax filing easier.

Calculating Taxes

Qualified dividends are taxed at a lower rate than interest. Your Form 1099 will tell you if any of your dividends qualify for this special treatment. Individual stock dividends and dividends passed through to you from ETFs are often qualified. Mutual fund dividends are seldom qualified—another appeal of ETFs if you pay income taxes in a tax bracket above 27 percent.

If you sell an investment within one year of buying it, your profit or loss is considered short-term; investments held longer than one year are long-term. Long-term gains are taxed at a lower, preferred rate than short-term gains, which are taxed at income tax rates. If you have both gains and losses in one year, you can count them against each other, dollar for dollar, under a strategy called harvesting your gains. If you need to sell investments to rebalance your portfolio or to withdraw cash, paying attention to the capital gains and losses can save you money. The IRS website, *www.irs.gov*, has more-detailed information on how this works. Tax laws vary from state to state. Check with your state's treasury department's website or counselors for the tax laws in your state.

CHAPTER 10

Finding the Perfect Investment Recipe

You may feel intimidated by the prospect of selecting the right investment mix—one risky enough to pay rewards that can keep pace with, or even slightly beat, inflation, but not so volatile that you dread checking your monthly account statements. Take heart: it's easier than it sounds. Many studies have shown that the asset allocation—the mix of stocks, bonds, and cash—in your investment accounts has greater effect on performance than individual investment choice. Fortunately, modern web tools and professional investment management options make picking an asset allocation easier than ever.

Find Your Risk Tolerance

Thinking carefully about your risk tolerance before investing will save a lot of stress once you've made your investments and start watching your account balance change. Consider your time frame and whether the goal you're investing toward will stretch across many years, such as retirement, or whether it will be a one-time purchase or a short-duration expense, such as college tuition. It's important to stick with your asset allocation through market ups and downs, but it is also okay to start conservatively and increase the risk you take as you become more experienced.

Importance of Time Frame

Online asset allocation tools often depict your investment mix graphically as a colorful pie chart. Most brokerages, including Schwab, Fidelity, and E-Trade, present your current asset allocation on your statement or on their website. This is helpful because it clearly depicts the proportions of your portfolio assigned to each asset class—the most basic being U.S. and non-U.S. stocks; bonds or other fixed-income investments; and cash. Over time, each of the various asset classes swings through periods of growth or decline. In any given period, your stocks may be performing well while your bonds are not. Then it could reverse. Sometimes neither the bonds nor stocks gain value and you're glad you have some cash in your mix. Deciding how large each slice of the pie should be is dependent on your time frame and your risk tolerance.

QUESTION?

When does an investment become a long-term investment?
Once you've owned the investment for one year, it is considered a long-term investment and enjoys the lower tax rate on profits if you sell. Beware the wash-sale rule! If you rebuy the exact same investment within thirty days of selling, you erase the previous sale for tax purposes.

In a perfect world, risk-taking is rewarded with higher return. But because this isn't a perfect world, the trick is to make sure that the return you're expecting is going to happen within the time that you'll need to start withdrawing your money. For instance, remember that, historically, stocks have grown faster than cash or bonds. The problem is that stocks are risky and can lose value over short periods of time. Because of this, stocks are a better choice for longer-term investments. If you need your money to grow over a short time—say five years or less—you're smart to invest in bonds or cash.

ALERT!

Investing for college is different than investing for retirement. Your asset allocation for retirement can remain aggressively invested in stocks even after you've actually retired. College investing needs to be more conservative because you're using the money over a very short period.

Stick with a Plan

The asset allocation you arrive at should consider how best to mix risk with return, considering your time frame and the amount of risk you're willing to take. You have a higher risk tolerance if you're not upset to see dramatic swings, downward as well as upward, in your account balances each month. If the goal you're investing toward is also long-term—say seven years or longer—then these short-term fluctuations probably won't bother you as long as the general trend is upward.

Sticking with your asset allocation may sometimes seem counterintuitive. Most investment advisors recommend that you check your investments against your target asset allocation at least once per year, and rebalance your portfolio. Your annual review assumes that some of your asset classes have performed better than others. The result is that the value of one asset class, say the stock portion, will have grown beyond the percentage that you originally targeted when you created your asset pie chart. At the same time, other classes will have been proportionately shrunk by the size of the larger sector, and you'll have to adjust the balance.

Assuming your target allocation remains unchanged, rebalance your portfolio by selling investments that are in the higher-performing, overly large class or classes and buying more of the lower-performing, undersized classes. You only need to sell and buy enough to restore the percentages you originally assigned to each class. Rebalancing helps ensure that you're taking profits when you should and that you are selling at a profit and buying low-priced assets whenever possible.

Changing Risk Tolerance with Experience

Don't worry if, at first, you don't want to take as much risk as your time frame, your asset allocation tool, or your investment advisor recommends. Start with a more conservative mix—with fewer stocks and more bonds and cash—and then work up to your allocation target when you become more comfortable. If you're still not sure, try setting up a hypothetical portfolio online, and then track it as its value changes. Financial sites such as Morningstar.com and Women's Financial Network (WFN.com) have tools to help you.

Online Resources and Trends

There is a surprising wealth of online resources to help you arrive at your asset allocation. Some are better than others, so it's important to know what to look for and how to interpret each tool's recommendations. There is a list of good tools in Appendix B.

What to Look For

Most asset allocation tools will ask you some basic questions about your investment goals and your time horizon. Be sure you're using a tool you understand and compare the results of a few tools before deciding on your personal target asset allocation.

Don't "time the market" by selling and holding cash when stocks start to go down. Knowing when to get back into the market is very difficult, if not impossible. Timing the market requires that you're right twice—finding the right time to sell and to buy. It's better to plan your asset allocation and stick with it through the short-term ups and downs.

Be wary of a tool that recommends specific investment products. Selling these products may be more the focus of the tool than giving good allocation advice. And avoid tools that ask you to make investment return assumptions or recommend frequent trading. If you're inexperienced at investing, it can be difficult to be sure you're making reasonable return assumptions—the asset allocation tool should have a database of historical returns to do that for you.

Monte Carlo

Most good asset allocation tools use a function known as "Monte Carlo simulation" that helps predict future outcomes using a huge variety of statistical inputs. For instance, rather than assuming that the investment class returns the same amount each year—something that history shows is never the case—Monte Carlo simulation can create a more realistic scenario by projecting performance within a range of investment returns. With Monte Carlo simulation, your asset allocation tool can assume more realistically that sometimes stocks do well and sometimes they don't. Instead of giving you a specific expected return, most tools will give you a more realistic range of returns to expect from a particular asset allocation.

ALERT!

Monte Carlo simulation is a very complex process, but it's not foolproof. As with other computerized programs, you can get bad information out if you put bad information in. Run several different simulations using software programs or web-based allocation tools and compare their results before deciding on an approach for your portfolio.

Getting Advice: Whom Can You Trust?

Investing is complex, and beginners and novices alike should get independent advice every once in a while. It's important to make sure that, as an amateur investor, you're not missing something important that professional investors might know. Money exerts very powerful psychological influence on investors, so it's often smart to ask the opinion of someone who's not emotionally involved with your portfolio. With all the investment advisors out there, whom should you trust?

Resources at Work

Most companies with retirement plans have administrators or human resources staffers available to answer your questions about investing in the plan and how to choose an asset allocation. These folks are generally onsite at your workplace on a regular basis and are very helpful in explaining the plan investments and details about the account itself, including how to log in to the plan's website and how to modify your investment choice. Their expertise is usually limited to the employer plan itself, so you'll need to find another advisor for an opinion on your other accounts.

Many companies retain employee assistance programs (EAPs) that provide access to investment and financial planning professionals. These programs are offered at no cost to employees by the employer as a part of their benefits package. Through your EAP, you may have access to a financial advisor to help with your investments. Just because your employer is making the referral to the EAP advisor, don't assume that the employer has interviewed the advisor; you should still ask the advisor all the important questions about expertise and conflict of interest that you would ask any professional before engaging him.

Many advisors who work for programs through employers are compensated by salary, so they have no conflict of interest in the advice they give you. Others may have a bonus program based on the amount the employees invest in a particular fund. Be sure to ask your advisor how he is paid.

Investment Advisors' Effect on Asset Allocation

Don't be afraid to ask questions of your investment advisor, especially if you're a new investor. Regardless of your experience, your advisor has been doing this longer than you and may feel more comfortable with an asset allocation that is riskier than you would be comfortable with. Be sure to ask how much the investments could gain or lose in a period of time. The advisor should be able to show you historical research on how much similar investments have gone down over time frames of three months, one year, and five years. Do the math with your own portfolio and decide if you would be comfortable with a similar decline. Remember, asset allocation only works if you can stick with it. If you can't sleep peacefully knowing the loss potential, select a more conservative allocation with fewer stocks. Later, you may feel comfortable with more risk.

Make sure you understand what your advisor is recommending to you. Now, that might sound obvious, but investing is complex and it can be easy to just take the advisor's word for it. This isn't always smart. Many people have gotten caught investing in assets that were riskier than they understood. Don't feel as if you need to give your advisor the third degree each time she makes a recommendation—after all, you're paying for her expertise. Instead, try these simple steps to help make sure you understand her recommendations:

- Read financial and investing websites and magazines.
- Save clippings or web articles to discuss with your advisor.
- Get opinions from several resources—e.g., your accountant, lawyer, and financial planner.
- Talk to your friends whose financial opinions you trust.

Talk to your advisor about how she is paid. There are three basic financial advisor compensation schemes: commission, fee based, and fee only. Some advisors may offer a choice or a combination, but in most cases the advisor will fall into one of the three categories.

Commission advisors are paid by the company whose financial product you buy from them. Fee-based advisors are often focused on providing investment services and are compensated as a percentage of the account you maintain with them—often called an assets under management, or AUM, fee. Fee-only advisors typically charge by the hour or on an annual retainer basis. Since their compensation is not focused on your investment account size or the products you buy, their practice can range from holistic financial planning advice to offering expert advice in a specific area such as retirement or college planning. Talk to any advisor you choose about potential conflicts of interest that her compensation scheme might create.

Investment Clubs

Investment clubs can be a fun way to learn about investing. Usually created by a group of friends, your investment club will assign each member a particular stock to research. Most club-support organizations provide educational resources for members to follow and help with bookkeeping and record-keeping. Members deposit a monthly investment amount into a pooled account that is then invested by the group.

FACT

Your investment club will need to decide what type of business entity suits it best. Many clubs become general partnerships by default because they are easy to create and require no paperwork or special tax knowledge. A limited liability company (LLC) might be a better option because it adds a measure of liability protection for the members.

You probably won't get rich investing in your investment club, but these clubs are a great way to learn and to cultivate a group of friends that you can talk to about investing and other financial planning issues. Check Appendix B for websites that can help you get started.

Target Date Funds

Target date funds make asset allocation easy by creating the investment mix and investment choices automatically. These funds are created by mutual fund companies or other managers and are made up of funds picked to match a specific allocation. The fund names usually indicate the time frame or the risk tolerance they're oriented to.

What They Are

Some target date funds are based on a time frame. Examples of these are Fidelity Investments' Freedom funds. As the name designates, the Fidelity Freedom 2015 fund is meant to provide an asset allocation and mix of Fidelity mutual funds that would be appropriate for an investor retiring around 2015. Fidelity decides on the asset allocation and picks the funds to match. As 2015 approaches, the asset allocation is automatically modified to reflect the shorter time frame.

Other target date funds suggest an allocation based on a risk tolerance. These funds feature names with words such as "aggressive," "moderate," or "conservative" to show which risk tolerance they are targeting. Vanguard Investments' LifeStrategy funds are examples of these funds. For example, Vanguard LifeStrategy Moderate Growth fund means to provide a portfolio for an investor with a moderate growth risk tolerance.

Target date funds sound effortless, but you still need to research them before you invest. Check to see if there are additional fees created by the so-called fund-of-funds structure of target date funds. If there are, it may be better to pick individual mutual funds yourself outside of the target date fund. Compare asset allocations among fund companies. What the fund company thinks is conservative or appropriate for a 2015 retiree may be dramatically different than the practices of another company. Check independent resources such as Morningstar.com for reviews of the funds and, as with any investment, read the prospectus before you invest.

ALERT!

Target date funds make great gifts. Once the minimum initial deposit is met—check the fund prospectus for this amount—even small additional deposits are instantly diversified across all the investments in the fund. A target date fund would be a better gift for a child or student than an individual stock because of the diversification.

Best Times to Use Them

New investors like target date funds because they can be a good way to get started. If you're starting with a small account or a small monthly deposit, the target date fund will offer instant diversification and automatic rebalancing to keep the right asset allocation. Many employers who automatically enroll employees in a company retirement account have started using target date funds because of these advantages. If your employer has done this, check the fund to be sure it's appropriate for you. If you're planning to transfer a large amount of money—from a previous employer's plan or from another account—a target date fund might be the easiest place to start, but might not be the best option for a large amount of money over a long period of time.

Managed Accounts and Money Managers

Many investment managers and investment companies offer a managed account option that can work well for investors with large accounts. Advisors are usually compensated under the fee-based model—in which they earn a fee based on a percentage of the size of the account. Some managers offer managed portfolios of mutual funds for smaller accounts, but you'll more commonly see managers offering individual stock portfolios with larger account asset minimums of $500,000 or more.

Advantages over Mutual Funds

Managed accounts offer a service advantage over mutual funds because you have direct access to the investment managers themselves. Managed accounts, also called separate accounts, are like private mutual funds. You give your money to a manager, who then invests it in a variety of individual securities—stocks, bonds, or other investments—under a policy statement similar to the investment objective your mutual fund manager outlines in the mutual fund prospectus.

Most managers offer a limited choice of account styles, such as moderate, aggressive, or even more specifically, small-cap value, for example, that capitalize on their particular investing expertise. Just as you might invest in a variety of different mutual funds, individual investors, using separate accounts, will own more than one account in order to take advantage of the expertise of managers with different specialties. Often this group of separate managers is overseen by a financial planner, or even the investor herself, and can include managers whose accounts cover a variety of asset classes such as small cap U.S. stocks, non-U.S. stocks, municipal bonds, or a special sector such as, for example, alternative energy companies.

When to Use Them

Managed accounts can be helpful if your account is large and you're an inexperienced investor. If you're more comfortable managing a team of people than you are a large portfolio, you may find the special service option of separate accounts appealing. If you are an educated but not an expert investor, and you'd rather pay the fee than become a do-it-yourself investor, then a fee-based or fee-only manager may be a good investing partner.

What to Look For

Most separate account managers work on the theory discussed earlier that active investment picking will be more successful over time than a passive approach or investing in market indexes. If you also subscribe to this opinion and can find a successful manager with exceptional customer service, the added expense might be worth it.

The experience of your separate account manager is very important. Often, you'll find a manager who has begun his career managing funds at a large firm such as State Street Global Advisors or Morgan Stanley, and then decided to open his own shop. This new company may be small, but the size of the firm matters less than the manager's expertise, track record, and resources. Ask prospective managers to provide historical performance reports of accounts they have managed. Ask them to outline the resources at their firm's disposal to help them continue their large-firm track record when managing your account. Many managers move clients into preset accounts, selling the client's current assets and buying new investments that follow the manager's predetermined portfolio. If this is the case, be sure you've planned for any tax consequences of selling your current investments.

By far the most important part of working with separate accounts is your relationship with your money manager. Ask about his business plans. Will you continue working with him as he grows? Have other associates in the firm, who may do the day-to-day, hands-on work of managing your assets, had the same investing success that the principals have? Ask about fees and how they might change as your account changes in value. Separate accounts typically charge an annual fee equal to 1 percent of the assets they manage for you, up to a certain dollar limit that reduces as your account grows.

Annuities

Annuities are products provided by insurance companies with special tax and insurance benefits. Annuities usually bundle a variety of investment choices, called subaccounts, that bear a resemblance to mutual funds. The earnings and investment profits in the annuity aren't taxed until they're withdrawn. When you do make withdrawals, you pay income tax on the amount you take that is over and above your original deposit. This doesn't matter whether the earnings were from capital gains or from interest earned by the investments within the annuity. Your investment in the annuity is only as secure as the insurance company itself; be sure to check the financial-strength ratings of the insurance company you're considering.

QUESTION?

My annuity is six years old and has performed poorly. How do I calculate the fees to close the account?
The prospectus lists the percent fee for withdrawal during each year. Check the annual fee, too. If it is the same as the year-six withdrawal fee, it might be worth closing the account without waiting another year.

Annuity Features

There are two phases in the life of an annuity—the accumulation phase and the payout phase. During the accumulation phase, the investor makes one or more deposits into the annuity. During the payout phase, the annuity makes payments back to the investor and, if directed, the investor's beneficiaries for a specific period of time.

Investors like annuities because the insurance company invests the money and promises an income payout for a specified duration of time. That time period could be for a set number of years—called a "term certain"— or for the investor's entire life—"lifetime income." The regular amount paid for lifetime income is lower than that paid for term certain in most cases, but the marketing appeal of income for life is very powerful. Be extra sure you review the payout options on your annuities very carefully to see which would work best for you.

Annuities are also used by governments and private entities to provide pensions, and there are a few very low-fee annuities like those provided by TIAA CREF—Teachers Insurance and Annuity Association, College Retirement Equities Fund—that have successfully accomplished what they have promised. Unfortunately, too many annuities are purchased by people who don't fully understand how complex and expensive they can be.

Annuities generally carry higher fees than mutual funds because of their insurance features. This insurance feature is what created the higher-cost tax characteristics of annuities. The benefit offered is that beneficiaries might receive more than the value of the account if the investor dies and certain requirements are met. The disadvantage is that recent tax laws have made the payments from annuities more expensive by being taxed as income rather than lower-rate capital gains.

Immediate and Deferred Annuities

Annuities that start the payout phase immediately after one deposit are called immediate annuities. Deferred annuities start paying after an accumulation phase and accept deposits over time. You may never decide to annuitize a deferred annuity—meaning to start taking payments. Many investors hold the deferred annuity like any other investment account and then plan to take periodic withdrawals when needed in the future. Annuities can be changed just like other investment products. You can sell your annuity and buy another—a tax-free transaction called a 1035 exchange. Or you can withdraw the money from your annuity and reinvest or spend the funds. The amount of your withdrawal above and beyond the amount you deposited is taxable as income. If you withdraw money from your annuity before you turn age 59½, you may also have an early withdrawal penalty of 10 percent.

Fixed and Variable Annuities

Annuities that are invested by the insurance company and earn interest are called fixed annuities. Be careful: the back-end sales charge on an annuity can make moving the account within seven years expensive. Many fixed annuities carry higher interest rates for the first year, with subsequent years being paid lower interest. The fees may make moving to another account quite expensive.

Variable annuities have subaccounts that invest in stocks and bonds like mutual funds. There are also new annuity products called equity-indexed annuities. In both cases, investors are seeking to earn returns similar to the stock market. Annuities have become a less desirable way to do this because you're shouldering all the same risk of investing in stocks without the lower-rate capital gains tax benefits. Equity-indexed annuities have become controversial because they seem to offer the chance at stock market returns without the stock market risk by promising a minimum annual return. Many investors have bought these complex investments without realizing that, after fees and expenses and tax charges, they have fared worse than if they had invested outside of the annuity.

CHAPTER 11

Buying Investments

Once you've decided how much to invest and the right mix of stocks, bonds, and cash for your particular goals, it's time to plan out how to buy the investments. Your choice to buy them yourself or use a broker can affect fees, convenience, and performance. Planning whether to hold your stocks in taxable or retirement accounts, planning for withdrawals, and making sure your noninvesting partner is kept in the loop are very important, especially when you're in your 40s and 50s. Finally, keeping good records and dealing with inherited or gifted accounts are a big part of investing success at your age.

The Ins and Outs of Buying

Getting your accounts organized can seem an insurmountable task. By the time they reach age 40 and beyond, many people have accumulated a couple of 401(k)s or other employer-sponsored accounts from previous jobs, a few IRA accounts, several savings and bank accounts, and maybe a stock option account, employee stock purchase plan, or cash balance plan from an old pension. But the time spent getting your accounts and records organized will pay dividends as you work though your retirement planning and will give you the chance to make your account more tax efficient.

Direct Purchase

Most people originally start investing by purchasing individual investments directly—that is, without the help of a broker. They buy mutual funds from the fund company itself. They might invest in stocks through a direct investment program—known as a DRIP account—or they might own the stock certificates themselves. Investing separately may save them commissions or fees associated with a brokerage account. But by the time they're in their 40s or 50s, this can translate into a large number of small accounts to track.

Brokerage Services

Brokerage services have become popular, in part because they help organize accounts and records. Brokerages provide a single account that aggregates a variety of stocks, bonds, mutual funds and index shares, and other investments. You must keep separate registrations—or ownership—for accounts under their special ownership or tax rules, but at least you can minimize the number of individual accounts you hold.

Organizing accounts by ownership rules means separating assets into accounts such as joint, individual, and transfer-on-death accounts. Joint accounts are held by more than one individual and can be accessed equally by any of the owners. Individual accounts are only accessible by the owner. Transfer-on-death accounts are handy because they become readily available to the beneficiary upon the death of the owner. There's no probate process for beneficiaries to go through, so money is available quickly, while the value isn't exposed to the risks and liability of a joint account.

FACT

If you have several small accounts, try consolidating them with one broker. Ask your broker to consolidate your statements for easier tracking, and the higher overall balance should save you fees. If the broker has an online asset allocation tool, having all your accounts on that one site will make analysis easier, too.

Organizing by tax rules means that you combine all of your retirement assets into accounts that are divided by special tax rules for how deposits are treated. Your IRA, rollover IRA, Roth IRA, SEP, SIMPLE IRA, and other similar accounts have to stay separate from one another, in most cases, because of tax rules, but if they are at least held by one broker, your account and tax statements will come from one provider—and in most cases on one statement. Holding more assets at one provider will usually gain you lower fees and maybe even waivers of some fees altogether.

What to Look For and How to Compare

Finding a good investment among the huge number of available choices is easier than it might initially seem. Statistics describing investments are standardized, and most resources categorize investments following Morningstar's style boxes. By breaking down your asset allocation into the appropriate styles and following a few simple steps to compare performance, cost, and convenience within each style, you'll have your portfolio set up in no time.

Morningstar's Stock Style Boxes

Morningstar created their style box model to visually depict the type—or style—of an investment. The style box is made up of nine small squares—three rows by three columns. Style boxes are depicted with one square darkened to show the style of the investment.

If your stock investment has a style box with a square in the top row darkened, it's a large-cap stock investment. If the middle row has a darkened square, it's a mid-cap company stock, and if the bottom row has a darkened square, it's a small-cap stock.

If the darkened square is in the left column, your investment is in value stocks. The middle column is for blend stocks, and the right column is for growth stocks.

Your asset allocation should seek to fit each of the squares in the stock style box. That means you'll have large, mid-cap, and small-cap stocks that are value-, blend-, and growth-oriented. By sorting your investments by their style boxes, you'll be sure that you make an apples-to-apples performance comparison.

QUESTION?

Do I need to find an investment to fill each of the squares in the Morningstar style box?
No, you don't. You may meet your asset allocation with a blend fund instead of a growth or value stock fund, or you may decide on an allocation that uses only high-quality bonds and ignores riskier low-quality, high-yield bonds.

Morningstar's Bond Style Boxes

Bond investments also have a Morningstar style box with nine squares. The top row of squares shows that the investment is in high-quality bonds, meaning that principal risk is minimal; the middle row indicates medium-quality bonds; and the bottom row is low-quality, or junk, bonds. The left column of squares is for short-term bonds, the middle column for medium term, and the right column for long-term maturities.

For example, if the upper right box is darkened, the investments would be in high-quality, long-term bonds. If the lower left square is darkened, the investment buys low-quality, short-term bonds.

Performance

Performance statistics are standardized and are available from the investment companies and from independent sites such as Morningstar. com, Google Finance, and Yahoo Finance. Use the style box to check the performance of your investment against others with the same style and the securities index it most closely matches. The best stock indexes to compare to are the S&P 500 for large-cap stocks, S&P 400 for mid-cap stocks, and Russell 2000 for small-cap stocks. The MSCI EAFE index is a good index with which to compare non-U.S. stocks.

Common bond indexes are Lehman Aggregate Bond Index for high-quality, medium-term bonds; Lehman 1–3 Year Treasury Bond for high-quality, short-term bonds; and the Credit Suisse First Boston (CSFB) High Yield Index for lower-quality corporate bonds.

ALERT!

Watch the fees in your retirement accounts. Retirement accounts have restrictions on the amount you can invest each year. Don't waste too much of this precious money on fees that don't do anything to increase your nest egg. Don't put annuities and mutual funds with high fees in your retirement accounts.

Performance numbers are given one-, three-, and five-year terms. If your investment has a sales load, be sure you're comparing performance numbers that include the effect of the sales load—look for the "load-adjusted return" to be sure the performance information is realistic.

Cost and Convenience

Cost and convenience are very important. If you're spending all your time and too much money managing your investments, it will be hard to stick with your plan. Mutual funds are best if you're investing a certain dollar amount every month because you can set up your accounts to invest automatically and you can use a fund that doesn't charge a transaction fee for deposits. If you're investing a lump sum of money, index shares, which have lower ongoing fees but charge a small commission per transaction, will be better.

QUESTION?

I'm busy. Do I really need to read the prospectus before I invest?
Yes! The prospectus is the only place where you can be sure the information is correct. Use Morningstar.com as a resource to help choose the investments so you can limit the prospectuses you review to just the investments you're planning to buy.

The investment prospectus will outline the fees in the investment. This information is repeated on Morningstar's investment reports and on the summaries—called tear sheets—provided by the investment companies. Pooled investments such as mutual funds and exchange-traded funds carry three types of fees: sales, management, and advertising fees, the last called 12b-1 fees. You don't pay the fees directly, so they can be difficult to calculate.

The fund pays the fees before calculating performance, so higher fees can result in lower performance. Not all funds charge all three types of fees. Funds that pay a commission to the broker who sold them are called A shares if they charge the fee when you make a deposit to the fund, B shares if they charge on the amount you withdraw, or C shares if they assess an annual fee. No-load funds don't charge a sales load; every fund charges an annual management fee. Small funds, or ones that pay broker commissions, collect annual 12b-1 fees to cover ongoing advertising costs.

FACT

A, B, and C shares are the basic classes, but you may find other share classes named after other letters in the alphabet, or called institutional or investor shares. Different classes usually mean different fees or minimum deposits—for example, institutional shares usually have much higher initial deposit minimums than investor shares. These differences are described in the fund prospectus.

Beware the Tax Man

Your investments are taxed in two ways: profits are taxed at capital gains rates and most dividends and interest are taxed at income tax rates. Tax rates can change almost yearly based on new or sunsetting tax laws, but for your planning purposes it's okay to assume that capital gains rates are lower than income tax rates. Any money you pay toward taxes on your investments counts against your overall returns. By thinking ahead about which investments to hold in tax-sheltered retirement accounts and which to hold in regular taxable accounts, you can help your portfolio be more successful.

Strategies for Taxable Accounts

Your taxable accounts are accounts whose funds are available to withdraw at any time. There are no tax restrictions like the ones on retirement accounts that limit the amount you deposit or restrict when you can withdraw money. Interest, dividends, and capital gains from investment sales from taxable accounts are taxable in the year they are realized. Your bank accounts, money market accounts, and individual or joint investment account are all examples of taxable accounts.

Use your taxable accounts to hold liquid money for emergencies or for upcoming expenses. Try to concentrate your stock investments in your taxable accounts to take advantage of profits being taxed at the lower capital gains tax rate. Stocks are more volatile than bonds, and if you have losses in your taxable account, you'll be able to count those against your capital gains to save tax.

Pooled investments such as mutual funds and exchange-traded funds don't pay their own taxes. When they have a taxable transaction such as interest earnings or capital gains, they pass it through to their individual shareholders. In your taxable account, this income is taxable to you on your next tax return.

Strategies for Retirement Plans

Retirement accounts—for example, your IRAs and employer retirement accounts—are called tax-deferred accounts. This means that you don't pay any tax on the activity in them until you withdraw money. Retirement plan withdrawals are taxed as income, meaning you can't take advantage of lower capital gains rates for stock investments in these accounts.

Remember, your asset allocation is the mix of investment classes over your entire portfolio—not just in one account. With that in mind, put more of your bond allocation into your retirement accounts to shelter the current income they are creating. Hold more of your bond mutual funds, CDs, and individual bonds themselves in your retirement accounts than you do in your taxable accounts.

Think of it this way: If you're in your 40s or 50s, you probably have about 30 percent or so of your asset allocation targeted to fixed income. By putting as much of that fixed income as you can in your retirement accounts, and then holding the remaining 70 percent of your portfolio in your taxable accounts, you will save tax money.

Contribute to a Roth IRA in the years you're eligible; they are a great tax planning tool. Withdrawals are tax free and can be delayed past age 70½. You don't get to deduct your deposit on your tax return, but the tax free withdrawals in retirement can be a great source of liquidity.

Planning for Withdrawals

Avoid limiting your tax planning flexibility in retirement by overfunding your retirement accounts. This doesn't mean you shouldn't save for retirement! Just think carefully about which accounts to invest your retirement savings into. Remember, money withdrawn from accounts such as IRAs and 401(k)s or other employer accounts is taxed as current earned income. Granted, contributions to retirement accounts will often get you a tax deduction at the time you make the investment, but imagine being retired with your only source of cash being an account that carries a tax on withdrawals. What would you do if you needed to buy a car after you're retired? With only retirement accounts to draw from, you would either incur the interest costs for a car loan or pay income taxes on the money that you withdraw from your IRA to buy the car. Be sure your retirement savings is going into retirement accounts and taxable accounts that bring tax-planning flexibility in the future.

Some risks you can see—such as the stock market going down—but others sneak up on you—such as inflation over a long retirement. Taking enough market risk by including stocks in your portfolio is an important way to reduce inflation risk—the chance that your nest egg won't keep up with the cost of living.

Patching Up Old Mistakes

Not all portfolios are perfect, and if you're in your 40s and 50s, you probably have a variety of old accounts or have inherited accounts that need some polishing up. Merging gifted assets and inherited assets that were meant to meet someone else's goals into your portfolio can be a tax challenge unless you know where to find important information. Making sure you have all of your accounts well organized will save you money, as well.

Gifted Assets

You don't owe tax when assets are given to you—though, depending on the size of the gift, the giver might—but you do receive the giver's basis in the asset. Remember, the basis is the amount originally paid for the asset, plus any additional deposits, including reinvested dividends, interest, and capital gains. Don't forget to ask the giver for his basis when you receive the gift. You'll need to know your capital gain amount when you sell.

Once you know that basis, you can treat the gifted asset like any other of your investments. Do an investment review, and if it doesn't fit your asset allocation or if it's underperforming comparable investments or the most appropriate index, it's time to sell.

Inherited Assets

You have some tax planning to do if you inherit a retirement account such as an IRA or a 401(k), but other than those special accounts, you don't owe tax when you inherit money. In some cases, the estate of the person you're inheriting from might owe tax; hopefully, she has paid the tax before distributing your inheritance to you. The advantage of inheritances over gifts is that you get what's called a stepped-up basis on the asset—instead of inheriting the giver's basis as you would with a gift, your new basis is the value of the asset on the day the giver died. Some large estates are valued as of six months after the day the individual dies—ask the executor of the estate whether this is the case in your situation.

If you've inherited a retirement account, it's important to get tax advice. If the individual who owned the account was over age 70½ and was taking withdrawals, you will need to continue making withdrawals of a certain minimum amount. If the account owner was younger, you may be able to delay taking withdrawals or you may be able to take small withdrawals over your lifetime. If you inherit your spouse's retirement account, you can roll the proceeds over into your own account and in many cases delay taking withdrawals. The reason for trying to delay withdrawals is to save taxes and continue the tax-deferred growth in the retirement account. This doesn't mean that you can't take money from the account if you need it; you'll just owe taxes on the amount if you do.

Your Own Accounts

It's never too late to fix a neglected investment or portfolio. Start by gathering your account statements and listing the account name, total balance, investment values, investment basis, and the amount you're contributing regularly to the account. Most brokers and investment companies keep track of the basis in the investments you bought through them for as long as you still hold the account with them. If you're not sure of a basis, call the broker and see if they have that information before deciding to move the account. If they don't know your basis, they should still be able to mail you copies of past statements. From these statements you should be able to add up all your deposits—remember to include reinvested dividends and interest as well as cash deposits.

If you're missing accounts or can't find statements, look at back tax returns for records of interest, dividends, or taxable capital gains. The tax return schedules that report these incomes will list the investment name. Call the investment company and check for accounts using your social security number.

Keep It Simple: Record-Keeping

Good record-keeping doesn't need to be complex. Something simple and easy to keep up with is best, and if your process is simple you'll more quickly notice if something is wrong with your accounts.

What to Keep and How Long

Keep records of your investment purchases until you sell the investments. Keep the transaction confirmation until you get the monthly statement. Then—since the transaction is on the statement—you can shred the confirmation. Most year-end statements will show the total deposits and withdrawals for the year. If this is the case, you can shred the monthly statements once you've received the annual statement. Since investments are often tax related, it might be easiest to keep your investment and tax information together. Tax returns and related records need to be kept for at least seven years. Be careful not to shred your investment information along with tax information you're discarding, unless you've already sold the investment.

Be sure you shred your investment statements when you throw them away. They contain lots of personal information—such as your name and address, account number, and invested balances—that could make you a target for identity theft. Many brokerages offer to provide online statements and transaction confirmations, a much safer option than working with paper.

Keep information about whether you were able to deduct the amount you deposited in your IRA account. Everyone with earned income is eligible to deposit money into a personal IRA account, but if you have an employer-provided account such as a 401(k) and you make more than a certain amount of income, you may not be able to deduct the amount you deposit in your IRA on your tax return. Keeping track of these after-tax deposits, as they are called, is important. These deposits become your IRA basis and are not taxable when you withdraw them in retirement.

Simple Systems

There are web-based systems for keeping track of your investments, programs that are downloaded to your computer's hard drive, and paper filing systems. Many banks and brokerages offer account aggregators that pull account information from all of your different investment account websites and consolidate them on one website. These are often powered by Yodlee. Yodlee has its own aggregator available at *www.yodlee.com.*

Software-based bookkeeping systems such as Quicken and MS Money will also help you track your investments and will calculate your asset allocation for you and create a pie chart showing your investment mix. Most of the brokerages—including Vanguard, Fidelity Investments, and Schwab—offer this as well.

Many investors use a simple three-ring binder to organize their investment statements; indeed, most statements come three-hole punched for this purpose. Adding a tab to list your financial goals and notes from your money meetings is a great way to keep all this information accessible and easy to use.

CHAPTER 12

Kids and Money

12

Money is often a taboo subject in families, but teaching your kids by example can be the best way to get them off to a strong start with their own finances and help instill a healthy, open attitude toward discussing money. As soon as you think they're ready, take the opportunity to get them involved in their own personal finances as you think about yours. Regardless how old they are—whether they're teens or even older—it's never too late to help them get savvy with their money.

Passing along the Planning Ethic

Your kids are going to have the same learning curve to climb as you did when you first tried to get your finances under control. If they are young, present their money education in phases that mesh with lessons they're learning in school. If your kids are older or grown, bring them up to speed by sharing your own financial planning story.

Many money attitudes seem to be hardwired from birth. Your children may be natural savers or natural spenders. If your kids are savers, encourage them by teaching them about investing. If your kids are spenders, help them manage a budget—and resist the urge to bail them out.

Money Education in Stages

Whether you're educating your kids or your grandkids, be sure the lessons you're offering fit with their understanding of planning and delayed gratification. Even if they're older, don't try to pile on too much all at once. Take it one step at a time: Start with the basics of budgeting and money management, managing credit cards and debt, and buying insurance. Next, progress to investing and retirement planning. Try to make conversations about money natural and commonplace.

You can set up a money market account in your child's name and social security number by making the account a Unified Transfer to Minors Act (UTMA) account (also called a Unified Gift to Minors Act (UGMA) account in some states). Alert family members who like to give your children gifts that a deposit to the account would be appreciated.

What Impression Does Your Lifestyle Make?

What message is your lifestyle sending to your children? Remember that appearances can be deceptive. People who appear to have a lot of money may in fact simply have a lot of debt. Make sure your kids understand that. If you're financially comfortable and have many personal assets, be sure they realize that it was good planning—not high credit-card balances—that got you there.

Many people are faced with difficult life changes in their 40s and 50s. If you're dealing with widowhood or divorce, don't be afraid to let the kids know that this has affected your financial situation. Use this difficult situation as an example of how strong financial planning and disciplined habits can help anyone weather even the most difficult storms.

Grade School Thrift Lessons

The earlier you start teaching children money lessons, the better. Starting an allowance as soon as children can understand delayed gratification and planning, and then adding on a savings account, is a great way to start.

Try to mirror your children's money lessons to adult financial realities as closely as you can. Make allowances consistent, like your paycheck. Avoid linking them to the household chores that the kids are responsible for. (After all, chores are an everyday reality of sharing family responsibilities.) It's helpful to pay the allowance in increments that are easily divisible. Try 25 cents or $1 per year of age, to start. And work with your child to decide how to invest, save, and spend the money. You could also consider a base allowance with an extra 10 percent bonus if certain incentive milestones are met, such as scoring good grades or completing special home projects.

ALERT!

Allowances are more effective when they're received consistently. Don't let the rush of the day interfere with getting the allowances paid. Remember, this is your child's payday. Setting up a direct deposit from your account to her account—when she gets one—is a good way to be sure these payments aren't missed.

Get your kids involved in shopping and comparing prices. Have them create savings plans for larger-ticket items that they want to buy, rather than you picking up the tab. If you need to, help them reach their goal more quickly by matching their savings deposits.

Finance and the Adolescent

Once your kids are teenagers, they're ready for investments and credit cards. Introduce investments first as a natural add-on to their savings account. Then add the credit card so that they have good spending and debt-management habits established before they leave home.

Investments

Teaching kids about investing is fun. Whether you're a beginner or an advanced investor yourself, getting your kids involved can be a great learning experience for both of you. Start younger teens with simple mutual funds. Try a target date fund so that their smaller deposits are allocated automatically across the diversified investments in the fund. Include kids in the investment review part of your monthly money meetings and ask them to do research on new funds.

Older teens and college students are ready for brokerage accounts. Have them set up accounts using your address as the residence so statements are not chasing them around their colleges; they can access the account online. You can list yourself on an account as the guardian without it being a joint account. Remember that colleges consider the child's assets in calculating for financial aid benefits, so much of his account will be tapped for tuition.

Credit Cards

Your teens will start receiving credit card solicitations almost immediately upon arriving at college, if not earlier, so it's wise to start teaching them good credit management while they are still home. Telling them to use a card only for emergencies, or not to get a card, is not an option. Credit cards are a fact of life like all the others you've taught them by now. You need credit to rent an apartment, turn on utilities, and rent a car. Most kids go from the college financial aid office, where they've just received what feels to them like play money to pay for college, to the bookstore, where the credit card applications are waiting. This can make credit cards feel like free money, too, unless they've already learned sound credit card habits from you.

Start your child with a low-limit credit card. Check *www.bankrate.com* for a list of issuers, and look for a card with no annual fee. You may need to cosign for the card. Be vigilant with banks that will try to increase the credit limit. If you're on the card as cosigner, you'll be able to keep close track of the account.

Sit down with your child and explain how to read the credit card statement online and in hard copy. Decide what charges will go on the card. Focus on using the card for convenience—e.g., to charge DVD rentals or order merchandise online—and insist that the balance be paid off each month. Be ready for your teen to start receiving solicitations in the mail as she gets close to her eighteenth birthday. Once she has a card of her own, close the one you cosigned. Make sure she keeps your address as the residential address for the credit card and have her reconcile and pay the card using online access.

The First Job

Your kid's first job is a huge boost to his self-esteem and his money savvy. Now that he has an income separate from his allowance, you can build on the saving and planning lessons you started when he was younger. Having his own income makes his investing and credit card education more meaningful.

It's important to insist that your teens work at least part-time while they're living at home. Dealing with a work environment is much different than volunteering or the dynamics at school. Having them work while you can still teach them to manage the work environment—as well as their paycheck—is key to their financial success.

Part-Time and Summer Work

No matter how overscheduled your kids may seem, adding any kind of paid work is going to be a huge advantage to their future money-management skills. Many colleges are starting to stress teens' work histories in their admissions decision as much as extracurricular activities and volunteer accomplishments. The type of work doesn't matter, as long as it's consistent.

Savings Programs

Talk to your teens about how much money they want to accumulate in savings for a particular need, or about basing their wage goals on a monthly expense such as their car payment or car insurance. Take them through the steps of budgeting the expenses they need to generate income for, targeting the job with the right pay scale and then setting up savings accounts as money baskets (see Chapter 1) to manage the salary.

Just as the younger kids did with their allowance, have your teens set up an account for current spending, one for long-term savings, and one for emergency savings. You may find that you want to encourage savings by matching money that stays in savings or investments for a period of time.

Budget Management

Help your child set up a simple income-and-expense tracking system. You might use a spreadsheet such as Microsoft Excel or simply start with her checkbook register. Have her categorize her expenses into fixed expenses that are difficult to change, such as car insurance; variable expenses that are easier to change, such as gas for her car; and extra expenses that are very easy to change, such as entertainment. By prioritizing the fixed and then variable expenses, you can help her decide how much income she has left for extras.

When to Cut the Strings

Most kids are anxious to leave the nest and cut their financial ties with their parents, but there are some who seem to never manage that transition. It's important to look at the role you play in helping your kids build financial independence. Be aware that you may be encouraging them to stay dependent on you without realizing it.

FACT

Cosigners on a loan are both responsible for the repayment of that loan. Avoid cosigning a loan for your child unless it's absolutely necessary. If you do cosign, ask to receive duplicate statements from the loan company so you can be sure the payments aren't missed.

When Is the Time Right?

The sooner you stop financially supporting your kids, the better for both of you. They need to learn to support themselves. If your kids are still in high school or college, this is the time to start communicating that their allowance ends when they graduate college—if not before. Remember, the key is to be clear and consistent. Many parents are surprised to find that the money they think they're giving the kids to help support them is actually keeping them from thriving. Allowances and gifts can send the message that you feel they still need your help. They'll continue to rely on you instead of making sure their career or work supports them.

Advice and education can go a lot further in helping your kids than simple cash handouts. If you think they're struggling, offer education and guidance before money. Pay the fee for them to meet with a financial planner. Offer to pay for financial planning classes or courses on money management. Buy them books on personal finance as gifts. Finally, share your own financial planning process with them.

QUESTION?

Can I lend my child money for a house down payment without making the money a gift?
Certainly. Your attorney can create an agreement that you both sign outlining the loan details such as interest and payment schedule. Beware: the mortgage company considers this loan part of your child's overall debt when they consider the mortgage application.

Helping and Gifting Through Life

Many parents and grandparents enjoy giving a regular annual cash gift to their kids and grandkids. This practice is often encouraged by the family's estate planning lawyer as a way of shrinking the elder's estate. The idea is to give the kids their inheritance early and to reduce potential future taxes on the grandparent's estate—saving everybody money. If this is your case, try to give the gifts in a way that enhances the recipient's investments instead of her lifestyle. Many givers simply write a check each year in the amount the tax law allows and their attorney recommends. A problem can arise when, after a cycle or two, the receiver starts to rely on the annual gift. By giving cash, the giver has encouraged the child to expand his lifestyle beyond his own income.

Instead of giving cash, ask your adult child to open an investment account for you to make your transfers to each year. Make it clear that you see this transfer as an addition to his wealth, not a supplement to his budget. Tell him you're making the transfer as part of your own financial plan, and be ready to stop the gifts if they are having an unintended impact on his finances.

FACT

If grandparents or other family members want to help pay for college, talk to the college's financial aid office about having them write a check directly to the school. In some circumstances, this direct payment won't affect the student's eligibility for aid, and payments made directly to colleges don't count toward the tax laws limiting gifts.

Instead of regular gifts, many parents look forward to one-time gifts to help kids with big-ticket items such as home down payments or college savings for grandkids. This can be a great way to help, as long as you consider the impact on your child's lifestyle. If you'd like to help with a house down payment, make the amount suitable for a down payment on a house your child will be able to afford, not to help him buy something bigger than he could on his own. If you'd like to help with college, give regular gifts to your grandchildren's college accounts instead of verbally committing to pay the full freight when they get to college age.

Kids on Campus

One of the most important roles you can play in preparing your kids for the lives ahead of them is to send them off to college with a strong personal finance foundation. Whether they're already in school or on their way soon, there are many things you can teach them about battling money peer pressure, cash management, and investing that will help them emerge from college with a sound financial frame of reference and the tools to help them build families and careers. If college applications are still in the future, include your child in the planning around her college nest egg, family gifts, and the asset allocation of her portfolios.

Building on Earlier Lessons

If you started your kids on an allowance when they were in grade school, this is the time to up the ante by having them contribute some of their allowance or their wages from a job to their education costs. Have them set up two online money market accounts with direct deposit from their paycheck or your allowance account. Treat one account as the college expense account and make the other a current expense account. This way—just as you would set aside money for a future household or family expense—you've planted the realization that part of each paycheck is allotted to paying current expenses and part to future ones.

Don't encourage your child to set up his dorm room to look like a photo from the college catalog. Shoot low on the economic scale and spend for the basics. Take advantage of the starving student stereotype, though starvation won't be an actual hazard, and let your kid start his college adventure with a focus on education, and without spending beyond his means.

Once the first semester of college starts, sit down with your youngster to plan the budget for the money in his college account according to the number of weeks in the semester. Most money market accounts will let you set up an automatic funds transfer so that each week—or every other week, as your student finds most convenient—an amount can be transferred into a checking account to pay for expenses. Have the student withdraw the cash each week to cover the expenses you have budgeted for.

Choosing the School

The process of choosing a school is the perfect time to teach strong personal finance lessons. One of the most important is: Don't waste the college savings by sending your student to a high-tuition school until they're sure what they want to study. Too often, parents will automatically start their kids at the school from which they ultimately hope they'll earn their diploma, without considering a less-expensive state school or community college for freshman credits. If the student isn't ready to declare her course of study, she might be frustrated by the pressure. What's worse, you've missed the chance to demonstrate deliberate and foresighted spending by frittering away more of the limited college fund on the first two semesters than was really needed.

Parent Planning: Balancing Accounts and Assets

Get your kids involved as early as you can in college financial planning by including them in a monthly discussion about your money and theirs. This is a variation on the monthly money meetings you learned about earlier. You don't need to share your whole financial picture with them; in these college money meetings you'll focus on their accounts and the accounts you own that are earmarked for their college costs.

Financial Aid

Financial aid generally takes three forms: grants that don't need to be repaid; low-interest loans; and work-study programs. As part of the college application process, you'll need to complete the Free Application for Federal Student Aid form that is universally known as the FAFSA. FAFSA information is used to calculate an expected family contribution, or EFC. Many families ignore the FAFSA form because they feel they make too much money to qualify for aid. Since most aid comes in the form of loans, completing the form regardless of what you expect the results to be is a good idea and a good learning experience for your student. Be sure your child fills out the form with information you provide; modern life is a process of paperwork, and it's time that your student is exposed to it.

Financial aid guidelines are likely to change, but there are a few things to keep in mind about accumulating assets for college costs:

- It's okay to save for college. Regardless of financial aid treatment, anything you save in an interest-generating account is that much less you'll need to borrow, and then repay with generally low but not insignificant interest.
- Spend the children's income and assets first. Student funds are counted at a higher rate than parents' assets where financial aid eligibility is concerned.
- Pay off consumer debt. Credit card balances are not considered on the FAFSA. Paying them off reduces your available cash and saves on the amount of interest you will eventually pay on the borrowed funds.
- Grandparents who would like to help pay college expenses should contribute to a 529 plan or to the parent, or wait until after graduation and then help pay down school loans. In financial aid terms, this equips the student to qualify for more aid than if the money were gifted to the student, increasing the assets that would reduce aid awards.

Don't completely deplete your savings in order to show fewer assets and therefore qualify for more financial aid. Annual salary and total income is a stronger factor in aid calculations anyway, and if you deplete your cash, you may get caught in an emergency. Most schools consider a means protection allowance that ignores the first $35,000 or so in parents' liquid assets.

Retirement and Home Equity

Fortunately, assets in retirement plans are usually not considered in the EFC calculation. Maximizing retirement plan contributions helps you prepare for retirement, saves income taxes, and helps you build assets that most schools regard as unavailable for college expenses. You'll have to report the retirement contribution you made in the year before you complete the FAFSA form, but don't let that stop you from saving.

ALERT!

Beware of organizations that charge large fees to help you qualify for more financial aid by transferring assets, by having the parent simultaneously enroll in college with no intention to attend, or by other fraudulent schemes. Check Appendix B for links to resources to help you research the financial aid process for free.

Home equity is also generally not considered available for college costs by most schools. It's wise, though, to keep equity available to you by opening an equity line of credit that can be tapped if you need it. Open the line and have it available, but don't take an equity loan and hold the cash payout in an account. That cash can be considered as part of your college tuition contribution, hurting the size of the aid award.

Getting a Jump on College

Any money that's saved for college will increase the student's school choices and decrease the amount of loans she needs to take. To help make it a little easier, the tax law allows for a few tax-advantaged account types that help protect the nest egg from taxes by allowing for tax deferral while the account is in force and in many cases not taxing withdrawals that are used for tuition. Additionally, colleges no longer consider these plans as student assets. This means that the assets are factored into the financial aid formula at the beneficial parental rate—or not counted at all, in cases where the account is owned by another family member.

Prepaid Tuition

Prepaid tuition plans are the more conservative of the college savings accounts. Under a prepaid plan, you minimize the impact of tuition inflation by buying into the current costs of college, below the inflated costs that will be charged years from now when your child is ready for school. Prepaid tuition plans are set up by each state and cover the major public colleges and universities in their state. In some cases, they cover a consortium of private colleges. The difficulty with these plans is that they limit the number of schools students can choose among. If the student picks a school not included in the plan, plan assets can be withdrawn, but there is no guarantee that the assets will cover costs at the chosen school. In fact, the assets in prepaid tuition plans are invested very conservatively, since they only need to stay ahead of schools' tuition increases. A student opting out of the covered group may find that his nest egg doesn't cover as much as he anticipated.

If you're concerned about a divorce, or are going through one, don't invest in a college fund at the expense of your own savings. Money in children's names—in UTMA or UGMA accounts—or in 529 plans is usually left protected in divorce negotiations. Besides, saving is even more important if you think you may be helping your child through college as a single parent.

529 Plans

529 college savings plans are a far better option than prepaid tuition plans because they're not limited to a specific group of schools and they allow for a broader range of investments—usually mutual funds following a specific asset allocation. These plans are also sponsored by the state, but participants are not limited to plans run by states in which they reside, or where they plan to attend college.

529 plans are organized as a basket of mutual funds managed by a fund company. They are distributed through brokers or directly to the public. Each fund company decides on the type of accounts it offers, but most give the investor the choice of choosing an age-based account or a style-based account. The age-based account acts much like a target-date mutual fund, with a specific asset allocation that is adjusted to be more conservative as the child gets older and closer to starting college. Style-based accounts assign a fixed asset allocation to fit the style they're tracking, whether it's conservative

by owning a small amount of stock, or none at all; moderate; or aggressive by being invested almost completely in more risky stock mutual funds.

The research website *www.savingforcollege.com* does a very good job helping compare 529 plans. Be sure to compare sales charges, annual costs, asset allocation, and performance. Some states offer tax benefits to residents who contribute to state-sponsored 529 plans. Beware of high sales charges—as with IRA accounts, you are limited in the amount you can deposit into a plan each year. Don't squander this limited contribution amount on sales fees.

FACT

Contribution limits are linked to gift tax rules. In 2008, you can contribute up to $12,000 to a 529 plan if you're single, $24,000 if you're married. Plans allow five years' worth of deposits to be made in one year under a special rule. If you decide to make an up-front deposit of $60,000 in one year, this will preclude you making additional gifts to the child for five years.

Reward Cards

Reward cards, most recognizably the one offered by UPromise, offer to add to your 529 plan when you buy certain merchandise or shop in specific stores. This may or may not be a benefit to your account, depending on whether you already buy the items that earn rewards under the program. Check the fine print and decide whether it's better to buy lower-cost items and bank the savings, or whether the reward card will benefit you.

Tweaking the Asset Allocation for College

Investing for college is different than investing for retirement because college covers such a short period of time. Your retirement assets can stand to fluctuate quite a bit, even after you retire, because even at age 60 or 70 you're still investing for a long period of time. College money gets spent quickly, leaving very little room for large value changes.

How other Assets Affect College Asset Allocation

A strong college nest egg involves more than just a college investing account such as a 529 plan. In many cases, parents planning for financial aid will try to limit their cash on hand to less than $30,000 or so to stay below the means protection allowance dictated by the school. If this is your case, be sure you have a home equity line available so you can easily access the equity if you need it.

QUESTION?

I have an Employee Stock Purchase Plan at work. Is this a good way to plan on covering college accounts?
It absolutely is, especially if you think you may not qualify for financial aid. If your employer allows you to sell your stock right away and offers a discount on the market price, this is a great way to supplement your college nest egg.

You may have decided to simply earmark some of your own assets in a taxable account to your child's education. If you're planning on financial aid, realize that selling the taxable assets generates income that may reduce the aid. Consider moving enough assets to pay for two years of college into a 529 plan in this case, while your child is still in high school. If you do, sales and withdrawals won't increase your income for financial aid purposes. If you're not planning on aid, keeping the assets in your name with enough in fixed income to cover the next three years' tuition will keep the nest egg safe without hurting long-term performance.

ALERT!

Your employer may offer loans against the value in your retirement plan. While available, this isn't the preferred way to build assets for college. Better to borrow against your child's future earnings with a school loan than against your retirement.

When to Increase Fixed Income

The allocations of many 529 plans keep 10 percent or 15 percent of stock in the account even after the child has started college. Remember, the stock market can decline in value for three years in a row, or sometimes more. If you're concerned about saving enough for school and don't have other resources to cover costs if the account declines, move out of the age-based choice in the 529 plan and into the income or conservative choice when your child is a high school sophomore or junior. The account growth will slow to simply earning interest, but if the stock market declines your principal will be safer.

How Wedding Plans Affect Your Financial Plan

Your children's weddings can be an exciting part of being in your 40s or 50s, but they can also be a financial challenge. You may be just finishing paying for college tuition, and the added cost of a wedding could strain your current finances and your future planning. On the other hand, you may be excited about the chance to help pay for a huge celebration. It's important to think about how your financial contribution to your child's wedding helps or hinders her future financial security—and your own.

Establish Expectations Early

Try not to imply to your kids that your contribution to their wedding costs is going to be different than what you can really afford. In many cases, the best approach is to offer a fixed dollar contribution to the budget, and then to step back and let the kids plan the event themselves. By doing this—and sticking to it—you avoid the surprise of a bigger expense than you can afford and the kids can plan their budget around the resources they know they have. Remember, your own financial security is more important than impressing the neighbors with a big wedding—be realistic about what you can give.

Consider giving your kids the choice of using your gift to pay for their wedding or to add to their investments or build a down payment on a house—or a combination. Generations have different value systems; you might be surprised by how highly they value the investment or down payment instead of the wedding.

Money-Saving Strategies

Encourage your kids to manage costs by prioritizing their goals for the event. Suggest that the bride and groom start their plan by listing their priorities on individual sticky notes. Then have them work together to arrange the notes in order of priority. For example, one of them may prioritize a small venue for the ceremony and the other may prioritize the honeymoon trip. Once the priorities are listed, assign a dollar figure to each. This will start as an estimate that can be refined with additional research. Finally, check the financial resources and fill out the budget, from the top priority down. This guarantees that the important issues are accounted for and you've minimized the focus on the details that are less important to the couple.

CHAPTER 13

Inheritances and Estate Planning

Estate planning in your 40s and 50s goes beyond that simple will you might have created when you were younger. Now it's time to update your will not only to consider family changes, grown kids, and older parents you might be caring for, but also to plan for leaving or receiving inheritances. Take this chance to talk to your parents and your kids about their own finances and estate plans. Talking through family members' wants and priorities if they die or get sick can be difficult, but having the conversation—before anything unhappy happens—can make dealing with crisis much easier.

Do It Right: A Lot Is at Stake

A carefully thought-out estate plan can help you protect your lifestyle and standard of living when you or a family member gets sick or dies. Your plan could also be designed to save money on taxes and direct how your money gets divided after your death. You can't complete your estate planning alone—a general practice attorney who does estate planning will be able to help you in basic circumstances. You'll need to hire—and pay a higher fee to—an estate attorney who specializes in complex planning and trusts if your situation is more complicated. Start with the general practice attorney; she will refer you to a specialist if you need it.

Set Your Priorities

An estate attorney will tell you that you can't guarantee the management of your affairs from the grave, but by employing certain trusts, ownership designations, and power-of-attorney designations, you can come close to controlling your assets both during your lifetime and after your death. Take time now, before beginning your plan or meeting with an attorney, to make a list of your priorities. Here are a few points to consider:

- How important to you is sole control of your assets?
- At what point of declining health would you consider asking a family member or friend to help you manage your money?
- Under what health or family circumstances would you decide to change your living situation?
- Who are the people your plan would affect—as caregivers, dependents, or beneficiaries?
- Whom do you want to include in the planning process?

Wills are easy to update if you change your mind and need to make a change to the beneficiary, executor, or any other part of the document. In many cases your lawyer will attach a codicil to the will with the changes you want instead of rewriting the whole document.

Direct Asset Control Versus Saving Taxes

In addition to regular income tax planning, your estate plan might need to consider whether or not to try to manage estate taxes. Estate taxes must be paid on assets above a certain value limit that are owned by the person who died and are not left to his or her American citizen spouse. If your spouse isn't an American citizen, or if your assets are being left to another individual such as a child or a friend, then the estate tax might apply to your estate. The estate tax laws are expected to be rewritten, so check with your advisor or the IRS website (*www.irs.gov*) for updates. Under current rules, a person dying in 2008 can leave an estate up to $2 million without having to pay tax. That limit is expected to increase to $3.5 million in 2009.

Remember that gifts are permanent. Once you give money away, it becomes the asset of the receiver and could be considered as asset by his creditors, or a marital asset in his divorce. If you manage to get the asset back, it won't be considered a gift for estate tax purposes.

If you're concerned about your beneficiaries losing part of their inheritance to the estate tax, you can take steps to reduce the tax by giving them assets while you're still living or giving up direct control of the asset by transferring it to a trust. Watch the tax rules if you decide to give assets away while you're still living. Just as with the estate tax, if you're giving assets to someone other than your spouse you need to watch the value of the gift. In 2008, you can give up to $12,000 to an individual without incurring a separate gift tax. The limit counts for all the gifts in a year, so be careful if you like to give birthday or holiday gifts—they apply to the limit as well. Since gifts and inheritances are transfers from one person to another, the gift and estate tax are linked. If you'd like to give more than the $12,000 annual limit to an individual, you can do it, and then file a gift tax return either paying the tax due on the gift or applying it toward the total amount your estate can leave.

Keep It in Trust

"Trust" is the name given to legal entities that can be created to hold assets. They can be irrevocable—or unchangeable—or revocable. They can be created while you are alive, called living trusts, or they can come into being at your death. In the latter case, they are created by instructions in your will and are called testamentary trusts. Trusts are managed by trustees who follow the trust's instructions, and often their own good judgment, to manage the assets in the trust.

Trusts can be simple or complicated. Your estate attorney will help you decide whether you need a trust as part of your estate plan, but the most frequent uses of trusts are to reduce estate taxes, to manage assets for an individual who can't manage the assets himself, or to smooth the financial bumps for a family as an individual's estate goes through probate. Some people place their assets in revocable trusts so that they can name additional individuals as joint trustees—including themselves, in most cases—so that those trustees can be called on to manage the assets if they become incapacitated.

Taking Care of the Basics

All adults need an estate plan, especially in their 40s or 50s. Your plan can be very simple; without one, you're subject to the laws of your state. This could make managing your finance and health decisions difficult if you're incapacitated, and state laws could result in unintended consequences at your death. Most general practice attorneys can help you with a basic estate plan, and in much of the country they may charge less than $1,000—less than you might spend on a vacation or a piece of new furniture.

Minimum Need

A basic estate plan includes a will, a power-of-attorney document, and a health care proxy or living will, depending on your state. Your will is basically instructions to the probate court regarding what to do with your assets and whom you name as guardian for your young children. The power-of-attorney document gives a specified individual the power to legally act in your stead. The health care proxy is like a power of attorney for your health care and can govern medical decisions made on your behalf. These decisions may be as simple as consulting with your doctor while you recover from anesthesia after a simple operation or as complex as making the decision about your life support. Some states make provisions for a separate living will in which you can dictate end-of-life choices; other states expect that these instructions will be spelled out in the health care proxy.

ALERT!

Beware of estate planning software and websites; you could end up doing yourself more harm than good. Remember, your estate plan will come into action at a difficult and emotional part of your family's life—not a good time to discover an error, or that there is something missing from the plan.

Alternative Ways to Control Assets

Being married creates some rights regardless of whether you have a formal estate plan. These include the right to inherit a portion of your estate and receiving unlimited gifts and inheritance without estate or gift tax. Your spouse would also be able to continue living in your joint home if you're incapacitated and could have a right to your pension benefits. Remember that in many states, your children would be inheritors if you die without a will—called dying intestate.

Not all assets pass to inheritors according to the directions in your will. Retirement accounts, life insurance, and annuities should have appropriate beneficiaries listed within those particular documents. Be sure to keep these up-to-date as your children grow and your relationships with your family change. The original designation you might have listed—"to all my children equally," for example—may not still be appropriate if one child is dealing with a difficult divorce or another child is receiving government benefits that could be affected by an outright inheritance. If you're helping your parents manage their estate, don't forget to review their beneficiary designations as well. Each account should have both a primary and a contingent beneficiary—to receive the inheritance if the primary beneficiary isn't alive—to avoid having the funds revert to the estate to be distributed through the will. An advantage to assets being distributed through beneficiary designations is that they are available almost immediately, without the delays of the probate court having to read the will.

FACT

The probate process allows for the will to be read, for creditors to present themselves for payment, and for assets outlined in the will to be distributed. The cost to have an estate probated varies by state. People with large estates often try to avoid living in states that dictate probate fees related to the size of the probate estate.

The Players

There are several different roles that you'll need to assign in your estate plan. The executor moves your will through the probate process and makes sure your instructions are followed. Your power-of-attorney designee has the right to act for you while you're alive but unable to act for yourself, and is nominated under either a durable power of attorney, which takes effect immediately upon your signing the document, or as a springing power of attorney who takes over for you after a number of physicians have declared you incompetent. Your health care proxy is charged with making medical decisions for you. If you have children, you'll name a guardian to care for them if you die.

If you've created a trust to manage your assets while you're alive, it's likely that you have assigned a trustee, possibly with a co-trustee, depending on the laws in your state. The trustee has a fiduciary duty to manage the assets in the trust according to the trust's instructions. You would also name a trustee if your trust doesn't take effect until after your death. For these trusts, many people name a family member who will understand the needs of the family in addition to an institutional trustee such as a bank trust department or attorney who, in conjunction with the family member, would manage the trust assets.

QUESTION?

Will a trust protect my estate from creditors?
Most trusts don't offer protection from creditors, but this feature is often advertised by unscrupulous advisors. Be sure to speak with an experienced estate attorney if you're concerned about protecting your assets from creditors.

Life Insurance: The Right Amount

Life insurance can be an important part of a balanced estate plan, no matter what your age, but it's an especially important consideration in your 40s and 50s before old age increases the premiums or failing health renders you uninsurable. If you had a divorce agreement requiring you to maintain coverage, or if your estate plan would simply be helped by life insurance coverage to pay taxes or protect your family after you die, now is the time to look at your current policies and decide whether you need to buy more.

Protect Your Family

Make sure to consider all the support relationships you have with friends and family when reviewing the amount of life insurance coverage you need. Chapter 4 details the different types of insurance available to you and will help you decide which type of policy to buy and how to check the strength of a policy you already own.

As part of your estate planning, it's important to be sure you have enough coverage to support your family or other dependents; that the beneficiary designations are worded correctly; and that the policy is owned by the right person, or even by a trust, if necessary.

If you have a pension, the spousal benefit works very similarly to a life insurance policy. Under this provision, you take a lower monthly benefit so that when you die, your spouse can continue to receive an income. The reduction in your benefit works much like an insurance premium on your life, reducing your monthly income so that a benefit can be paid if you die first. Many insurance agents suggest buying a policy separately and taking the maximum pension benefit, so that if the spouse dies first the pensioner isn't stuck at the lower pension income, especially paying to insure a benefit that's no longer needed. Fortunately, most pensions now take this possibility into account and will bring the pensioner's benefit back up to 100 percent if her spouse dies first, eliminating the need for additional life insurance coverage.

If you have a child or family member who relies on you but who also receives a government disability benefit, you'll need to consider this in creating your estate plan and deciding whether to use life insurance as part of his benefit. A disability and elder law attorney can guide you in setting up your estate plan and adjusting your beneficiary designations to fit with your plan.

Tax Savings Strategies

If you have a large estate (over $2 million in 2008 and over $3.5 million in 2009 and beyond) and would like to reduce the estate taxes you might pay on your assets, your estate lawyer may suggest buying life insurance and having the policy owned by someone besides yourself—to avoid having it subject to estate taxes as well—an irrevocable life insurance trust. An ILIT, as it's called, is an irrevocable trust that once created can't be changed. Using an ILIT, instead of putting assets in the trust that you would prefer to keep under your own control, you put a life insurance policy into the trust with enough benefit to pay the estate taxes, when due. You'll need to gift money to the trust each year so that it contains sufficient money to pay the annual life insurance premium, but that inconvenience and the cost of the premium could be small compared with the estate tax liability you would have had.

Divorce Requirements

Divorce settlements often require life insurance coverage to protect a support order such as alimony or child support. If you're required to carry coverage under an agreement, you might consider negotiating—in the case of a child support obligation—a beneficiary designation that leaves the benefit in trust for the child rather than outright to your ex-spouse. If you're the benefiting spouse looking to insure a benefit you are receiving, you should negotiate to own the policy yourself, with your ex-spouse paying the premiums, so that you can control the policy benefits and be sure the policy is kept in force. If this negotiation fails, insist that you receive a duplicate insurance statement directly from the life insurance company so that you would be made aware of any changes.

Keeping the Family in Mind

Don't create your estate plan in a vacuum. Even though you will make the major decisions yourself, it's important to include your family and close friends who may be affected in the process—or at least let them know the details of the plan and how they're affected.

Young Kids

If your kids are forty or more years younger than you, consider the impact on them of losing a parent when they are still young. Pay special attention to your life insurance and trusts that could be used to manage their inheritance until they are old enough to manage their money themselves. Money doesn't need to be left to them immediately upon your death or even when they come of age; your attorney can help you consider whether you should leave your money in trust for your children, with payouts to them for education and other necessities, then structuring final distributions to them at staggered ages, say age 25, 30, and finally age 35. Using this method, you avoid the sad situation of the child squandering his money when he is too young to understand better financial management.

Adult Kids

If your kids are adults and are all doing well on their own, your estate plan might simply state that your assets should be left to them equally. If for some reason you decide to do something different, it's important to meet with them all—either together or individually—and explain your decision.

Remember, your estate plan comes into effect after your death and is then irreversible. Don't try to teach your kids a lesson from the grave. It may be misunderstood, and you won't be around to mend hurt feelings.

Second Marriages

Second marriages can pose some interesting estate planning problems. Many individuals with children from a previous marriage use a strategy called an A/B trust to make sure that their new spouse is supported without cutting their children out of their inheritance. This strategy—also a helpful estate tax planning tool—leaves some assets to the current spouse in a trust for her benefit called an A trust. A second pool of money is placed into a B trust, whose income is usually accessible to the surviving spouse, and whose principal passes to the children from the first marriage after the second spouse's death.

Getting Your Parents to Talk about Money

Getting your parents to talk about money when that hasn't been the family custom is tough, but necessary. Just as it's important to let your own kids in on your estate plans, knowing what your parents have in place is essential to making sure you can support them when they need you. Many people who were concerned about bringing up the topic are often surprised by the positive reaction they got from their parents. In this case, it's simply a matter of bringing it up at a time when you have the privacy to talk about it and you're not under pressure to hear the whole story immediately.

Your parents' social conventions are related to the norms of their generation, not yours. Be sure to give them time to warm up to the idea of discussing their finances with you. If you start early, you'll have time to plan before anything serious happens.

If your parents are resistant, try sharing your own estate planning process with them. Use anecdotes from the news to impress upon them that sharing information is important. Remember that you don't need to know their financial affairs down to the penny, but having a general idea of where their affairs stand and what their wishes are can save a lot of stress and mistakes later on.

Leaving an Inheritance: Avoid the Pitfalls

It's wonderful to be in a position to leave your kids an inheritance. But with this benefit also comes a responsibility that many parents don't always consider. Avoid the unhappy circumstance of suppressing your children's own abilities and financial success by setting the expectation that they can bank on a sizable inheritance and won't need to provide fully for themselves.

The Psychology of Inheritance

The greatest legacy you can leave to your kids is the confidence and ability to earn a living and build wealth for themselves. Multiplied over their working lifetime, their earnings can amount to a huge nest egg, just as yours has. No one ever received a large inheritance and regretted that he had worked over his lifetime without having to. Unfortunately, too many have waited for their inheritance without fully applying themselves to work and career, only to be disappointed that their inheritance was too small to support them—or even nonexistent.

It doesn't take a huge nest egg to set up the expectation in your kids that they will inherit a lot of money. Remember that they will watch your behavior and make inferences from what they see in your behavior and attitudes. Talking to them early and getting them involved in money management are effective ways to pass on your values.

Bring your kids into a discussion about their inheritance as soon as you can. Time spent talking to them about your expectations and theirs will be time well spent and will give you the opportunity to gauge the psychological effects your wealth is having on your kids. If you think things are developing in a way that's different than what you hoped, don't hesitate to reach out to a family therapist with expertise in the area of inherited wealth.

How Much Is Too Much?

Your 40s or 50s is the perfect time to start gauging how much money to leave for your kids. This is also the perfect time to get kids involved in the business and investment decisions you are making and start teaching them your money values through example. No matter what their age—grade school, teens, or adults—they can be involved in what you're doing. You're young enough that your estate plan doesn't have to be set in stone yet, but can be set up in revocable trusts or still in your own name so that you can watch how they deal with their potential inheritance.

Forewarned: Avoid the Biggest Mistakes

Estate planning mistakes are tragic because they often go undiscovered until it's too late—the person has died or suffered a major incapacitation. Fortunately, with care and regular review, you can avoid many of the most common pitfalls.

Lack of Planning—Communicating Too Little Too Late

Start planning and start communicating now. It's never too early or too late to start implementing your estate plan and talking to affected family members about it. A basic estate plan takes about two months to implement from the time you start thinking about it to the time you first meet with your attorney to the document signatures. This isn't a heavy time burden and there isn't any reason why you can't fit it easily into your schedule.

You may have special instructions you would like your family to know, things that don't need to be in the will—which technically becomes public information as part of the probate process—but should be understood. Write a letter with these details and let your children or executor know where the letter is. Making it a separate document doesn't make it as enforceable as the will but for wishes such as, "Please give my daughter my wedding ring," a letter can be easily changed and updated.

Tax Basis Planning

As mentioned in Chapter 11, many people forget to keep track of what they paid for an investment—their tax basis. This can cause particular problems in an estate plan. Remember that if you give assets while you are alive, the receiver also receives your tax basis. If they inherit that same asset, they get what is called a stepped-up basis to the value of the asset when you died.

This is an important consideration. If your parents are elderly and are planning on gifting assets to you now, you might consider whether they have a large enough estate to be taxable for estate tax, and the difference between your tax bracket and theirs, and then decide whether it's better for them to hold a particular asset until death or to gift it to you now. This might seem a tacky discussion to have with them, but it's important not to pay taxes needlessly, when guidance from an advisor familiar with the situation could help keep the money in the family and out of Uncle Sam's pocket.

IRA Withdrawals and Your 401(k)

There are special tax rules that relate to inherited retirement accounts. Basically, if the inheritor is a spouse, he will be able to transfer the account to his own name and continue as if it was initially his account. If the inheritor is an entity other than a spouse—such as a child, a trust, or the deceased's estate—then the payout options are more restrictive. In many cases, if the inheritor or beneficiary is a person (not a trust or the estate) he will have the option of taking distributions from the account over a long period of time— usually at least five years, or if the estate plan was completed correctly, over his lifetime. The longer the distribution period, the greater the income tax savings because the beneficiary won't generate a tax obligation until money is withdrawn from the account.

Be careful if you inherit a retirement account from an individual who is over age 70½. Distributions need to be made soon after the person's death. Get advice from a financial planner or tax professional to be sure you take distributions on time.

Putting Kids' Names on Assets

Well-intentioned families often try to simplify estate planning by putting adult children's names on assets such as bank accounts and the family home. Don't use this strategy unless you've been advised by an estate or elder law attorney. Remember that the asset is exposed to the creditors of the named owners and that could subject the asset to liabilities that weren't intended, including bill collectors or lawsuit beneficiaries. Additionally, the act of putting the adult child's name on the house could have damaging gift tax ramifications.

QUESTION?

Would putting my name on the deed protect my parents' house from nursing home costs?
You should meet with an elder law attorney to discover whether any part of her estate can be protected from medical costs. Putting your name on the deed may not have the result you're looking for, even if you also live in the home.

A life estate is an interest in a home for a person's lifetime without being a full ownership. This strategy is often used to give a second spouse continued residence while the children from the first marriage own the home. But beware: Strategies like this can create a conflict of interest between two parties. In this case, the children may have no incentive to maintain the home for their stepparent's benefit.

CHAPTER 14

Working for Yourself

Many people in their 40s and 50s have reached their career prime. They've found something they enjoy, and they're good at it. Others discover that they're ready to take the career skills they've perfected and strike out on their own. Whether you'd like to freelance or consult within your current industry, buy a franchise, or build a small business, your 40s or 50s is the perfect time to do it.

14

A Freelance Approach to Your Career Track

People working in management or in executive jobs often feel as if they spend as much time managing their career track as they do doing the job itself. Consulting to your current employer or to companies in the same or similar industries can be a great bridge to the next position after a layoff. Or you might decide to pursue self-employment to grow a small business or even stretch your way into part-time retirement.

After the Layoff and Between Jobs

Dealing with layoffs, whether you're the one delivering the bad news or the one leaving the company, can be wearying. Chances are that by the time you're in your 40s or 50s, you've been through a few. If you have the financial safety net of a severance package and an emergency fund, a lay-off at this time in life can be a good opportunity to expand your horizons to other, similar jobs in different industries.

Start your planning by listing the pros and cons of the position you're leaving or a recent job that you enjoyed more. Notice the trends in both lists and use these patterns to summarize what an ideal consulting relationship would look like. Next, connect with your colleagues from your last job and previous jobs. If they were laid off too, this will open doors to new companies where those people now work and create new relationships. Continue networking until you find a relationship that aligns with the trends contained in your list of pros and cons.

Check out Appendix B for sites that will help you develop consulting relationships.

As a Business

If you discover you're good at finding and cultivating consulting opportunities, you may be able to develop this skill into full-time work. You'll need to treat it just like any other professional services business and devote time to business planning, operations, and marketing in addition to delivering the consulting service, but it may be a great way to feed your interests and make a living without going back to the same type of job you left. Follow the business planning suggestions below just as if you're starting a new business from scratch.

Stretch Income into Retirement

Many consultants are able to continue in business with average prospecting and sales skills for three to five years after they are laid off solely on the strength of their old corporate contacts and network. Additional marketing and business development skills could extend this period. If this time frame is enough to get you to retirement—and the income is high enough to be sure you can still invest for retirement as you've planned—then this could be a great transition for you. You may even find that if the consulting is less stressful, you will be able to work at part-time consulting longer than you initially planned to work in your full-time job. With a little planning and budgeting you can trade a little more time in the work force for a more enjoyable lifestyle by consulting part time into retirement.

Investing in a Franchise or Buying a Business

If you decide that you'd like a complete break from your current industry, you might consider buying a franchise or a business that's already operating. Laying out some cash to buy a business in exchange for the time you would have spent starting and building it may be a good fit for you if you have the means and are anxious to get up and running. The support of a good franchise or training from the selling business owner can also bring you more quickly up to speed.

Business in a Box

It's surprising how many different types of franchise opportunities exist. Franchises such as senior home care and lawn and home maintenance, and business services such as signs and advertising, provide a huge array of business sectors to choose from. Initial investments range from a few thousand to hundreds of thousands of dollars. The franchiser—the company or individual that owns the rights to the business and grants licenses to run its franchises—generally provides the business plan and regular support and training to the franchisees. Franchisers usually receive a portion of gross sales or a regular fee that pays for marketing and support.

Buying a business that is already running skips the steps needed to build the business and business processes. A going concern will have already refined the service or product offering and should have an established brand in the market. Buying a business from a retiring founder or business owner will give you more autonomy than a franchise, but less support. The buyer usually makes an initial payment, and then the seller continues to work in the business for a short period of time for an income called an "earn out." This earn-out period gives the buyer time to learn the business and allows for a smoother transition from seller to buyer, and hopefully better customer retention.

Things to Consider

Franchisees often complain that the support they get from the home office is small compared to the franchise fees they are expected to pay. As a franchisee, you'll have limited say in the marketing plan and budget of the parent company. A successful franchisee is one who can negotiate and bargain with the home office when needed. Be sure to interview a number of current franchisees about their experience with the company before buying in. Be sure to learn about the training and hiring support and ongoing marketing expectations of the company. Newer, less-proven franchises will have lower initial fees. Consider your ability to build on the foundation they have created if you're considering a younger, riskier franchise.

FACT

Businesses are often sold through business brokers. A good broker can be helpful in finding the business and negotiating a sale. Make sure you understand whether the broker is negotiating for you or the seller. Hire an attorney to represent your interests.

Buying a business is a lot like entering into a short-term partnership. Be sure to create your own team of advisors to help you with the negotiation and purchase of the business. A business attorney experienced in the field and an accountant who works for you exclusively—not both you and the seller—is crucial. Check with your local Small Business Administration office for referrals to advisors.

Due Diligence

You need to interview other franchisees and the customers and employees of the business you're planning to buy. Your accountant will help you review the books of the franchise or business. Reviewing the last three years of financial reports will help you see whether the business is growing, is shrinking, or has plateaued financially. If growth has been flat, you'll need to decide whether you have the energy and time to commit to reinvigorating growth or whether you're better off looking for another opportunity.

Check out *www.score.org* for access to volunteer business executives and owners who can help you with your business planning. SCORE—originally standing for Service Corps of Retired Executives, now known only by its initials and tagline "Counselors to America's Small Business"—provides volunteer business counselors to help with every aspect of your business.

Be sure to test best- and worst-case financial scenarios with your CPA so you can understand what effect the investment might have on your retirement plans. A business risk you might have been willing and able to take in your 20s might be unreasonable in your 40s or 50s.

Starting a Business

If you're ready to go it alone and have the financial means to reduce your income for a time, starting your own business may be a great new life chapter for you. Especially if the new business will help you create a lifestyle to keep you employed longer into your 60s and maybe 70s, taking a few years off from investing in an employer's retirement plan to invest in a small business could be a great opportunity.

The Planning Process

Working for yourself may sound like a great idea, especially on the days when your boss is driving you crazy and your coworkers are trying your patience, but it's important to remember that starting a business will probably be much harder than continuing what you're doing now. Writing a business plan and engaging in the tedious projections of cash flow and investment return is the perfect test to see whether you'll be able to commit the energy and time needed to start from scratch.

If you're still working or consulting, now is the time to enroll in a business planning class or engage your advisors (see *www.score.org* or *www.sba.gov* for help) and start planning on your own. The business planning process will step you though defining your product or service offering, pricing, marketing, and cash flow. You'll get the chance to think through your operations and staffing needs and will get a good understanding of your financial commitment. Many advisors suggest you decrease your earnings expectations by one-third and double your expense projections to "stress test" your projections.

Financing

Almost all small businesses are started with a large part of their funding from the founder. You can supplement your own contributions with bank loans, credit cards, and lines of credit, but be ready to personally guarantee repayment of anything you borrow.

Some businesses take on financial partners early in their growth. If you're skilled in these types of negotiations and have sound contacts, this could be a good way of reducing your risk while still meeting the business's capital needs. Silent financial partners—if they're willing to remain so—could also present a way for you to continue receiving a salary while you're starting the business.

As Part of a Retirement Plan

At the start of your planning, consider whether your business will be a salable asset that could supplement your retirement nest egg, or whether it's a lifestyle business that will help you to earn income into your 60s and 70s—

beyond the age you would have worked for another employer. Understanding which type of business you're creating will help you make decisions about growth and investment that otherwise might seem unclear. For example, if you're planning on building a lifestyle service business, you might minimize the number of other principals you hire so that you can focus on building your own customer base. If you're planning on selling the business, you might increase the number of principals to give the business more value after you retire.

Don't overestimate the value of your business as a retirement asset. Some business types that might be very salable now may not be later due to the business climate when you want to sell and retire. Find a good mix of investing in the business and taking money as salary and investing in a retirement plan.

Recovering from the Usual Mistakes

Planning on starting or buying a business, or investing in a franchise, is always risky, but taking on this transition in your 40s and 50s adds a little more importance to the situation. If you're not careful, you could risk the financial security you have worked to develop over the bulk of your working life. On the other hand, you have the maturity, self-understanding, and business expertise to make a business very successful. If this is your first foray into business ownership, it's important to keep a few things in mind so you'll have the chance to reach this success.

Mistake: Not Creating a Plan

Many business owners start their business without a plan. Your plan doesn't need to be volumes and volumes in length, but it does need to contain all the aspects of a business plan and needs to be carefully thought through. Flying by the seat of your pants when you're in your 20s and 30s might be recoverable. It's much less so when you have the financial obligations and shorter time before retirement that you have in your 40s and 50s.

It's never too late to plan. If you started your business a couple of years ago and are frustrated with the growth and amount of work you're doing, contact SCORE or the SBA, or check your contacts for referrals to a CPA and financial planner now.

Outside Financing: What They're Looking For

Most business owners seek outside financing at some point in their business growth. Financing is usually structured as debt or as equity financing.

Debt financing usually comes first for most businesses. Owners often default to personal credit cards and home equity loans because they're easy to establish and many owners don't have the business plan and financials that banks require before making a large loan. Debt that is mixed up with your personal finances can make tracking the business finances difficult. A better option is a business loan and/or a business line of credit that is related to the business. Many banks will lend up to a certain amount—$50,000 in many cases—to a small business on nothing more than the business owner's personal guarantee and good credit. Rates are usually lower than credit card rates and higher than home equity loans. These business loans are preferable to both credit cards and home equity because they help to build credit under the business.

QUESTION?

I'm grooming a key employee to take over the business when I retire. When should I add him as a partner?
It depends on your business plan. Professional service firms such as law and accounting firms have an established partnership track for associates. Make your employee a partner when you are ready to start sharing the decision making—and not before.

Owners looking for equity financing—involving selling a share of the business to a backer—need to be ready to share control in the company—not something all owners are ready to do. Equity financing is more complex than debt financing because agreement needs to be created outlining the ownership benefits and responsibility of all parties. In some cases, your attorney might recommend structuring your business in a more formal entity such as a corporation or a limited liability company so that shares can be transferred to others. All of these things could be worth the effort if the capital offered by the equity investor is enough to help make your company grow.

Working with a Partner

Some business ideas are difficult to implement alone, and there are other times when it may be appealing to have a partner in the business. Partnerships are created automatically when two individuals decide to work together—there are no legal filings or special forms required. This, unfortunately, often leads to a situation where a partnership has been created with little planning or communication. When you're working on your own, you don't have the problem of not meeting or understanding another's goals or impressions of the business direction. Working with a partner requires that you both go out of your way to communicate. The best first step for this is to create a written partnership agreement defining your expectations and dissolution plans when a partner dies, is disabled, or wants to leave the business. Your business attorney and accountant can help you with this, and then each partner should have her individual attorney review the document for her benefit.

Pricing in Employee Benefits

If you have worked for a large company, you may have been given a booklet touting the dollar value of all the benefits they give you beyond your base salary. If you've never had the opportunity to see it all added up in this way, it's hard to imagine how much money health and life benefits, disability insurance, payroll taxes, and paid vacation and sick time add up to. It's important to plan for the extra costs if you decide to go into consulting or open your own business.

Paying FICA

You and your employer share responsibility for paying state and federal income taxes as well as social security and Medicare taxes on your income.

If you are self-employed, you are responsible for all the same taxes you had when you worked for someone else, plus the employer's half of the social security and Medicare taxes. This self-employment tax takes many by surprise because they are accustomed to their taxes being withheld automatically from paychecks.

When you're self-employed, the temptation is often to live on the entire amount your customers pay you and then to try to come up with the tax money when it's due at tax time. Avoid this temptation by automatically deducting 30 percent from all customer receipts and depositing the amount in a separate savings account earmarked for taxes. Check with your accountant at midyear to see whether the 30 percent rule of thumb is the right withholding target, and then make adjustments. Once your business is established, a good rule of thumb is to withhold 40 percent to pay taxes and to allow for a retirement contribution. You can reduce the need to plan for these taxes if you structure your business so that you are paid as an employee and taxes are withheld from your paycheck before you receive it.

FACT

The self-employment tax rate is 15.3 percent, which includes 12.4 percent for social security and 2.9 percent for Medicare. Regular federal and state income taxes (if your state has an income tax) are also due on self-employment income up to a certain level that is adjusted for inflation.

Health Care Benefits

Under current laws, self-employed individuals are able to make a deduction on their taxes for the cost of their health insurance. Your premium may be higher than when you were part of a large group at a bigger company, but the health insurance deduction can help a little. When comparing the earnings you would have in a large company as an employee versus being self-employed, don't forget to include the cost of health insurance.

States that require everyone to carry insurance will have resources to tap for coverage. If your state doesn't require health insurance, consider joining an industry or business organization that makes group coverage available as a member benefit.

Contractors Versus Employees

The added cost of FICA taxes and the responsibility of keeping new hires busy makes adding staff under informal contractor agreements instead of employees very tempting. Be sure to review the IRS's rules regarding contractors before you hire. Workers who are working under your control with performance guidelines could be considered employees, whether you pay them as employees or not. Don't risk owing back taxes and penalties by trying to skirt the rules.

Keep the Books Straight for Uncle Sam

Unless finance is already your background, there are few small-business owners who look forward to maintaining their books and dealing with tax preparation. Save yourself time and frustration by retaining a business accountant in your planning and business process. Many accountants are happy to act as advisors, even if you are doing a lot of the number crunching to save on their fees.

Don't spend all your time doing your bookkeeping if you're more skilled at another part of the business. Free up your time by hiring a competent bookkeeper so you can sell, manage, or provide a revenue-generating service. Use monthly meetings with your bookkeeper to stay up to date.

Drawing Salary Versus Building Equity

Your accountant will help you strike a balance between drawing a salary from your business and reinvesting. A small business is likely to show a tax loss for the first few years, even with positive cash flow, because money is being reinvested for growth. Tax losses should only be a factor supporting growth—not a business strategy. Unless your business is a hobby, be sure that you are either creating an income that you can draw, pay taxes on, and then invest for retirement, or that your business is growing into an asset that you can sell profitably. Better yet, why not plan on creating the best of both worlds by drawing a salary and building a valuable business?

Planning for Self-Employment Taxes

Self-employment taxes are a part of doing business. Whether they are considered true self-employment taxes because your business is small and you're the only one drawing income, or they're coming out of your business revenue as the business's and employees' shares of the FICA taxes, planning ahead to minimize surprises is important. In addition to making regular quarterly reviews of your business performance, plan on having your accountant review your business income and expenses in the early to mid-fall of each year. She can help you calculate whether you're on track toward a larger or smaller profit than last year. She can check whether you're having too much, too little, or the right amount of tax withheld from your income, and she can help you plan for any year-end retirement plan contributions or purchases to save taxes.

Passing Expenses Through the Business

Many business owners lose track of their true personal expenses because their business does so much for them. They attend conferences, take clients to dinner, drive a company car, and might have a beautiful home office that the business pays for. Your accountant will back out the disallowed expenses and you'll pay tax on them. Unfortunately, unless the business owner is writing the checks, he often loses track of his true living expenses. Not knowing your lifestyle costs can make retirement planning difficult. Be sure to account carefully for the added lifestyle perks that the business provides you so you're not surprised after you retire.

Working from Home

Check the IRS rules before you decide to claim a home office for tax purposes. Although recent cases have relaxed the treatment of a home office deduction, you still need to be sure taking the deduction is in your best interest. Assuming that your office meets the IRS definition of a home office—including exclusive business use and being required for the business—if your house has a large capital gain or if you're planning to sell and move soon, it may be better to ignore the home office deduction altogether. The home office deduction gives you an expense against your business income, but it also creates a small piece of business property—your office—that is now embedded in your home. When you sell your residence, the home office portion might be considered commercial property and would be excluded from the capital gains tax advantages enjoyed by your residence.

CHAPTER 15

Real Estate

Sound decisions about what real estate to buy, own, or rent are important at any life stage, but especially when you're in your 40s and 50s. The benefits, costs, and emotional characteristics of real estate make it different than any other type of investment. Whether you upsize or downsize your home, buy a vacation property, or gift a down payment to help your kids get settled, the decisions you make about property now will have an important effect on your retirement plans, nest egg, and future lifestyle.

15

A Home of Your Own

There are a lot of fun real estate choices to make when you're in your 40s and 50s. If your kids are grown, this may be your first chance in a long time to pick where you want to live without having to worry about school districts, bus routes, or day-care commutes. You can pick your location and home style based on your lifestyle now and what you want it to be in the future.

Choosing a Location

Spend some time thinking about your home location relative to how long you'll be living there and lifestyle factors that the location affects. If you're planning to live there just until you retire, a long commute to work may be a bad idea. If you're planning to put down roots and build your retirement support community of neighbors and friends, having a long commute to work for a few years might matter less to you.

Other things to consider if you're planning to stay long term include:

- Access to health care and community support systems
- Proximity to your kids and friends
- The style of the home you prefer, including whether a one- or two-story home will work best for you in retirement, given mobility and health concerns

Weather and seasonal conditions are a more important factor in choosing a long-term location than you may realize. People move to warmer climates after they retire for a reason—the older you get, the less tolerant you become of cold temperatures. And snow and ice become increasingly irksome for walking and driving as you age.

Real Estate as a Retirement Asset

If you're planning to make your current home an investment for retirement, it's important to disregard the emotional ties that many people feel toward their home and treat yours like an investment. Make sure you're budgeting toward keeping the property maintained and equipped with up-to-date amenities. Keep personalization to a minimum and avoid being too trendy in your permanent structures and design. Consider the costs of selling the property at retirement, and have a plan B that includes assets unrelated to real estate that can provide income so you don't have to sell in a down market.

ALERT!

If your house is in a good location or on a large lot, you may not need to keep it meticulously up to date. Your buyer may buy for the location rather than the house or plan to tear down and build new. Don't invest in upgrades if your house isn't as valuable as the lot it sits on.

Additions to Add Value

In most housing markets, there are only a few additions and upgrades that you can make to a house that add value. Builders and designers are fond of calling some projects "investments" in the property, but if your plan to sell coincides with a downward trend in the market, even proven upgrades such as adding a bathroom might not yield a return upon sale. Make additions to your home cautiously to avoid wasting money that won't be recouped.

Homes need to be kept up to date, and that is part of the cost of owning them. A house on the market in 2008 that still has the same small, avocado-colored refrigerator your mom had isn't going to sell as quickly as one with more current appliances. Plan a regular, budgeted contribution to your household fund to cover upgrades, just as you do to cover maintenance. If you plan something more than a basic upgrade—such as changing from that avocado refrigerator to a modern, stainless-steel one—and you're not selling right away, beware that styles might change dramatically before you sell. The upgrade might make sense, as long as you budget the upgrade as something you will enjoy, knowing you might not recoup your investment upon sale.

Planning for an Empty Nest

This is your chance to plan your home around you, without having to consider your kids and their needs. Give yourself a chance to welcome this transition; it's an exciting time for both you and your spouse or partner. Be thoughtful and deliberate about what you do with your home after the kids are gone. Some parents will be happy to change the locks and convert the kid's room into a home office. But others may want to build an addition so that the kids can come back with their own children. Take this opportunity to strengthen your personal finances and theirs by ending your direct financial support and begin making financial decisions without the kids' goals in mind. You may choose to help them later under certain circumstances, but for now, this is the perfect chance to cut the apron strings.

Home decorating magazines will have a current list of additions or home upgrades that are adding value in your market. Historically, changes that add space or convenience are your best bet. Adding a downstairs bathroom to a house that doesn't have one, paving a gravel driveway, and adding a garage have been good bets in the past.

Planning for the Vacation Home

If you love to vacation in the same place each year, or like to visit a favorite destination more than once a year and would rather not lug suitcases with you each trip, you've probably considered a vacation home. If you have the funds and the plan, buying a vacation home in your 40s or 50s can be a great help to your retirement nest egg.

How to Buy

The decision whether to buy a vacation home or continue renting is about lifestyle and disposable income. As with a year-round home, owning your retirement property means that part of your vacation budget is being applied toward maintaining and updating your vacation home. That will work fine if that's what you're planning for. But if owning the vacation home eats into other things you'd like to be doing, then it might not be your best option.

Fortunately, your vacation home purchase won't need to be made under the same pressure that went with your residence purchase. You can try before you buy, by visiting the location as a renter before you commit as an owner. As much as possible, make your rental visits mirror what you're planning for as an owner. If you're planning to buy because you'd like to visit the location more often, try multiple visits as a renter first. If you're buying to become part of the community, rent and start your involvement before you purchase. Dollar for dollar, you might spend a little extra doing this due diligence, but a little extra research will help you choose the type of situation you want.

Costs to Plan For

Make sure your vacation home purchase stays exciting and enjoyable by planning ahead for extra costs. Just because you're only there part time doesn't mean you can ignore regular maintenance and the costs of keeping the place up to date. If your second home is a condo, be involved in the condo association just as you would be at home. Set aside funds to cover off-seasonal chores and to open and close the house if your place isn't year-round. If you plan to have seasonal renters, allow for housekeeping, extra maintenance, advertising, and an accountant to help you work out the tax return—at least for the first year until you learn how to do it. The best times to rent are usually the times you probably want to be there, too. Make sure the finances work without factoring in rental income.

FACT

Joint ownership of property can expose the property to the creditors of any owner. Your real estate attorney will help you decide how to protect a family vacation home from divorcing spouses, nursing home costs, and legal judgments against an owner.

Tax Advantages

Don't take equity out of your residence to buy a vacation home. This might be attractive at a time when home prices are rising, but it is something like financing a vacation on your home equity line—a risk that could leave you hanging if and when the market falls. If you decide you can afford a loan to buy your second home, use the second home itself as collateral. Taxpayers who can itemize their deductions can deduct interest on mortgages against a second home the same as they do the mortgage on their first home.

Keeping It in the Family

If your family owns a vacation property that all would like to share, or you're thinking of buying a property with other family members, talk to a real estate lawyer or your estate attorney to see whether it would be better to own the property as partners or whether a more formal arrangement such as a limited liability company might be a better idea. Your attorney will help you assess the amount of liability the property might create for each owner and will help you draft a use agreement that outlines everyone's rights and responsibilities regarding the property. Try to set up an agreement as soon in the buying process as you can to avoid misunderstandings and hard feelings later on. If you already own a property with family, a visit to an attorney should be a top priority.

American Dreamin': Renting Versus Buying

Owning a home has become so closely linked to defining success and the American dream that many people would never consider renting once they can afford to buy. Good planning in your 40s and 50s means disregarding social norms and deciding whether owning or renting is right for you based on your life stage and retirement plans.

Your Life Phase

There are life phases when you may consider renting over buying. Recovering from a divorce, starting a job in a new part of the country, and moving to a new area that you're unfamiliar with are all temporary life phases that warrant living someplace that can be temporary. It's okay to be in a life phase that's in a little bit of flux. Allow yourself the time to settle into a new place or a new lifestyle. Think realistically about how long you will want to live in certain circumstances and then add up the numbers. Mortgages are amortized so that the payments in the beginning years are mostly interest.

This interest can feel like paying rent to the bank instead of the landlord if you're not also gaining equity in the home. After mortgage interest, real estate taxes, maintenance, and selling costs are factored in, are you better off buying or renting in your current situation?

QUESTION?

Don't I need to reinvest my money from my old house into a new house within two years to avoid capital gains taxes?
Capital gains tax rules no longer require that you reinvest in a new home within two years of selling an old one at a profit, so you're free to do what you want with your cash.

For the Kids at College

Paying your kid's rent while he is at college—especially if it looks like he's on the five-year plan, or is planning for grad school in the same town, or is in a high-rent market—can feel like money down the drain. This could be a buying opportunity if the situation is right—that is, your child is able to manage the property; the space is small and cheap enough that there would be only one additional roommate, if any; and the college is in a growth real estate market. If all these things are true, apply the same "put down roots" calculation you would for yourself if you were deciding to buy or rent. After factoring mortgage interest, taxes, maintenance (especially maintenance, if this is going to be a college residence), and selling costs, are you better to buy or rent while they are in school?

As a Retirement Strategy

Start thinking now about whether you will want the luxury of owing no mortgage when you retire or whether you'll be ready for a little change and relocation when you stop working. Your choices should factor into your decisions now. Regardless of what you do—rent now, buy now, or continue to own—it's important that you keep growing your retirement nest egg. If you're renting because it's cheaper than owning and fits your life stage, you still need to be disciplined enough to continue investing. Set up a mutual fund or other investment account so you're still building wealth as you rent.

Common Mistakes and Myths

Don't be overanxious to buy if you're not settled or if you're feeling pressure to buy. This advice often goes unheeded when it comes to real estate—primary homes and vacation homes alike—because of the emotions involved. Keep in mind that homes are constantly coming onto the market; there is no reason to buy under pressure as if the property you're looking at is the last one on earth.

Timeshares

Timeshare residences are notorious for their high-pressure salespeople, and the interesting thing is that you're not even buying real estate with a timeshare—you're buying time. Most timeshares are very difficult to sell, making them liabilities when you need to sell or when you tire of a particular location. This illiquidity qualifies timeshares as purchases, not investments as their sales presentations would have you believe. If you love to vacation and the timeshare maintenance fits in your budget, then timeshares might work for you—just don't consider them part of your retirement nest egg.

The number of communities restricting residents to those over age 50 is growing rapidly. This lifestyle may seem appealing at first glance, but many 50-somethings who have moved into one have later lamented the loss of diversity and activity of an unrestricted community. Be sure to try before you buy into an over-50 community.

Location, Location, Location

Give yourself ample time to decide where you want to live when you retire. Your kids and friends might move, you might decide you want warmer weather or a more rural or urban environment. In most cases it's best to plan your initial retirement—the first two or three years—in the residence where you initially retired. That will give you time to transition out of work and into your new lifestyle without also having to change locations. Then, if you still want to move, plan some long visits to the places you would like to move to. People often retire and immediately buy in a new location without giving themselves time to try it out. Having to sell after a short time because you don't like where you are can be a nest egg–buster.

Investing in Real Estate

If you are a skilled businessperson, investing in real estate can be a great opportunity. Unfortunately, many people take real estate investing too lightly. Real estate is a business. Many people have rental property that they manage as a lifestyle business. They might live in one of the units or rent out an old family property or a previous home, but they don't consider these formal businesses. They should, because the rest of the investors in the real estate market do.

Best Strategies

Whether you own one property or several, it's important to treat real estate investing like any other business. Establish a business plan for each property. Decide what income you need to be profitable, including the time you spend managing the building. Plan in advance the price that you would eventually consider selling at. Create separate bookkeeping and bank accounts for each property to make the income and expenses of each easier to track. Don't use equity from one building to invest in another unless you've decided to own the properties as a group and have analyzed the risk. Be diversified—don't buy too many of the same type of properties in the same geographical area or that cater to the same demographic.

If running a business wasn't what you had in mind, but you would like to add real estate to your investment portfolio, look for real estate investment trusts, called REITs and pronounced "reets." REITs are pooled accounts that invest in real estate such as apartment buildings, office complexes, and strip malls. The income earned by the REIT is passed through to the shareholders. Professional management and diversification is a big appeal of REIT investments.

Risks

Pricing a home is easier than pricing an investment property. After all, you get to live in a home; the investment property doesn't offer that advantage. Income property is valued based on its annual net operating income, or NOI. The NOI equates to rent, less maintenance and other similar costs and an allowance for vacancies. The cost of your mortgage on the property isn't figured into the NOI. Divide the NOI by a rule-of-thumb number called a cap rate. The cap rate is akin to the annual rate of return on the property and will vary based on the location and amenities such as school districts and ocean views. Most advisors suggest dividing NOI by a cap rate of 9 percent or 10 percent to account for the risk.

QUESTION?

How do I calculate the value of the building I'm considering investing in if the cap rate is 9 percent?
Divide the annual NOI of the building by the cap rate. A building with a NOI of $14,000 would be worth $155,555 after dividing $14,000 by 0.09.

Remember that NOI doesn't include the mortgage costs of owning the property. Double check that you can cover your mortgage payments and still maintain the building if there are vacancies.

Helping Your Children Settle Down

How you help your kids get settled once they leave the nest will have an important effect on their future money habits and your financial relationship. Whether you encourage them to move back home to help shore up their finances or use your assets to gift or lend them money to help with a home down payment, it's important to make financial transactions with your grown children as businesslike as you would with a nonrelative. And the kids may not be the only ones who benefit when they move back home—planning to live with them in your old age can serve everyone's needs. If you think you may want to do that, this is the time to start planning.

ALERT!

If your kids are struggling financially, don't make a difficult situation worse by reverting back to the money roles you played when they were small kids. Resist the temptation to dig them out with cash gifts. Instead, hire a financial planner or encourage them to get advice from a professional.

Moving Back Home

Living together for a short time to help a child build up her finances can be a better alternative than simply giving her money when she needs it. People are always more careful with money they've earned than money they've been given. If your child has moved back home, help her set up a budget that includes covering her living expenses—including rent to you—and her savings plan and debt repayment. Have her create investment accounts for her home down payment or first and last months' rent and emergency fund. Also budget the period of time she is going to live with you; a specific expectation of the number of months or years before she lives independently is very important.

Down Payment Ideas

If you have the cash, it can be tempting to give your child as much as you can budget for his home down payment. This can be a problem if it gets him into a house he would otherwise not be able to afford. Getting your kid into a neighborhood where he is trying to keep up with the more-affluent Joneses or into a huge house that is too expensive for him to maintain is a recipe for insolvency and foreclosure. Instead, back into the amount you should give him by assuming he already has a 20 percent down payment. Then figure out how much he can afford for a monthly payment on a mortgage, real estate taxes, insurance, and maintenance. The total must be less than one-third of his income. Use his monthly payment target to calculate the mortgage he can afford, then gift him with what you want to give him toward a 20 percent down payment appropriate for his budgeted mortgage.

Private Mortgages

Many families are using private mortgages to help solve two problems: giving the child access to a mortgage at a reasonable interest rate and giving the parents a chance to invest their money at higher interest rates than they could make in other fixed-rate investment.

Don't lend money to your kids on a handshake. Your attorney or a service such as Virgin Money (*www.virginmoney.com*) can create loan documents and a payment plan that spell out the details of the loan and keep your transaction safe from the gift limit restrictions.

Before calling a mortgage broker, do your own calculations online. Check *www.bankrate.com* for current mortgage rates and various mortgage types and to calculate payments. Be sure to include closing costs, escrow deposits, and moving expenses in the budget.

In-Law Planning

In-laws and their kids can live together and still give each other privacy. Sharing a duplex or a house with an in-law apartment are two of the more common ways kids and their parents live together while keeping their own space. Talk to your real estate attorney about whether you should own the property jointly or whether the property should be owned by a separate legal entity such as a real estate partnership or limited liability company. Your attorney will help you work out the liability and estate-planning issues, and your CPA will help you with the tax planning. These professionals will be an extra cost to setting up and managing this relationship, but don't skip consulting them and risk having a problem later.

Beyond the technical aspects of buying into property together, plan several business meetings with your family before you make the change to understand what everyone's wants and needs are. Set boundaries about who is going to take care of what household chores, and even how many evenings per week you are going to take care of your grandchildren. Having it in writing helps assure that no one misunderstands when the time comes to actually take action.

CHAPTER 16

Taxes in Your 40s and 50s

If you're like most people, you don't open a chapter about taxes and start passing out high fives. But making sure your taxes are paid—and not a penny overpaid—is particularly important in your 40s and 50s. If you're making great money, good tax planning will make sure your nest egg benefits you more than it does Uncle Sam. If you're in a life transition, careful planning will help you get the most from limited resources.

Are You Paying Your Fair Share?

Don't fall into the trap of only thinking about your taxes at the tax deadline in April. Keep your taxes on your radar screen year-round so you can plan for how your taxes affect the rest of your financial life, including mortgage payments, money markets, take-home pay, and investments.

Alternative Minimum Tax

The alternative minimum tax, or AMT, was created by Congress in 1969 to make sure wealthy people were paying at least a minimum amount of tax based on their income. Before the AMT law, it was easier to use complicated strategies and deductions to reduce the tax bill well below normal, often permitting highly paid people to pay little or no taxes. Unfortunately, the AMT law wasn't properly indexed for inflation and now many unsuspecting middle-class taxpayers, who by today's standards are far from lavishly paid, are paying it. Check page two of your 1040 tax form to see if you are paying AMT.

QUESTION?

What items on my return cause me to pay AMT?
The AMT can be triggered by common deductions and exemptions such as personal exemptions for you and your dependents; taking the standard deduction; deducting state and local taxes paid; interest deduction on a second mortgage; and deductible medical expenses. Planning is hard because having these deductions don't always trigger the tax.

If you pay AMT, use an AMT tax-free money market account instead of a standard money market or tax-free money market fund. Also, realize that you're not getting as much benefit out of deductions for mortgage interest, real estate taxes, and personal exemptions for you and your dependents. You might also be paying more on capital gains than you realize. Check Appendix B for more resources to help you plan for being affected by AMT.

Planning Withholding Versus a Big Refund

Getting a big tax refund from the IRS is a waste of money; the government has your money sitting in its account rather than yours, and it doesn't pay you interest on it while it has it! If your refund is over $1,000, go to *www. irs.gov* and recalculate your paycheck withholding. Check the website for help confirming that you're in what's called "safe harbor" so you won't owe a penalty for underwithholding, and then make the paycheck adjustments the worksheet suggests. If you'll feel bad about missing the fun of getting a big check in April, set up your own "tax refund" in a money market account. Make a direct deposit with the amount your paycheck grew by when you adjusted your withholding. Instead of going to the government as withholding, your money will go to your account and earn interest. Using direct deposit makes your paycheck look the same as it did when you adjusted your withholding in your favor, and you'll have a nice nest egg built up in your interest-bearing money market account come April.

You can use paycheck withholding adjustments at midyear to compensate for a cash windfall or minimize a big tax refund, or you can make estimated payments separately by sending the IRS a check. Adjust your withholding when you can to make extra tax deposits. The IRS doesn't apply deadline penalties to withholding that they apply to estimated tax payments.

Midyear Checks

Don't be surprised by extra taxes due on tax day or a big refund caused by a midyear cash windfall. Bonus checks are often treated by tax rules like regular paychecks—resulting in overwithholding that gets paid back to you as a refund after you file your return. Other checks, such as IRA distributions or self-employment compensation, often won't have taxes withheld at all, possibly surprising you with a big tax payment when you file. Fortunately, the IRS website (*www.irs.gov*) is very user friendly. Get in the habit of using the site to calculate your withholding at midyear, especially if you have additional midyear income you didn't plan for.

Itemized Versus Standard Deduction

Not everyone has enough deductions, such as mortgage interest, real estate taxes, and medical expenses, to make itemizing these deductions worthwhile. Check the IRS website to see whether your deductions will total more than the standard deduction. Don't spend time keeping records for things such as charitable deductions if you're not going to take them on your return.

FACT

Check Topic 500 on the IRS website for info and assistance deciding if you should itemize your deductions. Common itemized deductions include home mortgage interest, state and local taxes, medical and dental expenses, charitable contributions, home office expenses, and educational expenses.

Planning for Phase-Outs

The amount you can claim in total itemized deductions is limited by your income. As your income increases over a certain amount, the total dollar amount of itemized deductions you can claim is reduced. This is called phasing out your deductions. Check the bottom of last year's Schedule A to see if this problem affects you. Understanding whether you are getting the full benefit of deductions such as mortgage interest will help you budget for these expenses.

Who Says Taxes Are Certain?

Taxes might be a sure thing, but the rules offer some wiggle room. Right now, many tax laws are slated to change or sunset in 2011. Stay tuned for many changes and adjustments to current laws. Congress will need to raise money for a variety of big-ticket items in the future. Baby boomers drawing on social security, Medicare for the elderly, health care costs for everyone, military efforts, and reducing the deficit will all need to be paid for.

Currently on the Radar Screen

A number of tax rule changes are looming. Congress has looked at changing taxes on capital gains and adjusting the income tax brackets. There will be changes in the AMT and estate tax limits. New credits related to energy saving and alternative energy devices are on the agenda. Many deductions and exemptions that are already increasing with inflation are affected by rules that change in 2011. Make sure to stay on top of the laws defining how much you can put in your 401(k), 403(b), IRA, or other retirement plan each year. Retirement plan contribution limits are increasing in order to encourage saving. Contributions to many retirement accounts are deductible; make sure you take advantage of increased contribution allowances.

Where to Check for New Info

The most reliable source of tax information is the IRS website and your home state government website. The IRS site, especially the Newsroom link, is helpful, but even though it has been improved, it can still be dense reading. Use popular magazines and websites for tips (there's a list of them in Appendix B) and to see what's new, then come back and double check the IRS site and your state site to be sure you understand the rule or strategy correctly. Journalists can make mistakes, and ultimately, you are responsible for the accuracy of your own tax return.

Who Needs to File?

It may seem obvious, but just about everyone with income needs to file a return. It's important to check whether you, your kids, and even your parents are required to file. Search the IRS website using the term "Should You File a Tax Return?" for a page on current income limitations on who needs to file and who doesn't.

Kids' Tax Returns

Your kids may need to file if they have income—earned or investment—in their name. This is the case whether or not you use them for an exemption on your tax return. Under the "kiddie tax" rule, the IRS says that the child pays at the tax rate of the custodial parent. This is easy enough to deal with if you're married, but divorce agreements often state that parents will alternate taking the kids as a deduction on their tax return. Don't let tax planning steer your divorce settlement, but you can avoid needlessly wasting tax money by considering each parent's different tax and income situation when you negotiate.

ALERT!

Tax laws change every year; be sure to check the IRS website for updates. You're responsible for the information on the tax return you sign. Read it and ask questions if you don't understand something. Beware of tax preparers or information services that advertise to reduce your tax burden through confusing tax strategies.

Are Your Parents Dependents?

Many people support their parents and yet don't realize that, for tax purposes, their parent is their dependent. If your parent has very low non–social security income and you provide more than 50 percent of his support, he may be your dependent. Check the IRS website to confirm all of the IRS guidelines. If it turns out that you can't deduct your parents as dependents, you still may be able to deduct medical expenses you paid on their behalf.

Self-Employment Tax Options

If you're not already self-employed but think you might like to be, this could the best phase of your life to do it. Lots of 40- and 50-somethings realize that middle age is the best time to put the skills and talents they have developed in their careers to work for themselves rather than an employer. If this is you, there are a few special things you need to consider when it comes to taxes.

Self-Employment Taxes

The employer's half of social security and Medicare taxes, called FICA taxes, needs to be paid even when you're self-employed. The difference between working for somebody and working for yourself is that the self-employed pay both sides of the FICA tax—your half and the employer's half. Don't despair; in the end, some of the self-employment tax you pay is deductible. The deduction doesn't totally credit the amount you'll pay, but it eases the pinch.

Being self-employed requires a change in how you think about the money you receive for the work you do. When you get a paycheck from an employer, your FICA and income taxes are already withheld. When you're self-employed and your customer pays you for your work, taxes aren't automatically withheld. It's important to realize that a big chunk of their payment to you isn't really yours to keep—it's owed as income tax. Simulate the withholding your employer used to do by automatically putting aside at least 30 percent of what you get from customers (after expenses) as your withholding for taxes. Consider this tax savings account untouchable—just like the withholding your employer used to take. If you don't, and you use that money for expenses during the year, you'll get caught short of cash come tax time.

Once you've been self-employed for a while, you'll be able to finesse the 30 percent rule of thumb to a number that more accurately reflects your taxes due. If this change means reducing the amount you set aside, avoid the temptation to spend the extra—set up a retirement account and start investing!

Sole Proprietors

You are a sole proprietor if you have self-employment income and have made no effort to set up another business entity. Most people—especially people with consulting income and no employees—prefer to be sole proprietors because there are no setup fees or extra tax returns to file.

One of the negatives of a sole proprietorship is that the business dies with the owner. This might not matter to you if you're a consultant without employees, but it would be unworkable if your business needed to transition to another owner after your death or retirement. If this is a concern, consider creating a separate business entity such as a corporation, limited liability company, or partnership.

"Self-employed" and "sole proprietor" are essentially synonymous. At year-end, many of your customers will send you and the IRS 1099 tax forms reporting the income they paid you. You might hear self-employment sometimes referred to as "being paid on a 1099."

Sub S Corporations

If you have employees or are running a business where there is a level of financial liability risk that can't be cost-effectively covered by personal or commercial insurance such as a restaurant or a landscaping business—your lawyer might advise you to incorporate. A corporation is a separate legal entity with its own tax ID number. Being a separate entity from you means that the entity doesn't die when you do and that the money that is at risk in the event of a lawsuit is only the money in the corporation, not your personal assets. You may need additional professional liability insurance if you are selling advice—as a lawyer or a financial planner, for example—but for most other types of businesses, the corporate veil, as it's called, offers plenty of liability protection. When you incorporate, you'll be given the option to take a "sub S" election (if you qualify under the Internal Revenue Code subchapter S requirements). By doing this you retain the corporate structure, but the income or losses of your corporation will be passed through to your personal tax return rather than being taxed at higher corporate tax rates.

Your bank will probably require you to sign a personal guarantee for money that they lend your business. If the business fails or isn't able to repay the money, then you are personally liable. In this case, your personal assets are not protected.

You'll own shares of your corporation as a shareholder, and your corporation will pay you—even though you're the owner—as an employee with regular paycheck tax withholding. Your accountant might refer to this as "being paid on a W-2." At the end of the year, your accountant will prepare a K-1 report for your personal return and a separate corporate tax return.

LLCs and LLPs

Your business lawyer might recommend a limited liability company or a limited liability partnership instead of a corporation. LLCs and LLPs have members instead of corporation stockholders. They pass their income down to the members just like sub S corporations do, and they offer liability protection. Your accountant will prepare the same tax return for the LLC/LLP as she would for a corporation. Many people prefer LLC/LLPs because they are more flexible to manage than corporations.

How to File: The Right Option for You

Choosing how you want to get your tax return completed—whether you do it yourself, use a service, or engage a professional preparer—has a lot to do with the complexity of your financial life, the amount of time you have to spend on the return, and the support you want in an audit.

Online

If your taxes are straightforward and you understand what's expected on your return, preparing with an online service such as TurboTax or TaxAct can be very convenient. The service's website walks you though your return with a series of questions. Ignore boasts that some services make about the average refund their filers received. Since your refund is a function of the amount of tax you owe versus the amount you paid in during the year, it has little to do with the efficiency of their service. If for some strange reason you paid an extra $10,000 in estimated or withholding tax that you didn't actually owe, and then used a service to do the return, your extra payment and the resulting refund would skew their average. Online services are a convenience—they're not magic refund-finders.

Comparing Professionals: CPA or Enrolled Agent?

Some newly divorced or widowed people have never filed a return because their spouse formerly handled those chores. If that describes you, and you have a complex tax situation such as a business or rental property, or just can't spend the time doing the return yourself, hire a professional.

Certified Public Accountants, or CPAs, have an extensive education and often specialize in complex returns for businesses and business owners. If your situation calls for hiring these big guns—and paying them—they will become invaluable advisors to you.

QUESTION?

Is filing using the IRS's E-File safer than mailing my paper tax return?
Yes! Your return is full of personal information. Filing electronically minimizes the chances your information will be lost in transit; mailed returns are collected at lockboxes and then transported to the IRS to be entered into computers. E-filing also avoids typos that could happen when the information is inputted into the IRS computer.

If you're an individual with a straightforward tax situation, or are self-employed, hiring a CPA might be overkill. Enrolled agents are tax professionals licensed to represent you before the IRS. Since they specialize in tax preparation and planning, they may be better able to help you, especially if you are looking for a strong advisory relationship but have a more straightforward tax situation.

One important key to success with any professional is your relationship with them. The smartest professional in the world won't do you any good if you can't communicate with him. Don't be afraid to ask about his business, his future plans, how long he has been working with clients like you, and how he feels about answering your questions throughout the year rather than just at tax time.

Tax Preparation Chains

Retail chain tax preparation services such as H&R Block and Jackson Hewitt can be helpful if you're not sure how to complete your online return yourself and have a straightforward tax situation that could be simplified by having someone with training input the return for you. The downside of this service is that you don't usually get the chance to develop a relationship with a preparer over a number of years.

The tax prep chains may try to sell you additional services such as instant refund loans, investments, or financial planning services. Refund loans are a waste of the fees they charge. If you file your tax return electronically and have direct deposit you'll get your refund very quickly anyway—in many cases in only a few days. If they offer financial or investment advice, do your due diligence just as you would for another investment advisor or financial planner. It's rare that these offerings are better than those sold by firms that specialize in investments.

Surviving an Audit

Most audits are resolved simply by providing the information to back up entries on your tax return or by correcting information that was reported incorrectly. Most audits are handled by mail, so surviving an audit is mostly about keeping good records and responding quickly and accurately to an inquiry. If you're called to a face-to-face audit, it can be very helpful to have a professional representing you. Professionals will often only want to represent you on a return they prepared—another good reason to build a relationship with a pro if your tax situation is complex.

The Records You'll Need

Good record-keeping is the key to accurate tax planning and preparation. Don't overwhelm yourself with systems and don't spend a lot of money on organization. A simple system that isn't bogged down by unneeded records is all you need.

How Long to Keep Your Records

Tax returns should be kept indefinitely—who knows when you'll need them. Of course, that doesn't mean that you need to keep all the supporting documents for more than three years. The IRS won't audit a return that is older than three years, unless they suspect fraud. But there is still a lot of information on your return that will come in handy down the road: Your annual income can prove your social security benefit due; your reinvested dividends support your investment basis; and you'll need a record of your

IRA contributions when you calculate your taxes in retirement. Here's a tip: use Adobe Acrobat software to make digital copies of your tax returns that take up no space!

FACT

Keep investment statements that show your initial purchase until you sell the investment. If you buy through a brokerage firm, it may keep track of this information for you on your monthly statement as Cost Basis. If that's the case, you'll only need to keep a running cycle of the previous twelve monthly statements.

Systems to Manage

Add a file to your regular filing system—whether paper or electronic—for last year's tax return and this year's tax information. Drop tax-related documents into the file as you come across them: charitable gifts, real estate tax receipts, medical bills, tuition bills, your year-end pay stub, etc. Refer to last year's return to see what to watch for. For example, if last year's return has an interest payment from XYZ Bank, you should be looking for a 1099 for XYZ Bank again this January. Looking for documentation as the year progresses will keep you from scrambling at the last minute to find things.

Using a Personal Bookkeeper

If you're too busy or disorganized to gather documents or manage bill-paying, consider hiring a personal bookkeeper. Use e-mailed bills and an online bookkeeping service such as Quickbooks so you both can access your records without needing to meet face to face. Bookkeepers don't need to sign checks for you—in fact, it's safer if they don't have direct access to your funds. Have the bookkeeper print checks for your signature or have them tell you where to download them online and print them yourself.

ALERT!

Having a personal bookkeeper doesn't mean you don't have to review your checkbook and other records. It just saves you the time needed to gather and organize the information. Plan a monthly phone meeting with your bookkeeper to review accounts and income and expenses.

Check Appendix B for information on where to find a personal book-keeper. Paying the bookkeeper will be an extra cost, but if she helps you find time for the things you'd rather do or if she makes tax time easier or saves your CPA time, she could pay for herself.

CHAPTER 17

The Sandwich Generation: Planning for Parental Care

You're finally focused on building your own financial security, and possibly helping your kids get established, and now your parents need your attention, too. Helping your parents can be a big emotional and financial challenge if you're not ready. Fortunately, whether you're dealing with a crisis or trying to avoid one by planning ahead, there is a growing list of resources to help if you know where to look and how to use them.

Starting the Conversation

Money is not a common topic discussed by most families, but if you're concerned about your parents' financial security, now is the time to get it on the table. With good planning and frank conversations, many parents will be able to continue managing their own affairs with guidance or assistance from you or a professional advisor.

Set the Stage with Small Steps

Don't try to launch into a full financial audit with your parents on day one. Respect the family roles that you've established, and don't try to break the child/parent mold immediately. Instead, start small. Create credibility by sharing your experiences and financial planning process with your parents. Use examples from your own life as a way to start talking to them as peers. If they're looking for your help and see the benefit of planning together, they will start to share their experiences and concerns as well.

If your parents are still comfortably managing their financial affairs, you can limit your discussion to a summary of the planning they have done, exchanging the names of your respective financial advisors and attorneys, and sharing copies of your wills and estate documents.

ALERT!

Early warning signs that your parents' bills aren't being paid are checks that go uncashed, calls from creditors, and piles of mail that go unopened. Offer to help them check their credit report online at *www.annual creditreport.com*. Help them check for evidence of identity theft and check their bill-payment habits at the same time.

When to Take Control

If your parents are clearly not managing their finances well or if they've asked for help, resist the urge to drop your own finances and obligations too hastily. If you're dealing with an immediate financial matter, tend to it and then start thinking of your new role as managing the broad family finances. In your new role, you're managing your affairs and your parents' together, rather than two separate family situations. Losing sight of your own finances while helping them will hurt your future security and could make you resentful. Managing both situations as a broader project where neither takes priority will help you recognize when you need outside help.

QUESTION?

I don't have time to pay my own bills. How am I supposed to find time to pay my mom's too?
Have mom list out her bills and set up as many as you can for auto-pay or direct billing. If there are too many, or you need closer followup, hire a licensed, bonded bill-paying service.

Professionals to the Rescue

Just like you, your parents need a financial planner, attorney, and accountant for financial, legal, and tax advice. Follow the guidelines in Chapter 18 for help finding and selecting a suitable professional. If your parents needs advice about transferring their assets or giving you legal authority to manage their finances directly, you should talk to an elder law attorney. A geriatric care manager can advise you on issues related to disability, failing health, and health care choices. A personal financial organizer or bookkeeper can help with day-to-day money management. Check Appendix B for links to help find referrals to the professionals.

Don't hesitate to take advantage of free and low-cost resources your parents may be eligible for. Take the National Council on Aging benefits checkup at *www.benefitscheckup.org*.

Elder Law You Need to Know

At some point, you will probably need the advice of an elder law attorney. This specialist can help you gather and complete the needed documents and create a plan to help you manage your parents' assets and affairs while still protecting their interests. The elder law attorney understands, among other things, the ever-changing laws around asset transfers, the Medicaid application process, nursing home issues, and estate planning.

Where to Find Help

If you already have an attorney, describe your current questions that relate to your parents and ask her for a referral to an elder law attorney. Some firms will have an elder law attorney on staff, or they can refer you to another firm or an individual. Many elder law attorneys work in small or one-person firms. Don't hold it against an elder law attorney if she is a sole practitioner. As long as she is qualified and has time to focus on your case, small size is not a negative.

Don't move your elderly parents' assets without talking to an elder law attorney. Get a referral from a friend or an advisor, or through the National Elder Law Foundation at *www.nelf.org* and the National Academy of Elder Law Attorneys at *www.naela.org*.

Establish Guidelines and Start the Discussion

Your elder law attorney will be representing your parents' interests, not yours. This is exactly what you want her to do, but it can create some awkward conversations if you and your parents haven't already discussed your role in managing their finances. Many parents won't say so, but there is often a suspicion that "my kids are just after my money." The fact that you're not after an early inheritance might not ease those feelings. Take an early opportunity to explain to your parents that your job is to help if you can and to help hire advisors to do the things you can't. Before going to the lawyer's office, talk together at least once or twice about your parent's goals, questions, and concerns.

Your First Meeting and Before

If possible, you and your parents should contact the elder law attorney together by phone before scheduling a meeting. Ask her how much of her practice is devoted to elder law, how long she has been practicing, whether there will be a fee for the initial meeting, and what materials you should bring to the meeting. Do some online research and a Google search of the attorney before meeting her and after your first meeting. Look for examples of her work in the community, her involvement in elder law, and the other professionals and professional organizations she is working with.

At your first meeting, you and your parents should both feel comfortable with the attorney and the process she recommends. If you're not, don't hesitate to interview another attorney. You will likely have quite a bit of contact with your elder law attorney; it's important that you like her and trust her.

The Documents You'll Need

Up-to-date documents that are accessible and organized are a key piece of anyone's financial management, especially someone such as your parent who is asking for outside support. Make a quick review and be sure everything is in place that needs to be.

Power-of-Attorney Versus Joint Accounts

Many older parents take adding their adult children's names to their accounts and their residential ownership records too lightly. The creditors of any of the people who have legal control of an account could get access to the money in that account to satisfy debts. This could range from divorcing spouses to insurance or legal claims, and even IRS liens. Money in joint accounts could even be counted as an asset when one of the account owners' children applies for college financial aid, decreasing the potential award.

Most people add names to accounts to make them accessible if something happens to them. Instead of joint ownership, though, look at adding a TOD—transfer-on-death—designation to nonretirement accounts such as bank and investment accounts. The TOD provision would make the money in the account accessible to beneficiaries without the delay and complications of the probate process. If your parents want their adult children or others to have account access while they're alive, a power-of-attorney over that account or financial affairs in general makes it possible for you and other caretakers to mind their affairs.

Using the Health Care Proxy

A health care proxy gives a caretaker the power to make health care decisions for aging parents if they're incapacitated. In many states, a health care proxy outlines a person's end-of-life wishes. Make sure both the primary person who is assigned the proxy powers and the secondary, or contingent, person have a copy of the document. Your parents' primary physician should have a copy on file as well. Review the document each time there is a change in your parents' health status, or the status of a named proxy, once every year.

Watch for other signs of your parents' unhealthy financial habits, such as problem gambling. Gambling can provide a form of temporary relief to seniors by distracting them from poor health and other concerns. If a parent is experiencing depression, gambling that started as entertainment could escalate to problem gambling if not treated. Contact the National Council on Problem Gambling at *www.ncpgambling.org*.

Getting Copies of Account Statements

Most investment managers, banks, mutual funds companies, and insurance companies are prepared to provide duplicate copies of account documents to people other than the account holders, if requested in writing by the account holder. This is a handy way to keep track of your parents' accounts and to make sure insurance premiums get paid on time and statements are available when it's time to file tax returns. Use online access and e-mail alerts whenever you can to save yourself time and make record-keeping easier. Using a separate e-mail address will help you segregate e-mails that pertain to your parents' accounts, and your parents can monitor mail to that address, too. Using an online account aggregator such as *www.yodlee.com* or *www.mint.com*, or an aggregator provided by a brokerage firm, provides access with a simple login.

Role Reversal and the Family Money Dynamic

It's critical that you acknowledge that everyone brings his or her own money hangups and "baggage" to the table when family members try to co-manage money. If relationships get strained, seek help from a family therapist or financial planner experienced in helping families communicate with each other about money.

How You Can Help—Sensitively

Use technology and the growing number of elder care options to help you help your parents without taking over their lives (or letting their care overwhelm yours). Financial accounts can be accessed online; houses can be cleaned and organized by cleaning services and professional organizers; yards can be tended by landscaping services; and basic and not-so-basic health care needs can be managed by home health aides. Face it: Maintaining a good relationship with your parent will take some money. It's important to budget carefully, but remember that what you're really buying is your parents' dignity and your sound relationship with them.

FACT

Not all services that will help your parents at home need to cost a lot. Check *www.eldercare.gov* for links to resources near your parents' home. Contact the National Council on Aging at *www.ncoa.org* for resources to help them in their home. Ask local church and youth groups if they have volunteers available or programs to help with elder services.

Three Pitfalls to Avoid

First, don't fall into the trap of thinking of yourself as your parents' parent. This will put too much pressure on you, and your parents will rightly resent being patronized. If you find yourself slipping into this thinking, step back and find someone else to take the reins for a while.

Second, avoid thinking that your way is the only way. Remember that even if your parents are completely unable to manage their own financial affairs, you are still only there to help. There will be few circumstances in which you'll be the only one with an opinion on how to go about it. Keep an open mind, communicate with your parents and other family members as much as circumstances allow, and keep a thick skin.

Finally, seldom is any action set in stone. Your elder law attorney will guide you—because there are a few things related to asset transfers that actually *are* set in stone—but most of the decisions you'll help your parents make are not. Keep your choices in the "let's try this" category, and you'll be better ready to deal with change when it comes.

If you decide to employ a home health aide—even if she comes through an agency—you are responsible for payroll tax withholding and reporting for her. Ask the agency you're using, your insurance agent, or your accountant for a referral to a payroll service that can help you.

Three Key Things to Remember

First, you're an important gatekeeper. A big part of your role is to help find competent and trustworthy advisors for your parents and to ask questions. Elders are often the target of unscrupulous salespeople and scammers.

Second, keep communicating. Your parents' generation learned to be very self-reliant and independent. Keep the communication lines open as best you can, and make sure they are open when your parents are ready to talk.

Finally, record-keeping is important. Having accurate information to give financial advisors and attorneys is vital.

Planning for Parents Who Live with You

Having your parent move into your house, moving in with them, or buying a new property together may be a great way to achieve all your goals. Creating a business relationship with clear communications and clear objectives for your joint living arrangement is a big part of making sure it works.

Buying into Your Home

Your elder law attorney may recommend that your parents buy into your house. In many cases, parents have the assets to afford the buy-in, and can contribute to household upgrades needed to accommodate them. The attorney will advise you on how the house should be owned—jointly with rights of survivorship, as tenants in common, or as a partnership. Check with your accountant before deciding on the ownership form and to understand the tax ramifications of owning jointly and then of inheriting your parents share later on.

Sharing Expenses

Create a clear outline of who is going to pay for which expenses based on how closely your day-to-day lives overlap. If you eat together, plan a grocery budget that you can both share. Set up a monthly home maintenance fee and a utility account based on the square footage each part of the family occupies. If you're managing your parents' bill-paying for them, maintain a separate credit card and bank account for their expenses. When you're shopping, ask the clerk to run your purchases through separate from your parents'. This may seem like a troublesome extra step, but it will make tracking expenses and reporting easier.

Contracting for Care

Don't hesitate to look for professional caregivers if your parents need care, even if they are living with you. The fact that you share a home shouldn't mean that you and your family must care for them full time. In fact, that could be the worst thing for both parties. Check Appendix B for information about free and paid programs for home care.

Is a Reverse Mortgage a Smart Solution?

Your parents' home may be their biggest asset, or perhaps second only to their retirement nest egg. Most people want to live at home for as long as they can as they get older. The mortgage industry has obliged by offering homeowners a product called a reverse mortgage.

What They Are and When They're Right

Unlike a typical mortgage loan, a reverse mortgage, which is usually available only to people age 62 and older, doesn't need to be paid back as long as the borrower lives in the home. Money from a reverse mortgage can be paid to the borrower as a lump sum, in monthly payments, as a credit line that can be accessed as needed, or in a combination of these ways. As funds are paid, they become a debt against the home's equity.

FACT

Many reverse mortgages are guaranteed by the U.S. Department of Housing and Urban Development and the Federal Housing authority. They often include a line of credit that can increase if the value of the house increases. It's important to seek the advice of an independent financial planner before buying a reverse mortgage.

What's in the Fine Print

Since the loan isn't paid, in the form of a sale by the bank, until the homeowner leaves the home, the bank won't offer a loan equal to the full equity in the property. That's because, although resident homeowners don't need to make payments while they are living in the home, interest still accrues against the home value. The loan plus the interest is then paid off when the house is finally sold. Any value remaining after the sale goes back to the original homeowner or his estate.

Since the resident still owns the home, he is still responsible for maintenance, real estate taxes, and insurance on the home. Because these are often the biggest expenses paid by retirees, many people decide that selling the home—and getting the full value instead of the discounted reverse mortgage value—is a better option.

Trends to Watch

Reverse mortgages have only been around for about twenty years. This may seem like plenty of time to shake out the bugs, but that period is insignificant for a financial product that relies on the kind of complex mortality and economic projections and estimates that reverse mortgages do. At the moment, the fees and limited size of these loans are serious deterrents from making them appropriate for most people's circumstances. Stay tuned; fees could drop and features improve enough that they will soon become a viable way of accessing the value in your parents' home.

Medicaid Planning

Medicaid planning for most people means planning to protect personal assets prior to applying for very expensive medical care such as in a nursing home or assisted living facility. Medicaid applications don't consider certain assets and a certain amount of income. Elder law attorneys use the rules to their best advantage in Medicaid planning to reposition the elder's estate into these uncountable assets or to give the assets away completely so that they can't be considered available to pay for nursing home costs.

What Is Medicaid?

Medicaid provides medical coverage for poor people. Many people become poor while paying for help with long-term chronic illnesses such as those associated with old age—needing help with necessary daily living activities such as dressing, eating, and personal care. This level of care is usually delivered in a nursing home or assisted living facility, so many people think of Medicaid coverage as an inevitable part of living there.

Medicaid and Medicare are often confused. Keep them straight in your mind by thinking of Medicare as the retiree health insurance policy. Medicare pays when you need care that will help you get better, but it doesn't pay for everything. There are copays and limits on spending for specific procedures—especially the procedures or care that will improve your daily lifestyle but not necessarily make you better again. For example, Medicare may pay for an operation to repair a broken leg and a certain amount of restorative physical therapy, but no more; Medicaid would pay if you had no money left to have an aide help you get dressed.

When Medicaid Planning Is Needed

Medicaid planning is hugely controversial. Many people claim that individuals should pay for their nursing home care the same as they paid for medical care when they were younger. They maintain that individuals should not seek to appear poor in order to receive government benefits.

Other people want to transfer an inheritance to their kids or have a partner or spouse that they want to protect who is still living in the community, meaning that presenting a low-asset appearance for the sake of Medicaid is important to them. In either case, it's important to talk about Medicaid with your elder law attorney if you're concerned about nursing home or other high medical costs.

Who Can Help?

Some insurance agents advertise that they can help you with Medicaid planning, and they may be experienced enough to help you work out potential strategies and to understand some concepts. But in the end, you should rely on an elder law attorney for the most reliable legal advice.

QUESTION?

My attorney suggests investing my dad's money in an annuity before he enters a nursing home, while my mom remains at home. Is that a good idea?
Maybe. One strategy for helping the spouse who's still at home is to convert some assets into the income payments provided by an annuity. Done correctly, it could help stretch your dad's finances and help your mom continue to live independently.

Pitfalls to Guard Against

Don't be frightened into moving assets or buying financial products or annuities because you're told "the nursing home will take everything." This is a common high-pressure sales pitch that has led to many poor financial decisions. Make sure that the person giving you advice has no financial stake in the transaction, such as a commission on the financial product or strategy they're recommending. Make sure you understand the strategy that is recommended and that you're comfortable implementing it and sticking with it. Attorneys will sometimes suggest a transfer of assets into trusts or other transfer strategies that require that a certain time elapse between the transfer and the Medicaid application.

What the Future Might Hold for Medicaid

Medicaid's future is high on the priority lists of politicians and policy-makers as baby boomers age toward retirement and as health care costs continue to rise. Look for restrictions on government benefits such as Medicaid to tighten and for waiting periods for benefits and "look backs"—the time between asset transfer and Medicaid application—to increase.

CHAPTER 18

Do You Need an Advisor?

When you were younger you probably collected an assortment of informal financial advisors as different needs came up, whether it was buying insurance, opening an investment account at work, or starting an IRA at your bank. Now that you're in your 40s or 50s, it's time to get serious about your financial team. A good team of advisors who work well together is the best assurance that your money and time are being best spent to reach your goals.

What You Need in Your Planning Toolkit

Whether you're just now getting serious about managing your finances or have felt pretty confident with your planning and research all along, realize that the planning you're doing at this phase of life is complex enough and critical enough to warrant asking for advice from a professional.

Getting advice doesn't mean giving up control. You always have the final word on what you do with your life and with your money. There are six tabs in your financial plan: goal planning, insurance, investments, taxes, retirement planning, and estate planning. Find the combination of do-it-yourself and teaming with outside advice that works for you within each tab.

If You're a Do-It-Yourselfer

Doing it yourself is a lot easier now than it's ever been, thanks to the proliferation of online resources. If you have the time and interest, you can make enormous progress on your own, with only occasional specialized help. You can run goal-planning projections, buy insurance, research investments and open accounts, prepare and file your tax return, calculate how much you need to retire comfortably, and even prepare a will. If you're a do-it-yourselfer, you'll want to do as much as you can on your own and then ask for advice when you need it.

Don't try to skimp and save the fee by skipping the annual review with a financial planner. A simple one-hour check-in can save you costly mistakes and missed opportunities. Building a relationship with a planner will make dealing with emergencies and complications easier and cheaper because he will already be familiar with your situation.

When will you need advice? Partner with a fee-only financial planner who will function as a second opinion for you. An annual check-in with your planner to review what you're doing will uncover areas that need more attention or that need review by a specialist such as an attorney or a CPA.

If You're New to Finances or Too Busy to Plan

If you're new to managing your finances, too busy to plan, or really would rather be doing anything else but managing your money, you'll need a financial planner as a partner. It's important that your planner remain a partner and not the sole decision maker regarding your money—that should always be your responsibility. There are many resources to eliminate the tedium and time demands of researching investments, creating planning projections, preparing your taxes, and making a budget. Being in charge of your money doesn't mean that you are doing all of these things yourself. It does mean that you are overseeing the processes and staying educated about your plan as it develops and evolves. Pay attention to online magazines, blogs, newspapers, and books to keep learning and to stay on top of new financial issues that might affect you.

QUESTION?

What do the initials mean after advisors' names?
In personal finance, the most common designations are CFP, for Certified Financial Planner, and CPA, for Certified Public Accountant. Both these designations require a rigorous exam process, experience, and ongoing continuing education. Check the Financial Industry Regulatory Authority's website, *www.finra.org*, for details on the education requirements for your advisors' professional designations.

You and your personal financial planner are the primary members of your personal finance team, but from time to time you'll need specialists to help implement parts of your plan and to offer advice in specialized areas.

The Quarterback: Your Financial Planner

If you're the head coach of your personal finance team, your financial planner is your quarterback. Your planner should meet with you on a regular basis to update your goals, review your plan, and help guide you in implementing the to-dos in your plan. If you're a do-it-yourselfer, you'll decide which things you want to do and which things you want your planner to do for you. It's the planner's role to understand the big picture and how your financial life meshes with your personal and financial goals. She will also suggest referrals to other professionals when you need their expertise.

Insurance Agents

Insurance policies—life, health, disability, auto, and home—are sold through an agent or directly to the public via the web. If you know exactly the type of coverage you need, you can save the cost of the insurance agent's commission by buying direct online. Term life insurance is convenient to buy this way. But if you're not quite sure of the coverage specifics you want, or you're buying a product such as disability, home, or auto coverage that requires expert insight, a relationship with an insurance agent is important.

FACT

Agents often specialize in either property/casualty or life/health coverage. Your property and casualty agent provides car, home, and liability insurance, which should be reviewed once a year. You may only see your life and health agent when you need a policy. They provide life, disability, and health insurance.

Tax Planning Advice and Preparation

Completing your tax forms can be pretty straightforward if you are not self-employed and have a limited number of deductions. If this is your case, you could complete your tax return using an online service, with some spot advice from your financial planner. If you are self-employed, have significant investment income or a rental property, or have employee stock options or a restricted stock plan through work, you should consider adding a CPA to your team.

Investing Advice and Management

Financial planners often double as investment advisors or managers because investing is so integral to reaching your financial goals. You may manage your own investments and use your planners as a guide or a second opinion, or you might have your planner acting as your investment manager. Some financial planners will refer you to money managers who specialize in a particular type of investment.

Legal Advice and Estate Planning

A general-practice attorney can handle most of the legal issues that will come up. He can prepare a basic estate plan including a will, health care proxy, living will, and power of attorney. He will often handle real estate transactions or refer you to an attorney who can. If you're planning a divorce or starting a business, you will need to add a divorce lawyer or a business attorney to your team. If you have a complex estate or want to put your money in trust, your financial planner might refer you to an estate attorney.

Setting Expectations

You're responsible for the success of your own personal finances, but you don't have to do everything yourself. You're managing a team of people, including yourself, to make sure you meet your goals. How all these team-mates work together is an important part of your success.

Your Role and Your Team's Roles

Your role is to make sure that your best interests are the top priority and that you express your needs, goals, and questions at every step along the way. Your advisors will make suggestions and recommendations. They rely on you to give them all the information they need and to be realistic and truthful about your circumstances. They also rely on you to make all final decisions, unless you have given them this power, as is sometimes the case if a money manager is managing an investment account and has discretionary authority to pick investments within certain guidelines.

Even if you've given your investment advisor discretionary authority to make investments, your account statement should come independently from an investment company that holds the account, not the advisor. Deposit checks should be written to the investment company, not the advisor.

Advisors Working Together

Insist that your advisors work well together. If they aren't communicating or if they feel protective of their turf, you can't be sure your needs are being met. You may feel some conflict if your financial planner is recommending a different policy than your insurance agent is suggesting, or if more than one advisor provides a particular service. If this is the case, understand that you will probably get the most unbiased advice from the advisor whose compensation isn't influenced by whose recommendations you implement. For example, if your financial planner and your insurance agent are both recommending a different type of life insurance but the agent is the only one paid on commission, you should consider her bias.

Remember that your advisory team includes you, and relies partly on your web research, your reading, and any classes you might take. Your advisors should respect your questions and should not make you feel as though you're being dictated to.

When Is an Advisor Crucial?

In your 40s and 50s, you need at least a financial planner to review your personal financial plan with you and the steps you are taking to manage your money toward reaching your goals. Bypassing a planner is a little like skipping regular medical checkups and tests. As an amateur, you aren't capable of tending to all the important details concerning your plan. A good advisor will save you at least the equivalent of his fee by maximizing your resources, saving you time, and preventing costly mistakes.

Advisor Fees and Conflicts

Your advisor needs a free hand to recommend strategies, investments, and purchases without being constrained by the conflicts of interest that come into play if she's compensated when you take her advice. It's possible to get good advice from an advisor regardless of how she is paid, but to avoid conflicts, it's important to understand her compensation structure.

How Do Advisors Earn Their Money?

Financial advisors can be paid through product sale commissions or fees paid by the client. Commissions can be paid when you initially buy a specific financial product, and then "commission trails" can continue to be paid to the advisor as long as you own that product. Brokers often share their commission with the company they work for, and their earnings could be affected by the amount of that company's product they've sold over time. In other words, there could be strong pressure to sell you something you don't need, or that is less effective for your plan than a competing, perhaps lower-paying, product.

QUESTION?

My commissioned broker is suggesting an annuity for my IRA. Is this a bad idea?
Annuities carry higher costs—and commissions—than most mutual funds, and could raise a conflict of interest. Ask the broker to recommend a comparable mutual fund and ask what the fee/commission differences are and why the annuity would be better than a fund.

Advisors who are paid directly by the client usually base their fee on an hourly rate, an annual retainer, a fee based on the amount the client is investing with them—called an assets under management or AUM fee—or a flat project fee schedule with a menu of prices for each project. Some advisors charge a combination of fees and commissions, with the commission offsetting the fees that are billed to the client.

Danger Signals

There can be conflicts of interest in almost every relationship. Advisors compensated by commission are motivated to suggest products that make them the most money. Advisors who charge based on assets under management are motivated to suggest investing your money through them rather than paying down debt, for example. Advisors who are paid an hourly fee are motivated to pad the hours of work they do. It is important to remember that anyone you hire could have a conflict.

Very few advisors give in to these conflicts, and the ones with professional designations such as CFP and CPA, as well as your attorney, have taken an oath to always put the client's interests ahead of their own. You can further minimize the conflicts in your relationship with your advisor by asking the right questions.

Questions You Should Ask

Every advisor should offer a first meeting or phone call in which you can ask questions and get to know about him before making a commitment to work with him. Some advisors will charge a fee for this meeting, but most won't. After all, they want the chance to check you out, as well, and to decide if you're someone they would like to work with.

Expect to meet with your financial planner to review your plan once a year or more, as needed. Expect to meet with your accountant or CPA once during tax time and again in the fall for a tax projection, if your situation is complex. Insurance should be reviewed annually. Your estate plan should be reviewed every five years.

Ask about their fees and how they work. If they are fee-paid advisors, are they able to quote an up-front project fee? If they are commissioned advisors, can they describe the various commissions they receive from product sales and how they differ across various offerings and companies? The National Association of Personal Financial Advisors has a questionnaire on their website—*www.napfa.org*—that you can use as a guide when interviewing an advisor, as well as a form your advisor can use to disclose the commissions he receives.

Monitoring Progress

Part of managing your personal finance team is monitoring progress and measuring success. This includes your own progress toward continuing your financial education and completing the things you've assigned to yourself to implement.

What to Watch For

Having well-managed personal finances means having short-, mid- and long-term financial goals that you're working toward. Your goals—especially your mid- and long-term ones—should include intermediate milestones that let you measure incremental progress. For example, your long-term goal may be to retire in fifteen years. An intermediate milestone might be to increase your 401(k) investing through your employer by 5 percent. At your year-end check-in, make sure that you achieved this milestone.

Your advisors should be communicating with you on a regular basis about the tasks they're performing for you. They should return calls and e-mails promptly and not make you feel as if you're an interruption to their daily work. They should also set clear expectations about what they need from you as part of your work together. If these things aren't happening, you should talk to the advisor. If discussion doesn't fix the problem, it's time to find another advisor.

Online Education

Online financial information and advice should be easy to understand and clearly indicate who is providing the information. Understand how the site is making its money; consider whether its revenue model biases the site's advice and information. Make sure that you don't rely on the advice given on websites unless they are the regulatory sites themselves. You might read an interesting article about a strategy or a rule, but be sure you confirm it by researching it yourself or by checking with your advisor before relying on it. Check the Resources at the back of the book for good sources of online education.

Regulating Agencies

Ask your advisor who her oversight organization is. Lawyers are overseen by their bar association, CPAs by the American Institute of Certified Public Accountants, CFPs by the Certified Financial Planner Board of Standards. Advisors who sell investments for a commission are monitored by the Financial Industry Regulatory Authority; advisors who give investment advice and are paid fees are regulated by their state or the Securities Exchange Commission. Insurance agents are overseen by their state.

Handling Problems with Advisors

If you have a problem with an advisor, contact her first. Many problems are simple misunderstandings, and most advisors will work hard to clear things up. Keep personal notes from your discussions with your advisor and ask her to give you recommendations in writing to minimize possible misunderstandings. If your contact with the advisor doesn't clear up the problem, it's time to contact the agency that oversees her.

Finding the Perfect Advisor Match

Finding a financial advisor you're comfortable with over the long term is central to achieving your financial goals, and will make it easier to develop a strong, trusting relationship. Financial planning is an art, not a science; the better the planner knows you, the more effective his advice will be.

Asking for a Referral

Because your financial planner is the quarterback of your advice team, he may be the first person you start shopping for. By far the best way to find a planner is to ask friends you respect, and who are satisfied with their financial progress, for a referral to their planner. You'll still need to meet the planner before deciding whether to work with him, but having the personal reference from a friend is very helpful.

Your financial planner or other advisors can also refer you to great resources. Don't discount advisors whom you've only seen once; a good resource could be the agent who manages your car insurance or the attorney who handled your house-closing process.

Online Searches

Online searches are a good way to create a list of advisors to interview and a good way to learn about them before you do. Try a search through the various membership organizations such as NAPFA or the Financial Planner Association. Check the advisor's website. Then search the advisor's name through Google to learn more about his organizational memberships or public activities. Check Appendix B for online sites to research financial advisors.

FACT

Some associations charge advisors a fee to be included in their online searches. In this case, realize that you're only seeing a list of advisors willing to pay the fee. Associations such as NAPFA charge a fee for membership, and also require ongoing continuing education to maintain membership and to be included in the online search through their website.

Managing Advisor Turnover

Ask your advisor about his firm's succession plans. What are his plans to transition his clients to a new advisor after he retires or if he is disabled? If the advisor is planning to retire within the next year, ask to meet his successor well in advance to make sure you like her and to help make the transition a smooth one. Advisors in one-person shops may be planning to have a number of other small firms make themselves available as successor advisors. Large firms may be planning to assign clients to one of many younger advisors.

In addition to making sure you understand the people involved in your advisor's succession plan, make sure you ask how your personal information and records will stay secure in the transition.

CHAPTER 19

Breaking Up Is Hard to Do: Divorce and Separation

Divorce or the breakup of a long-term domestic partnership at your age can be especially devastating, both emotionally and financially. It's hard to start over at midlife and it's difficult to recover from the inevitable legal expenses without dipping into your nest egg. Reduce the negative financial consequences of your breakup with some clear, businesslike thinking about the money decisions you need to make now. It's not always easy, but it's possible. Making the hard decisions now, during the breakup negotiations, will help make sure you're secure later, when you're older.

19

Where to Start

Hopefully, you know everything there is to know about the finances of your household and will easily be able to create—or access—a net-worth statement with the list of assets and liabilities that you both own, and a budget or income-and-expense statement showing you what the household cash flow is. Many couples agree that one person will act as the family bookkeeper, pay the bills, and keep the accounts. This person should have all that information, but the non-bill-paying partner may not. If this person is you, you'll need to do some gathering to put together the financial information you need.

There are state-specific laws governing divorce for couples who are married, who are domestic partners, or who have common-law marriages. Your lawyer will help you understand how your state's laws affect you. Once you have your financial ducks in a row—as best you can—meet with an attorney to sort out the legal steps you'll need to take.

Information You Need

Refer back to Chapter 1 for help creating a net-worth statement and an income-and-expense plan or budget. Work out two statements and two budgets, one for the combined household and one for you alone. It's important to know what you own, what your partner or spouse owns, and what you own together. You'll need to understand what your current income sources are, what your expenses are now, and what they might be when you're by yourself.

Make a list of all the insurance policies you and your partner own. These include homeowner's or renter's, auto, life, health, and disability insurance. Chapter 4 will help you understand how each of these works.

Be sure to account for benefits that you both have through work. Employee benefits include 401(k) or 403(b) plans, stock options, restricted stock grants, and pensions. Chapters 6 and 7 will help you learn more about these plans.

Don't forget to gather information on real estate or other tangible assets such as works of art, boats, planes, and cars. Your county registrar's office will have copies of real estate deeds. Find purchase records or receipts for valuables such as art and jewelry or have them appraised. If the separation has just happened, don't pay for the appraisal out of your own funds or joint funds if it will be expensive and leave you short of cash. Instead, make a note that assets need to be appraised and include that in the negotiation discussions.

Where to Find Information

You can get plenty of valuable information from the investment statements, bank statements, and monthly bills. Remember that many bills may only be available online; if you have a category on your expense worksheet—for example, "electric bill"—but you haven't received a bill, call the company for help retrieving the online statement. Some investments such as annuities, employer retirement plans, and life insurance might have statements that arrive quarterly or annually instead of monthly.

If statements aren't mailed and you're not sure how to access e-mail copies or electronic statements, you can start your sleuthing in your tax documents:

- Check your tax return for a list of accounts that generate interest and dividends.
- Page one of the Form 1040 tax return will show the amount of a deposit that was made into an IRA or a self-employed retirement plan.
- The return will show income sources and possibly a list of deductions for real estate taxes and mortgage interest paid.
- There may be schedules in the return that show income from active or passive business ventures.
- If there is a W-2 form with the return, you'll see the amount contributed to an employer retirement plan and the income from that employer.
- The 1099s with the return will show nonemployment income such as interest, dividends, and retirement plan withdrawals.

FACT

Pay stubs will show income per pay period and year-to-date. Many companies—especially large ones—have stopped mailing pay stubs and now offer copies online. Some jobs may have more than one pay stub. Bonuses, commissions, or extra duties such as police details may be on separate stubs.

Develop Postbreakup Goals and Priorities

You'll have an easier time making financial decisions during the breakup negotiations if you spend some time now thinking about what your priorities are for your life afterward. Think far down the road: Where do you want to be in five, ten, fifteen, and even twenty years? Go back and look at Chapter 2 for help in developing your goals. Write down your most important goals and carry them with you. Refer to them when you're tempted to make a decision that will make the short term easier, but will hurt your long-term chances of reaching your goals.

Special Advisors

It's very important that you don't try to get through this without help. Too many people are hurt, especially financially, by not seeking professional help when they need it. Most people realize how important it is to hire a lawyer if they're divorcing their spouse. Many people will suggest it to them; their friends, their mediator, their therapist will probably all suggest hiring an attorney to represent their interests. Not being married doesn't mean that you shouldn't hire a lawyer, too. If you're separating from your partner, married or not, there are many legal and financial issues to sort through.

Unfortunately, lawyers cost money—sometimes a lot of money, especially if the two parties don't initially agree and their lawyers spend a lot of time researching and negotiating. Reduce this time and cost by getting educated about the separation process. Consider using a mediator to help maneuver you and your ex through as much of the negotiations yourself as possible without the expensive help of an attorney.

Online Resources

Financial savvy is important in any negotiation. You don't have to be an expert, but understanding the ramifications of your decisions is important. Review the general financial online resources in the Web Resources section of Appendix B. Study the sites that help with the parts of financial planning that you have the most uncertainty about.

A quick web search of the word "divorce" will yield a huge number of pages. Look for sites that are journalistic and not sales oriented. Check each site's About Us link to understand how the site makes its money. Check out blogs for information on how others are dealing with their divorce. And don't rely on legal information you find online; check with your attorney before making a decision.

Using a Mediator to Save Money

A mediator will meet with you and your soon-to-be-ex to facilitate a separation agreement. The idea is that meeting with a trained facilitator should help you work out many of the agreement questions on your own. A good mediator will help you do this quickly and will create an agreement your lawyer can review to be sure it protects your interests.

Anyone can claim to be a divorce mediator. Be sure the person you pick has experience and treats both of you with respect. Call the references they give you. Check the Academy of Family Mediators at *www.mediate.com* for a list of mediators in your area.

ALERT!

Stay in touch with your financial planner as you proceed through the separation negotiations. He'll help explain the financial ramifications of the decisions you're faced with and will make suggestions to help you negotiate. Check with the planner before finalizing the financial agreement.

Don't start or continue mediation if you don't feel able to work directly with your ex in a negotiation. Mediation won't work if you're not able to stand up for your interests. The power structure that dictated your roles in your relationship will still exist in mediation. If this will put you at a big disadvantage or cause you too much stress, it will be better to skip the mediator and have your lawyer negotiate on your behalf.

Tax Planning when the Accounts Have to Be Divided

Tax planning in a separation is one area where it makes a difference whether you are divorcing after a marriage or ending a long-term partnership. Spouses have legal rights that partners don't. The federal tax code was written with this in mind. In either case, it's important to understand the after-tax value and the true current value of the assets you're dividing to be sure you get your fair share.

Calculating After-Tax Value

After-tax value is the amount of money left over after selling an asset or liquidating an account, then paying taxes owed on the proceeds. Check Chapter 16 to review the different types of taxes that affect your assets. Remember, ordinary income is taxed at a higher rate than capital gains or profits on investments. These rates change based on your total income and filing status (married or single, for example). Check *www.irs.gov* to see what your rates are.

QUESTION?

How does the alternative minimum tax work into the after-tax calculations?
The AMT laws are very complex. If you have a number of deductions such as mortgage interest and dependents, or a complex tax situation that involves things such as stock options or a small business, you should ask your CPA to help with the after-tax valuations.

Retirement accounts, such as an IRA or a 401(k), are tax deferred. This means that the money in them isn't taxed until it's withdrawn. The amount withdrawn from a retirement account is taxed as ordinary income to the person who owns it. In a divorce, spouses can direct in the final divorce decree that money from one person's retirement account be moved into the other's account. This transfer under a Qualified Domestic Relations Order, or QUADRO, takes place after the divorce is final. Since the money moves from one spouse to the other, it isn't taxable. If you can QUADRO the account, the after-tax value would be the same as the current value, because there's no tax when the money is transferred.

If the ex-spouse receiving the money decides to take the cash rather than a transfer of assets directly into his IRA, then the amount is taxed as income to him. The after-tax value of the account would be the value less the tax they owe, in this case. Spouses don't pay the 10 percent early with-drawal penalty if they receive money from an IRA through a QUADRO.

None of these tax-deferred transfer benefits are available to nonspouses. For unmarried partners, the after-tax value of the account is the value less the tax due, less the early withdrawal penalty of 10 percent if your partner is under age 59½.

The after-tax value of nonretirement accounts doesn't hinge on whether you're a divorcing spouse or a separating partner. It is the value of the account less any capital gains taxes due on investment profits. Unmarried partners must beware of gift tax problems when transferring money from one ex-partner to another. There is a limit—$12,000 in 2008—that you can transfer between unmarried people per year.

Valuing Nonliquid Assets

Nonliquid assets are tougher to decipher because they don't issue reg-ular account statements showing their value. Start with an appraisal or a reliable estimate of the value, and then subtract the cost of selling the asset—regardless of whether you plan to sell after the separation. To get after-tax value, from net value subtract any capital gains taxes that would be due because the asset appreciated since purchase.

Valuing Income Streams

An example of an income stream is the regular payments from a pen-sion. The total potential proceeds from a pension are usually higher than the amount available if the pension is cashed out in a lump sum. This is the reason that many people opt to receive the payments instead of cashing out the pension. It's also the reason you can't rely on the current account value when you're valuing a pension in a separation.

Calculate the present value of the future pension payments using a spreadsheet program or a financial calculator. Your financial planner or accountant can help you with this, as well.

Value of a Career

Putting a value on the ability to work for an income each year is more difficult than valuing an income stream from a pension. Often, one person in a couple puts a career on hold to raise children or otherwise support the family's lifestyle. When you separate, it's important to consider the value of this work—even though it went unpaid. Compare the two partners' future income potentials. Calculate the present value of the difference between the two, and see what you get. Many people feel guilty about receiving alimony from an income-earning spouse after a long marriage spent raising kids. This present value comparison of ability to earn can be a very large number and might make you feel differently about making sure you get enough future support to help you get back on the career track.

Planning for the Kids

Money issues and raising kids before the breakup might have been difficult. The emotional and psychological aspects of the breakup are not likely to make things easier. Which parent the kids will live with, whether support is paid as alimony or child support, and especially the kids' lifestyle with each parent deserve special attention.

FACT

Separation agreements often include provisions for job training or school tuition for the partner re-entering the work force. Effort spent learning new skills that will increase your income potential can turn out to be one of your more valuable assets. Don't discount it.

Alimony Versus Child Support

If you're starting a breakup and you're just shy of ten years together, consider staying together until you reach the ten-year mark. Ten years is considered in many states a long-term relationship and could give you an advantage in the support negotiation. Alimony is taxable income to the receiver and a tax deduction for the giver. The amount of alimony you can expect differs from state to state, and often hinges on how long you were together. Child support is not taxable to the receiver and is not a deduction for the giver. Support is almost always limited to a certain period of time. Carefully consider how this timeline factors into your total budget when you plan what you'll do after the separation in your career and retirement savings plans.

ALERT!

You must make your financial decisions unemotionally during the breakup. Bad choices that you made quickly or in order to smooth the breakup in the short term can hurt you in the long run. Don't be tempted to agree with something simply because you want to get through the negotiations quickly.

How Will the Divorce Affect the Kids?

It's natural to want to shelter kids in a breakup by giving them the same lifestyle after you've separated as your family enjoyed before. The reality is that it's at least twice as expensive to run two households as it was to run one. Trying to spend like you did before just isn't realistic. It sounds cold, but you can use the divorce as a learning experience for your kids. This is the perfect time to teach them that safety, happiness, and security are not related to how much income you have. If money management was a strong suit of yours in the past, you have the opportunity to set a good example regardless of what your ex is doing. If you struggled with finances before, turn a new page. Include your kids in your money education and help them learn to stand on their own financially.

Restarting Your Financial Plan

Getting your financial plan back on track after a breakup in your 40s or 50s is tough because of the timing. Initially, you grew into your plan. You were young and the only baggage you brought to the planning process was the messages your parents had given you about money—and maybe a little bit of credit card debt. Now you're restarting a plan with diminished resources after splitting a household and maybe carrying significant debt from legal fees. You're older and wiser now, but there's also less time to build before retirement. You have less wiggle room to take chances and make mistakes.

Dealing with Post-Divorce Debt

Divorces can easily end up costing $50,000 or more. Unless you had the resources to cover that expense, you will probably have quite a bit of debt to face after the divorce. Avoid the emotional and financial paralysis this can cause by going back to your original notes about your five-, ten-, and fifteen-year goals. Get yourself out of thinking about where the debt came from and start from scratch. You have the debt—now what should you do to pay it off and start moving toward your goals? Don't carry the emotional baggage of how you got the debt on top of the debt itself. Go to Chapter 3 for help in creating a plan to pay down your debt and start rebuilding your nest egg.

Budgeting on Your Own

Managing money by yourself again can be invigorating or terrifying. If you're newly back to the necessity for personal money management, take extra care to set up the savings baskets discussed in Chapter 1. Be careful not to fall into the trap of careless spending to make yourself feel better in the short term—the weight of debt will make you feel worse in the long term.

Accounting for Extra Costs

Make a careful inventory of the things you need to do to enable you to move toward your life goals. If you need to increase your salary, decide whether to spend money on tuition or fees for more job training. If your kids are still young and are sharing time with their other parent, do you need to budget for their visitation travel? If you're maintaining the house on your own, do you need to pay someone to help maintain it? Look realistically at the expenses you'll have now that you're single.

Tax Planning Update

Any life change warrants a review of your tax situation, especially a divorce that will change your income and your filing status. Check the tax withholding from your pay, then in October or November make an estimate of what your final tax return will look like by having an accountant complete a tax projection for you. This will help you anticipate the expense of any extra taxes that might be due in April. If, instead, you're expecting a refund, reduce your withholding and take home more in your paycheck rather than waiting for a refund windfall.

Dodge the Most Common Financial Blunders

Emotional stress during your separation is inevitable. It's important to not let that stress impair your financial decision-making skills. Beware of common financial mistakes.

Staying "House Poor" for the Kids

Often the knee-jerk reaction to a breakup is to do whatever it takes to maintain the status quo for the sake of the kids. If your kids are still home, this often means feeling compelled to keep the house. Watch out! You may be giving up bargaining power for no benefit. Your kids may or may not have an easier time with the divorce if you stay in the house. That is hard to predict. What's easy to foresee is that keeping the house as an asset could put your future financial security at risk. It costs money to maintain a house. If you're dividing assets with your ex, and you end up with a lot of home equity but not much else in the form of retirement or in emergency liquid savings, it will be difficult to keep up the home maintenance. Strongly consider whether selling the house, splitting the proceeds, and buying into something new that you can afford on your own income is a better option.

Miscalculating After-Tax Asset Values

There are a lot of gray areas in separation negotiations; one of these is calculating the value of the family's assets. Investment accounts are easy, because the value is simply the total printed on the statement—give or take a bit of capital gains tax. There is room, though, for different interpretations of the value of retirement plans and pension incomes.

Income is taxed at different marginal rates depending on the other income received that year. An argument could be made to calculate after-tax value of retirement account withdrawals at different tax rates. The present value of a pension payment can be calculated differently depending on whether a higher or lower interest rate is used in the calculator. This is why it's important that you get feedback from a financial planner and that you educate yourself on how these calculations are made to be sure you're agreeing to a fair deal.

Not Planning for Cash Flow

Separations take a long time to sift out, and money can get tight if you're paying legal bills and counting on regular support from your ex. If you're expecting to separate, think about expenses before you start the process. Make sure you have liquid cash available in savings and that there are no outstanding bills that could drain that savings after the separation. Be sure the utilities and other household bills are current; check that income tax returns have been filed and taxes paid; make sure the real estate taxes and the escrow account through your mortgage company is up to date; and take care of any deferred home maintenance, especially if you're planning to stay in the home.

Undervaluing the Career

Staying home or working part time in order to act as the primary caregiver to children has a huge amount of value. An economics professor might calculate the value by comparing it to the amount of salary the caregiver is willing to forgo to stay home. This number is theoretical, but it makes a point. You give up a huge amount of future potential earning power by staying home. Many people discount this value by not insisting on the alimony they're due, or by making other financial concessions. This is a huge mistake. If you spent the years from your 30s to your 50s raising kids while your spouse continued on the paid career track, his earning potential will be stronger than yours after a divorce in your 50s. You'll never regret your decision to focus on raising your kids; don't discount your value by not insisting on the support you deserve after they're grown.

After long-term couples separate, one partner's standard of living often drops while the other's improves. Many factors affect this, including education and career opportunities, but one of the biggest effects on your life after divorce is your attitude. A therapist or life coach can help you get back on track toward your financial goals. It's money well spent.

Playing the Financial Victim

The emotional stress of separating from a long-term partner is enough to make anyone fall into the trap of playing the financial victim. Relationships seldom fail for any one reason. Don't let guilt over something you did—or think you did—or anger about your partner's behavior affect your financial decision-making process. Don't rush to make choices that you may regret later. Take yourself through the process at the pace you feel allows you to make educated decisions. If you're starting with little financial savvy, put things on hold until you have knowledge enough to work with your advisors to make the best choices for your future.

CHAPTER 20

Planning after the Death of a Spouse

Coping with the grief of losing your soul mate—whether that person was your spouse or your life partner—can make working through your personal finances difficult even if you're money savvy and financially prepared for the loss. There are only a few things that need to be handled right away. Once those things are done, avoid making any other permanent financial plans or investments until you're sure you're emotionally ready. This is the time to give yourself the space to reflect and grieve, do your research, and build a financial team to help you when you need advice.

The Nuts and Bolts of an Estate Plan

The will, the trust, or the probate court—if your partner didn't have a will—dictate the cast of characters that you'll be working with. Each person has a different role and a different set of responsibilities.

Executor

The executor is something like the estate's personal representative. He shepherds the estate through the process of being settled, which is not a speedy process. You're probably the executor for your spouse's estate. Don't put pressure on yourself to get through things quickly. Start by gathering your financial information—review Chapter 1 for suggestions on gathering information—and contact your current financial planner, accountant, or attorney for a referral to a lawyer who can help you with the probate process.

ALERT!

The executor can be personally responsible for managing the finances of the estate. Don't make distributions to beneficiaries until you're sure you have the bills and taxes paid. This delay could extend up to a year or more for a more complex estate.

Trustee

The trustee is responsible for overseeing a trust and managing the assets the trust owns. Typically, these include things such as investments or real estate, and the trust document outlines guidelines on how the assets are to be managed and how income or principal is to be distributed. You both might have acted as trustee for a trust set up before your partner died, or the trust may have been established by instructions in her will. Trusts are convenient because you take charge of the assets without having to wait for the probate court, but it is very important that you talk to your lawyer for help in understanding the requirements the trust places on managing the assets.

Some trusts have more than one trustee. You may be co-trustee with a professional manager such as a bank or a lawyer. Trustees are often paid for their expenses and a management fee by the trust.

A trust created while you're alive is called an *inter vivos*, or living or family trust. A trust created in your will is called a testamentary trust. The inter vivos trust keeps the assets from becoming public during probate and may save probate costs if your state law bases probate fees on the size of the probatable estate.

Beneficiary

Beneficiaries are the people or organizations that will be given a benefit from the estate. You are most likely the primary beneficiary of your spouse, but other charities or children may also be named. The will or trust document explains what each beneficiary should receive, and when, and it's the responsibility of the executor or trustee, as the case may be, to make the distributions.

Remaindermen

Remaindermen are the secondary beneficiaries of a trust after the death of the initial beneficiary. If you're the beneficiary of a trust, your remaindermen may be your kids, or your partner's kids, or family from a previous marriage. A charity that gets the trust principal after your death could be the remainderman. Remaindermen and beneficiaries can have conflicting interests; if the beneficiary uses all the assets in the trust, there could be nothing left for the remaindermen.

Trusts try to minimize conflict between beneficiaries and remaindermen by stating that the beneficiary can take interest from the trust but not principal, so that the principal is preserved for the remaindermen. The beneficiary in this case often asks the trustee to invest in high income-producing investments that may not be in the best long-term interest of the remaindermen.

Finding the Right Advisors

If you can, try to build a support network of trusted advisors before you're faced with having to manage your money alone. If you haven't been able to do that, start by interviewing the people your partner worked with. Don't limit yourself to them, and don't rush to make a decision. This new relationship with a past advisor or a new one needs to benefit you. Give yourself time to pick someone you're compatible with.

Where to Look

Review Chapter 18 for ideas on what type of advisors you'll need to help with your financial planning. If you haven't been introduced to your partner's advisors, check his account statements and insurance policies. The sales person who sold the policy will be named on the statement along with her phone number. Investment advisors will either send investment statements on their letterhead or they'll be named as advisors on the brokerage account statement. Look for cover letters enclosed with estate documents for name and contact information of the attorney who created them. Check e-mail accounts, address books, and check registers for other advisors your partner did business with. His pay stubs will have the company name and contact information you can use to get in touch with human resources officers at his employer.

Deciding Whether to Change

Your spouse or partner's advisors will be able to help you cope with the urgent matters that need attention right away. They're familiar with the financial information and will have access to the accounts. If the accounts were not joint or in trust, you'll need to be named as executor before you can access them.

You don't have to continue working with previous advisors. Observe how well they help you during this stressful process as a gauge to how well they'll work on your behalf later on. Don't work with anyone who makes you feel minimized or seems unempathetic, and absolutely don't work with anyone who is pressing you to make quick decisions on things that don't have firm deadlines, particularly investment changes or buying new investment products.

Expertise and Specialties to Look For

If you can't find any past financial advisors, or if you don't think your partner had any, talk to the lawyer who is helping you through probate—or even your funeral director—for referrals to a financial planner and an accountant. Certified Financial Planners and Certified Public Accountants both have the broad expertise to help you get started organizing the estate and getting your own finances in order.

Don't forget yourself in the process of focusing on your financial security. Money spent on therapy to help support the grieving process is money well spent on your future physical and emotional health. Take care of yourself.

Planning Priorities and Timelines

The financial priorities and deadlines that you need to be aware of relate to monthly household expenses and taxes. Your planner or accountant will be able to help you sort through these and prioritize what needs to happen right away, versus what you can put off until later.

QUESTION?

My partner died with more credit card debt than assets. His creditors are calling our home and harassing me about paying his bills. Should I pay them off?

No. You can't blame them for trying, but creditors must get in line to be paid according to a specific probate protocol. Many people die with more debt than assets; it's common for some unsecured creditors such as credit card companies to go unpaid.

No Quick Decisions

Resist the impulse to throw yourself into the process of managing the finances by making big, permanent, or expensive decisions such as buying or selling investments. Focus first on paying the daily household bills such as the rent, mortgage, utilities, and loan payments that are in your name. Check Chapter 1 for help understanding the types of statements and monthly bills you should be expecting and how to organize the information into an income-and-expenses worksheet and a net-worth statement. This will be the start of understanding the big picture so you can make longer-term planning decisions.

Planning for Cash Flow

Collect the bills that arrive solely in your partner's name, but don't pay them unless they are related to your housing, safety, or convenience, such as paying the car payment or insurance. Contact life insurance companies as soon as possible. As the beneficiary, you'll receive a check or a check-book to access your benefit.

You aren't liable for the debts of your partner or your spouse unless you cosigned, or the debt was assumed jointly. If you inherit an asset such as a house or a car that serves as collateral for a debt, then you'll need to arrange to take over the payments.

Long- and Short-Term Timelines

If your partner was over age 70½, then you need to confirm that the required minimum distribution was made from her retirement accounts. Contact her former or current employer to see if you need to make any decisions about stock options, restricted stock, or other employee benefits by a certain time.

If you're married, you'll still file your tax return at the regular time. If you're the executor for your partner's estate, you'll be responsible for filing her final tax return. If you plan to disclaim any inherited benefits so they can pass to the next generation, you'll generally need to do so within nine months. Check the Web Resources section in Appendix B for a list of links to timelines you need to watch.

Making the Right Adjustments to Financial Accounts

Over time, you can work on updating your accounts so that they are titled just in your name. This is important to avoid confusion down the road.

Update Ownership

Update the ownership of assets that were owned jointly by retitling them in your name. Most financial institutions and the registry of deeds will require a death certificate and a letter requesting the change, called a letter of instruction. Retitle your car and home, and update insurance policies so that they are in your name alone.

Update the beneficiary designation on your own retirement accounts and insurance policies. Decide whether you should put transfer on death designations on any of your bank accounts to give a friend or adult child access to cash if something happens to you. Don't make the account joint, because it exposes the money to his creditors.

Protect Your Credit

Check your credit report and your partner's to be sure you're aware of all the accounts held in either of your names. Close accounts that are solely in your deceased partner's name and that have zero balance. Accounts with a balance will need to be paid according to your state's laws with money from the estate. Check your credit report and your partner's to be sure there are no fraudulent accounts or transactions happening under his name.

Collecting the Benefits You're Due

Employment benefits such as pensions, retirement plans, and privately owned annuity contracts can often be paid to you in a lump sums or in regular payments. Take your time deciding which payment schedule works best for you and your beneficiaries.

FACT

Spouses are allowed to transfer retirement plan assets such as 401(k)s and IRAs directly into an IRA that they own. Other nonspouse beneficiaries may roll over funds to an inherited IRA or beneficiary IRA and take distributions over their lifetime if the original investment company allows it. Check the plan document at the investment company to research your options.

Pensions and Retirement Plans

Company pensions are usually available in a lump sum payment that can be transferred to an IRA if the worker hasn't already started taking payments. Contact the employer's human resources department for help with the distribution. If the pensioner was already receiving payments, she may have chosen a benefit amount for you as her spouse. The employer will send a letter letting you know what your benefits are.

QUESTION?

Can I continue under my late husband's health insurance, or do I need to buy a new plan?
You need to contact your husband's employer within thirty days of his death. You should be eligible for COBRA health insurance coverage for thirty-six months.

Annuities

Private annuity contracts give the owner the option to designate a beneficiary. The beneficiary can choose whether to take regular payments, interest, or a lump sum from the annuity. In most cases, at least part of this payment is taxable as income to the beneficiary, so it's important to have finished at least a rough financial plan and have spoken to a planner or accountant before deciding what type of benefit to choose.

Bringing Children into the Process

Don't harm your own financial security by trying to use money to soothe children after the loss of a parent. Even if the kids are grown, it can be tempting to use financial gifts to make their loss easier. Understand that they are grieving, too. If you're the stepparent or an unmarried partner, you may be surprised by some unexpected changes in your relationship with them.

Financial Security and Changing Financial Relationships

Losing a loved one is stressful for everyone involved. Adding money to the mix—a lot or a little—can add to the stress. Talk to your therapist about how your relationship with your children or stepchildren has been affected by the loss. Don't try to make things better with money or gifts, and absolutely don't give in to threats or pressure to give money that you can't afford.

Gifting and Estate Planning

Once things have settled enough that you've had time to think about your future financial goals and have created at least a general financial plan, you'll be able to update your estate plan. With your financial goals in mind, decide whether to gift money to family members now or in your will. Update your own estate beneficiaries and revisit your executor, health care proxy, and power-of-attorney designations.

APPENDIX A

Glossary

12b-1 fees
A hidden fee charged by mutual fund companies to pay for marketing expenses. It was named after the line of legislation that enabled the fees.

401(k) plan
An employer-sponsored defined-contribution retirement plan that accepts employee contributions from their paychecks, pretax. The plan is tax-deferred because proceeds are taxed only when they're withdrawn. Additional penalties apply for withdrawals before age 59½. It takes its name from a section of the Internal Revenue Code.

403(b) plan
A defined-contribution retirement plan that resembles the 401(k) plan but that can be used by public education organizations, nonprofits, and self-employed ministers.

529 plan
A tax-advantaged savings plan, also called a qualified tuition plan, that is state sponsored and designed to encourage saving for future college costs. Contributions may or may not be tax deductible. Proceeds are not taxed until withdrawn and are tax free if withdrawn to pay qualified tuition expenses. It was named after Section 529 of the Internal Revenue Code.

account aggregator
A web service that compiles account information from financial accounts such as bank, credit card, investment, and retirement plans into a single online application where they can be more easily managed. Aggregators are a handy way to save and compile site passwords.

active investing
The practice of managed buying and selling in an account based on research, quantitative models, and other principles. Active managers feel that this extra work will help them outperform the market. (*See also* passive investing)

alternative minimum tax
A tax that was created to prevent tax filers from using sophisticated tax loopholes and deductions to minimize or avoid paying tax. Because income limits in the law were not set to adjust with inflation, many middle-income taxpayers now pay this additional tax.

annuities
A contract between you and an insurance company, under which you make a lump-sum payment or series of payments into a tax-deferred account. In return, the insurer agrees to make periodic payments to you beginning immediately or at some future date. Most annuities have significant withdrawal penalties if money is withdrawn within five to seven years of being deposited.

asset allocation
The strategy of dividing an investment portfolio among different asset categories—such as stocks, bonds, and cash—that are affected by different economic factors, to minimize excessive risk that one segment will underperform in the current economy.

assets under management (AUM) fee
A fee that compensates advisors based on a percentage of the total assets being managed on a client's behalf.

bankruptcy
A legal status that is conferred on individuals or organizations unable to pay creditors. In bankruptcies filed under Chapter 7 of the Bankruptcy Reform Act, debtors are essentially given a fresh start. Some property is sold to pay debt, but most unsecured debt is written off. Chapter 13 filings create a repayment program, usually over three to five years.

beneficiary
The person or legal entity that receives assets from a deceased individual according to the terms of a will or established legal contract such as a life insurance policy, annuity, or retirement account.

bond ladder
A portfolio of bonds whose individual maturity dates are such that redemptions are spaced over a period of years. Ladders can be evenly spaced with bonds of equal value staggered over consecutive years.

bonds
Also called fixed-income investments, debt instruments that are sold to the public by governments and companies. Upon maturity, borrowers collect the face value and are entitled to stated interest payments. Bonds are as safe as the ability of the issuing company's ability to pay.

broker
An individual or institution that acts as an intermediary between investors and financial markets, facilitating the buying and selling of securities. Brokers are generally paid a commission on transactions.

budget
A list of planned expenses and income.

capital gain
A profit resulting from the sale of a capital asset that exceeds the total amount invested, called the basis. Capital loss results when the asset is sold for less than total investment.

Certified Financial Planner
A professional designation conferred by the Certified Financial Planner Board of Standards on candidates who meet education requirements, planning experience, and ethics requirements and have passed a rigorous exam.

Certified Public Accountant
A designation conferred on accountants who have passed the Uniform Certified Public Accountant Examination and who meet other education requirements.

COBRA
A provision in the federal Consolidated Omnibus Budget Reconciliation Act of 1985 that allows individuals to continue group health benefits for a period of time after the covered worker leaves the employer or dies.

Coverdell IRA
Also called a Coverdell Education Savings Account, a trust or custodial account with tax benefits if used to pay the qualified education expenses of the account beneficiary.

defined benefit plan
Also familiar as the traditional corporate pension, a retirement plan that promises a specified monthly benefit at retirement, either as an exact dollar amount or according to a formula that considers such factors as salary and service.

defined contribution plan
A plan under which the employee, the employer, or both contribute to the employee's individual account, sometimes at a set rate. These contributions are chosen by the employee from a limited list of choices. Accounts can be transferred to individual retirement accounts when the employee leaves the employer.

employee stock option plan
Not to be confused with an employee stock ownership plan, option plans are contracts between a company and its employees that give employees the right to buy a specific number of the company's shares at a fixed price within a certain period of time.

employee stock ownership plan
Also known as an ESOP, a form of defined contribution plan in which the investments are primarily in employer stock.

employee stock purchase plan

A program that allows employees to purchase shares of their employer company's stock, often at a discount.

equity

Any security, such as a stock or bond that carries ownership interest.

estate planning

The process of managing all the assets of an estate in a way that best accomplishes the goal of the individual, including minimizing taxes, simplifying probate, and passing as much of the estate as possible to beneficiaries.

exchange-traded funds

Baskets of securities that are designed to mirror the performance of a specific index, such as the S&P 500.

executor

The individual designated in a will to carry out the wishes of a deceased person.

FICO

A highly regarded credit-scoring system developed by Fair Isaac & Co. that is widely used by mortgage companies and other lenders.

financial planning

The holistic process of coordinating cash management, tax planning, insurance, investment planning, retirement planning, and estate planning to most effectively accomplish a person's financial goals.

harvesting gains

The process of selling investment securities at a loss in order to help offset the tax consequences of capital gains.

health care proxy

A power of attorney used specifically to enable a second party to make health care decisions on behalf of an incapacitated person.

incentive stock options

A type of stock option with preferential tax characteristics that encourages the employee to hold the shares of stock after exercising the option to buy them.

individual retirement account

Commonly called an IRA, a retirement account that encourages saving by offering tax deferral until funds are withdrawn. If certain conditions are met, contributions to IRA accounts are tax deductible. Eligible workers can make Roth IRA contributions after tax, and withdrawals are tax free.

inflation

The increase in the cost of goods and services caused by overall economic expansion.

life insurance

A contract under which an insurer pays beneficiaries a specified sum, if the insured dies while covered. Term life is in force for a specified period; permanent insurance has a savings component that is planned to support the policy forever.

liquidity

The capacity of an investment to be converted to cash quickly and without price fluctuations caused by economic conditions.

long-term care insurance

Insurance to cover the cost of a chronically disabling illness.

margin loan

Borrowing capacity secured by the value of investments in a brokerage account. A margin call can occur if the value of the securities drops below a specified threshold requiring the investor to add cash to the account to cover the call. Brokerage firms are allowed to sell investments in the account to cover margin calls if the investor does not deposit cash.

Medicaid

A government health care program for the poor.

Medicare

A federal health care program for people age 65 and older. Part A is mandatory and pays for inpatient services; Part B is voluntary and pays for outpatient services and regular health care; Part C combines the benefits of part A and part B into one policy and is marketed by independent companies. Part D subsidizes prescription drugs.

money market account

An interest-bearing account similar to a savings account managed by a bank or investment company that is highly liquid.

mortgage

A loan secured by real estate. Borrowers make regular payments meant to pay off the loan over a period of time. A reverse mortgage enables a property owner to borrow against the equity in a property, in which the lender earns an increasing ownership share in the property in exchange for regular payments to the borrower.

mutual fund
An investment pool managed by an investment company that invests the collective deposits in securities according to specified parameters outlined in a prospectus.

net-worth statement
A document listing all of a person's assets, including cash, minus all liabilities. The difference between assets and liabilities is called net worth.

passive investing
An investment strategy most often using investments based on broad market indexes. Passive investors believe that it's nearly impossible for an individual investor to consistently beat the market, so they buy indexes in order to meet market returns and rely on keeping expenses and taxes low to enhance their earnings. (*See also* active investing)

pension
See defined benefit plan.

personal finance
The holistic process of applying financial management strategies to the holdings of an individual or family, including budgeting, spending, and saving to meet a future goal.

power of attorney
Legal authorization permitting a second party to make decisions on a person's behalf.

prospectus
A document approved by the Securities & Exchange Commission that discloses all important information related to an investment.

rebalancing
Adjusting an investment portfolio back to the target asset allocation by buying and selling securities in the portfolio. Rebalancing helps ensure that investments are bought low and sold high.

REIT
Also known as a real estate investment trust, a pool of investor capital that is invested in income properties.

risk
Broadly, the likelihood that an investment will lose value over a period of time. Inflation risk is the chance that gains will not keep pace with the rising costs of goods and services. Market risk is the possibility that an entire asset class, such as bonds, will lose value. Company risk, or business risk, is the potential for a particular company to suffer an event that dramatically decreases its share value.

risk tolerance
The ability of an individual to cope emotionally with dramatic swings in investment value.

sales load
A sales fee added to the price of some mutual investments such as mutual funds and annuities.

SEP
Also called a Simplified Employee Pension plan, a relatively uncomplicated retirement savings vehicle that allows self-employed workers to make contributions on a tax-deductible basis to individual retirement accounts.

SIMPLE
Formally known as a Savings Incentive Match Plan for Employees, a retirement plan similar to 401(k) plans that's available to companies with fewer than 100 employees. SIMPLE plans have lower administrative requirements than 401(k) plans that make them less expensive for small companies to offer them to their work force.

social investing
A strategy to buy investments that support a person's social values.

social security
The universe of federal benefits programs that provide individuals and families with retirement income and disability benefits.

stock
Broadly, a claim on a proportional share of a company's assets and profits. In practice, a financial instrument that can be bought and sold for prices set by market demand and related to a company's financial performance.

tax planning
The strategy of making financial planning and investment decisions to minimize tax liability.

trust
An independent legal entity that can own assets and be managed by a person for his own or another's benefit.

will
A legal instrument that directs the probate court how to divide and distribute a person's property after her death.

workers' compensation
An insurance program funded by premiums paid by employers to compensate people injured on the job.

yield curve
A graphical depiction of bond yield over time that compares yield with maturity.

APPENDIX B

Web Resources

The web has become an indispensable resource for anyone planning his or her personal finances. If there is any compelling reason for a web-ophobe to embrace the medium, financial education is it. The web empowers you to research financial opportunities and waves red flags to signal danger zones. Don't view these resources as endorsements, and be sure you check more than one site as you seek answers to your questions. Because some sites are useful in many different areas, they may appear in more than one section.

Calculators

Choose to Save
www.choosetosave.org/calculators

KJE Computer Solutions Financial Calculators
www.dinkytown.net

Financial Calculators
www.fincalc.com

Credit Cards and Counseling
www.annualcreditreport.com

Fair Isaac
www.myfico.com

U.S. Citizens for Fair Credit Card Terms
www.cardratings.com

Credit and Debt Management at About.com
http://credit.about.com

How Stuff Works
http://money.howstuffworks.com/personal-credit-debt-management-channel.htm

U.S. Trustee
www.usdoj.gov/ust

Federal Trade Commission
www.ftc.gov

National Foundation for Credit Counseling
www.nfcc.org

American Consumer Credit Counseling
www.consumercredit.com

U.S. Dept of Justice, List of Approved Credit Counseling Agencies
www.usdoj.gov

Budgeting and Money Management
Living a Better Life
www.betterbudgeting.com

Financial Planning at About.com
http://financialplan.about.com

The Frugal Life
www.thefrugallife.com/finances.html

The Dollar Stretcher
www.stretcher.com

Yodlee Money Center
www.yodlee.com

Mint
www.mint.com

Bankruptcy
Bankruptcy Information
www.legalconsumer.com

U.S. Courts
www.uscourts.gov/bankruptcycourts.html

Nolo
www.nolo.com

Nolo's Bankruptcy Foreclosure Blog
blogs.nolo.com/bankruptcy

Insurance Resources
Insure.com
www.insure.com

Free Advice
http://insurance.freeadvice.com

U.S. Department of Health and Human Services
www.ahrq.gov/consumer

Centers for Medicare and Medicaid Services
www.cms.hhs.gov

LifeInsure.com blog
http://discussion.lifeinsure.com

Asset Allocation and Investing
U.S. Securities & Exchange Commission
www.sec.gov

Asset Allocation at SEC.gov
www.sec.gov/investor/pubs/assetallocation.htm

Iowa Asset Allocation Calculator
www.ipers.org/calcs/AssetAllocator.html

Securities Regulations Advice
www.sec-nasd-regulations.com

Financial Industry Regulatory Authority
www.finra.org

The Motley Fool
www.fool.com/investing.htm

Treasury Direct
www.treasurydirect.gov

Morningstar: Stocks, Mutual Funds and Investing
www.morningstar.com

American Stock Exchange
www.amex.com

Retirement Planning

Analyze Now!
www.analyzenow.com

Retirement Planning at About.com
http://retireplan.about.com

Financial Planning at AARP
www.aarp.org/financial

Social Security
www.ssa.gov

Bankrate.com
www.bankrate.com/retirement

The Vanguard Group
https://personal.vanguard.com/retirement

Fidelity Investments
http://personal.fidelity.com/retirement

Wiser Women Blog
http://wiserwomen.blogspot.com

Hiring Professional Advice

National Association of Personal Financial Advisors
www.napfa.org

The Financial Planning Association
www.fpanet.org

American Institute of Certified Public Accountants
www.aicpa.org

National Association of Enrolled Agents
www.naea.org

American Bar Association
www.abanet.org

Find Law Lawyer Directory
http://lawyers.findlaw.com

Independent Insurance Agents & Brokers of America
www.iiaba.net

The National Association of Professional Organizers
www.napo.net

American Institute of Professional Bookkeepers
www.aipb.org

Financial Websites, Newsletters, and Blogs

Smart Money
www.smartmoney.com

MarketWatch.com
www.marketwatch.com

The Wall Street Journal
www.wsj.com

MSN Money
http://moneycentral.msn.com

Women's Financial Network
www.wfnusa.com

Jim Lowell's Fidelity Investor
www.fidelityinvestor.com

The Independent Advisor for Vanguard Investors
www.adviseronline.com

WIFE e-newsletter "A Man is Not a Financial Plan"
www.wife.org/subscribe.htm

Jennifer's Compass blog by Jennifer Lane CFP
http://jenniferscompass.typepad.com

Online Money Market Accounts
ING Direct
www.ingdirect.com

Emigrant Bank
www.emigrantdirect.com

Bankrate.com
www.bankrate.com

Financial Aid Resources
FinAid
www.finaid.org

Federal Student Aid
www.fafsa.ed.gov

U.S. Department of Education
www.ed.gov

Real Estate
Zillow
www.zillow.com

AARP Reverse Mortgage
www.aarp.org/money/revmort

U.S. Department of Housing and Urban Development
www.hud.gov

National Association of Realtors
www.realtor.org

Taxes
Internal Revenue Service

www.irs.gov

Keeping Tax records
www.irs.gov/publications/p552/ar02.html

Tax Guide for Investors
www.fairmark.com/amt

Accountants World
www.accountantsworld.com

World Wide Web Tax
www.wwwebtax.com

Don't Mess With Taxes Blog
http://dontmesswithtaxes.typepad.com
/dont_mess_with_taxes

ID Theft
Identity Theft Resource Center
www.idtheftcenter.org

FTC Identity Theft Site
www.ftc.gov/idtheft

Sandwich Generation and Elder Law
National Elder Law Foundation
www.nelf.org

ElderLawAnswers
www.elderlawanswers.com

National Association of Professional Geriatric Care Managers
www.caremanager.org

Mayo Clinic
www.mayoclinic.com

National Council on Problem Gambling
www.ncpgambling.org

Nolo's Everyday Estate Planning Blog
http://blogs.nolo.com/estateplanning

Sometimes I Feel Like a Piece of Bologna Blog
http://generationsandwich.blogspot.com

Elder Law Answers Blog
http://hmargolis.typepad.
com/elderlawanswers_blog

Online Education

U.S. Financial Literacy and Education Commission
www.mymoney.gov

National Endowment for Financial Education
www.nefe.org

Federal Reserve Education
www.federalreserveeducation.org

Institute of Consumer Financial Education
www.financial-education-icfe.org

National Association of Investors
www.better-investing.org

Investment Clubs and the SEC
www.sec.gov/investor/pubs/invclub.htm

Divorce

Family Law Information
www.divorcenet.com

Nolo's Divorce, Custody & Family Law Blog
http://blogs.nolo.com/divorcefamily

Divorce Support
www.divorcesupport.com

Loss of a Loved One

Social Security Survivors Benefit Info
www.ssa.gov

Widow Net
www.widownet.org

AARP's Family, Home and Legal
www.aarp.org/families

When a Loved One Dies Checklist
www.printablechecklists.com/checklist87.shtml

Find Lost Life Insurance
www.mib.com/html/Lost-life-insurance.html

Index